WALLS,
CEILINGS &
WOODWORK

TIME
LIFE
BOOKS®

Other Publications:

FITNESS, HEALTH & NUTRITION

SUCCESSFUL PARENTING

HEALTHY HOME COOKING

UNDERSTANDING COMPUTERS

THE ENCHANTED WORLD

THE KODAK LIBRARY OF CREATIVE PHOTOGRAPHY

GREAT MEALS IN MINUTES

THE CIVIL WAR

PLANET EARTH

COLLECTOR'S LIBRARY OF THE CIVIL WAR

THE EPIC OF FLIGHT

THE GOOD COOK

WORLD WAR II

HOME REPAIR AND IMPROVEMENT

THE OLD WEST

WALLS, CEILINGS & WOODWORK

TIME-LIFE BOOKS
ALEXANDRIA, VIRGINIA

Fix It Yourself was produced by
ST. REMY PRESS

MANAGING EDITOR	Kenneth Winchester
MANAGING ART DIRECTOR	Pierre Léveillé

Staff for *Walls, Ceilings & Woodwork*

Editor	Kathleen M. Kiely
Art Director	Diane Denoncourt
Research Editor	Nancy D. Kingsbury
Designer	Solange Pelland
Contributing Writers	Beverley Bennett, Michael Kleiza, Nancy Lyon, Michael Mouland, Peter Orr, Brian Parsons, Phillipa Rispin, Jeremy Searle, Wayne Voce
Contributing Illustrators	Gérard Mariscalchi, Jacques Proulx
Technical Illustrator	Robert Paquet
Cover	Robert Monté
Index	Christine M. Jacobs
Administrator	Denise Rainville
Coordinator	Michelle Turbide
Systems Manager	Shirley Grynspan
Systems Analyst	Simon Lapierre
Studio Director	Daniel Bazinet
Photographer	Maryo Proulx

Time-Life Books Inc. is a wholly owned subsidiary of
TIME INCORPORATED

FOUNDER	Henry R. Luce 1898-1967
Editor-in-Chief	Henry Anatole Grunwald
Chairman and Chief Executive Officer	J. Richard Munro
President and Chief Operating Officer	N. J. Nicholas Jr.
Chairman of the Executive Commitee	Ralph P. Davidson
Corporate Editor	Ray Cave
Group Vice President, Books	Kelso F. Sutton
Vice President, Books	George Artandi

TIME-LIFE BOOKS INC.

EDITOR	George Constable
Executive Editor	Ellen Phillips
Director of Design	Louis Klein
Director of Editorial Resources	Phyllis K. Wise
Editorial Board	Russell B. Adams Jr., Thomas H. Flaherty, Lee Hassig, Donia Ann Steele, Rosalind Stubenberg, Kit van Tulleken, Henry Woodhead
Director of Photography and Research	John Conrad Weiser
PRESIDENT	Christopher T. Linen
Chief Operating Officer	John M. Fahey Jr.
Senior Vice Presidents	James L. Mercer, Leopoldo Toralballa
Vice Presidents	Stephen L. Bair, Ralph J. Cuomo, Neal Goff, Stephen L. Goldstein, Juanita T. James, Hallett Johnson III, Carol Kaplan, Susan J. Maruyama, Robert H. Smith, Paul R. Stewart, Joseph J. Ward
Director of Production Services	Robert J. Passantino

Editorial Operations

Copy Chief	Diane Ullius
Editorial Operations	Caroline A. Boubin
Production	Celia Beattie
Quality Control	James J. Cox (director)
Library	Louise D. Forstall
Correspondents	Elisabeth Kraemer-Singh (Bonn); Maria Vincenza Aloisi (Paris); Ann Natanson (Rome).

THE CONSULTANTS

Consulting Editor **David L. Harrison** is Managing Editor of Bibliographics Inc. in Alexandria, Virginia. He served as an editor of several Time-Life Books do-it-yourself series, including *Home Repair and Improvement, The Encyclopedia of Gardening* and *The Art of Sewing.*

Ron Straight has lived in and worked on century-old houses for most of his life and is, of necessity, an avid do-it-yourselfer. Most recently he has completely renovated an 1887 row house in Washington, D.C. In the process, he encountered and overcame nearly every problem described in this volume.

Evan Powell is the Director of Chestnut Mountain Research Inc. in Taylors, South Carolina, a firm that specializes in the development and evaluation of home equipment and building products. He is contributing editor to several do-it-yourself magazines, and the author of two books on home repair.

Stan Warshaw, founder of the United States School of Professional Paperhanging in Rutland, Vermont, has taught wallcovering installation and repair for 14 years, and has been a professional wallcovering contractor for 33 years. He is the author of three books and many articles on wallcovering installation.

Allen Williams, special consultant for Canada, is co-owner of Williams Plastering Inc. in Montreal, Quebec. Williams has been a professional plasterer for 40 years. He has plastered hundreds of new homes, offices and stores and has repaired plaster in more than 1,000 homes.

Library of Congress Cataloguing in Publication Data
Walls, ceilings & woodwork.
  (Fix it yourself)
  Includes index.
  1. Interior walls. 2. Ceilings. 3. Woodwork.
4. Dwellings– Remodeling. I. Time-Life Books.
II. Title: Walls, ceilings & woodwork. III. Series.
TH2239.W36 1987   643'.7   87-10149
ISBN 0-8094-6212-5
ISBN 0-8094-6213-3   (lib. bdg.)

For information about any Time-Life book,
please write:
Reader Information
541 North Fairbanks Court
Chicago, Illinois 60611

CONTENTS

HOW TO USE THIS BOOK

Walls, Ceilings & Woodwork is divided into three sections. The Emergency Guide on pages 8-11 provides information on how to cope with fire or flood damage, as well as safety tips. Take the time to study this section before you need the important advice it contains.

The Repairs section—the heart of the book—is more than a collection of how-to tips and techniques. It is a system for troubleshooting and repairing plaster, drywall, tile, paint and varnish, wallcoverings, wood trim and panels, and special surfaces. Pictured below are four sample pages from the chapter on drywall, with captions describing the various features of the book and how they work. If you have a hairline crack in your drywall, for example, the Troubleshooting Guide will offer a number of possible causes, ranging from shrinkage of the joint tape to shifting of the drywall panel. It will then direct you to page 19 for detailed, step-by-step repair instructions.

Each job has been rated by degree of difficulty and the average time it will take for a do-it-yourselfer to complete. Keep in mind that this rating is only a suggestion. Before deciding whether you should attempt a repair, first read all the instructions carefully. Then be guided by your own confidence, and the tools and time available to you. For more complex or time-

Introductory text
Describes the construction of walls, ceilings and woodwork, most common problems and basic repair materials.

Cross-references
Direct you to important information elsewhere in the book, including general finishing techniques and wall anatomies.

Tools
All the tools required for repairs in this chapter are pictured here. Other tools are described in the Tools & Techniques section *(page 132)*.

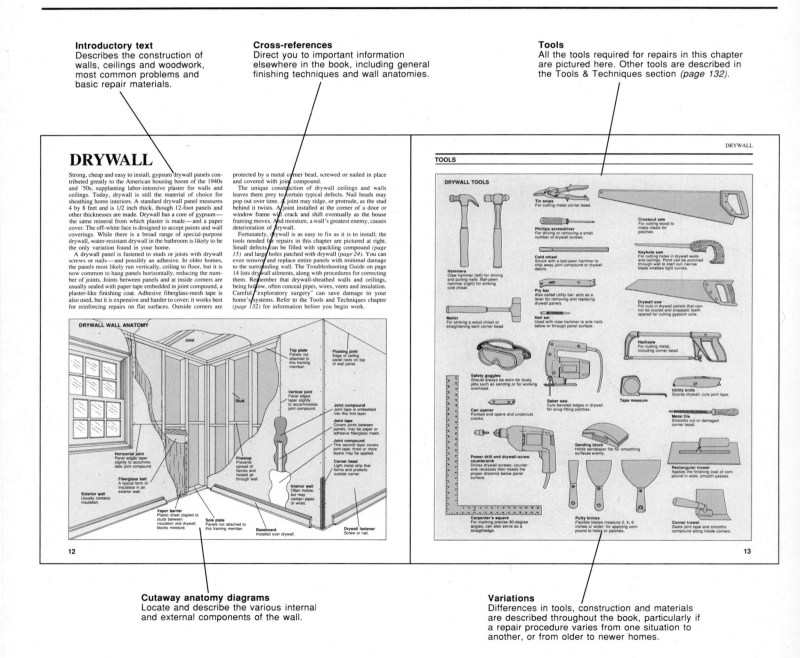

Cutaway anatomy diagrams
Locate and describe the various internal and external components of the wall.

Variations
Differences in tools, construction and materials are described throughout the book, particularly if a repair procedure varies from one situation to another, or from older to newer homes.

consuming repairs, such as replacing an entire wall, you may wish to call for professional service. You will still have saved time and money by diagnosing the problem yourself.

Most of the repairs in *Walls, Ceilings & Woodwork* can be made with simple tools such as putty knives and paintbrushes, along with basic patching materials such as spackling compound. The tools you will need for a specific job are presented in each chapter. General techniques for using ladders and protecting the work area are presented in the Tools & Techniques section starting on page 132. If you are a novice when it comes to home repairs, read this section in preparation for a major job.

Home repair can lead to serious injury unless you take certain basic precautions. Wear safety goggles when working on a ceiling or when cutting wood, ceramic tiles or fiberglass insulation. For dusty work such as sanding, also wear a dust mask or respirator. Rubber gloves will protect your hands from caustic chemicals such as paint stripper; heavy work gloves will prevent cuts and scratches. If you must remove an electrical fixture, turn off power by removing the fuse or tripping the circuit breaker at the main service panel *(p. 137)*. Most important, follow all safety tips in the Emergency Guide and throughout the book.

Troubleshooting Guide
To use this chart, locate the symptom that most closely resembles your wall, ceiling or woodwork problem, review the possible causes in column 2, then follow the recommended procedure in column 3. Simple fixes may be explained on the chart; in most cases you will be directed to an illustrated, step-by-step repair sequence.

Name of repair
You will be referred by the Troubleshooting Guide to the first page of a specific repair job.

Step-by-step procedures
Follow the numbered repair sequence carefully. Depending on the result of each step, you may be directed to a later step, or to another part of the book, to complete the repair.

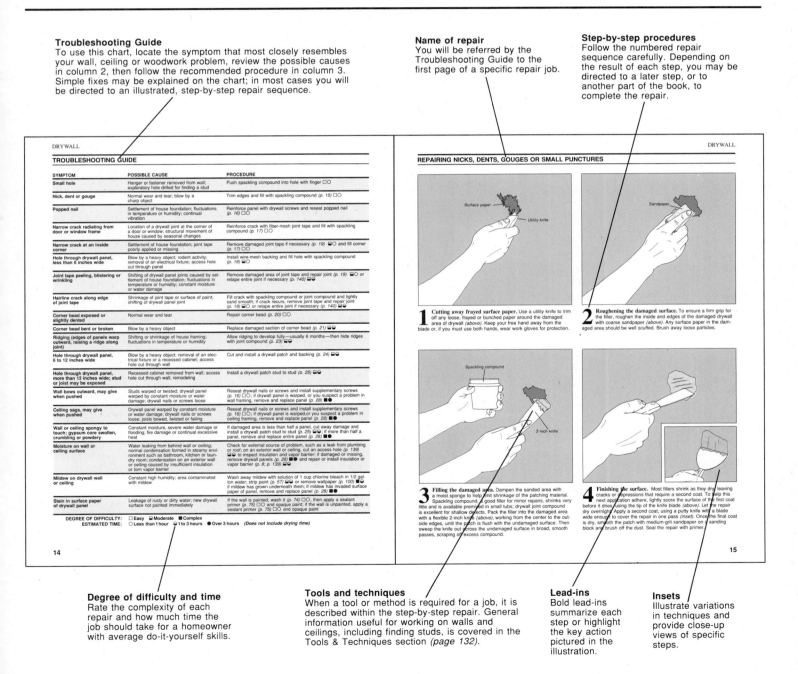

Degree of difficulty and time
Rate the complexity of each repair and how much time the job should take for a homeowner with average do-it-yourself skills.

Tools and techniques
When a tool or method is required for a job, it is described within the step-by-step repair. General information useful for working on walls and ceilings, including finding studs, is covered in the Tools & Techniques section *(page 132)*.

Lead-ins
Bold lead-ins summarize each step or highlight the key action pictured in the illustration.

Insets
Illustrate variations in techniques and provide close-up views of specific steps.

EMERGENCY GUIDE

Preventing problems with walls, ceilings and woodwork.
Your home's walls, ceilings and woodwork seem the most benign of its components. But the household systems they conceal, such as electrical wiring and plumbing, can damage them or injure you. In addition, many of the patching compounds, adhesives, paints and solvents used in making routine repairs can be hazardous to your health.

Wall and ceiling damage often points to more basic problems affecting your home. A broken pipe, a leaky roof or failing joists may first be revealed by defects in a wall or ceiling. When confronted with major or recurring damage to a wall or ceiling, find and correct the root cause before beginning repair; call a professional if necessary.

Do not break through a wall or ceiling without forethought. First, turn off power to the circuit or the entire house *(page 9)*; in the case of a plumbing leak, turn off the local water shutoff valves or the house's main shutoff valve *(page 9)*.

The list of safety tips at right covers guidelines for performing for the repairs in this book; refer to each chapter for more specific safety information. Keep a fire extinguisher nearby *(page 11)* if using solvents. The box below contains information about the use and repair of hazardous materials.

The Troubleshooting Guide on page 9 puts emergency procedures at your fingertips, and refers you to pages 9 through 11 for quick-action steps to take. Read these instructions before you need them, and consult the Tools and Techniques section *(page 132)*, which locates and describes the systems hidden within your walls.

When in doubt about your ability to handle an emergency, don't hesitate to call for help. Post numbers for the fire department, the water, gas and power companies and the poison control center near the telephone. Even in non-emergency situations, they can answer questions concerning the proper use of repair materials and household utilities.

HAZARDOUS MATERIALS IN THE HOME

Until the 1960s, lead was a major ingredient of wall and trim paints. Lead paint is dangerous only if chips of it are eaten, or if dust from sanding or fumes from heat-stripping are inhaled. See page 79 for information on identifying and removing lead paint.

Asbestos was outlawed as a building material in the 1970s. Before that time, it was an ingredient in fireproof ceiling coatings, textured paints, ceiling tiles and some spackling and joint compounds. Asbestos is safe unless it is damaged, cut or flaking, releasing asbestos fibers into the air. If you suspect that asbestos forms part of a damaged wall or ceiling, call in a specialist.

Formaldehyde insulation has been removed from most homes and it is no longer installed, but formaldehyde is still used as a binder in composite-fiber boards used to make wall panels. It is safe to handle and cut a panel. The main hazard is a leaching of formaldehyde into the air called "outgassing," but sealing unfinished wall panels with paint or polyurethane varnish will prevent it.

Toxic solvents used in painting and stripping include petroleum distillates, acetone, methanol and methylene chloride, a potent carcinogen. Do not use these chemicals indoors unless you open all windows in the room and aim a fan outside to vent toxic fumes. Tape sheets of plastic over doorways to prevent fumes from reaching other rooms in the house.

SAFETY TIPS

1. Before attempting any repair in this book, read the entire repair procedure. Familiarize yourself with the specific safety information presented in each chapter.

2. Carefully read the label on any paint, solvent, patching compound, adhesive or other material used to make a repair. Follow the manufacturer's instructions to the letter, and pay special attention to hazard warnings and storage instructions.

3. Label your electrical service panel with the locations of the circuit breakers or fuses that control wall outlets and ceiling fixtures, as well as the main power shutoff.

4. Before removing electrical outlets or fixtures, switch off power at the service panel *(p. 9)*. Leave a note on the panel so that no one switches a circuit back on while you are working.

5. Locate and label the house's main water shutoff valve *(p. 9)*, as well as the water shutoff valves for household appliances and plumbing fixtures.

6. Before cutting into a wall or ceiling, make careful exploratory holes to determine whether hidden electrical wires, pipes or insulation are in the way, and work around them.

7. Guard against electrical shock when using power tools. Plug power tools into grounded outlets only, and never cut off or bypass the third, or grounding, prong on a power tool's plug. A tool with a two-prong plug must be labeled "double insulated." Do not use any power tool in a damp area.

8. Wear long pants and a long-sleeved shirt when doing dusty repairs or when working with chemicals or fibers that are dangerous to the skin. Change after leaving the work area, and launder work clothes separately.

9. Wear the proper protective gear for the job: safety goggles when working overhead, operating a power saw, or doing dusty work; heavy work gloves to handle sharp metal, fiberglass or building materials; heavy rubber gloves when applying chemical strippers, solvents and cleaning solutions. Wear a hard hat when removing a large section of a ceiling.

10. Wear a dust mask or respirator when doing jobs that generate sawdust, plaster dust, mineral or glass fibers, or toxic fumes. Choose a respirator filter specially made to block the particles or vapors being produced. Replace filters according to the manufacturer's instructions.

11. Ventilate the work area well when using paints, solvents, adhesives, strong cleaners, chemical strippers and heat guns. Do not smoke while using flammable chemicals.

12. Do not drink alcoholic beverages while using paints, solvents, strippers or adhesives that produce fumes—the combination can cause illness. If you feel faint or sick, leave the room and get fresh air, then improve ventilation before continuing work.

13. Keep children and pets away from the work site. When you finish work for the day, store chemicals, tools and building materials out of their reach. If children or pets contact or ingest chemicals, call the Poison Control Center or veterinarian immediately.

14. Allow rags soaked in paint, solvent or adhesive to dry thoroughly outdoors, then dispose of them outdoors in a ventilated box or trash bag.

15. Do not pour paints, solvents, strippers, adhesives or patching compounds down a house drain or into a septic system.

16. When working with flammable chemicals or power tools, have on hand a fire extinguisher rated ABC or BC, and know how to use it before you begin work *(p. 11)*. Install smoke detectors in your home.

17. Post emergency, utility company and repair service numbers near the telephone.

TROUBLESHOOTING GUIDE

SYMPTOM	PROCEDURE
Water leaking from ceiling; soggy bulge in ceiling	Shut off valve to fixture causing leak, or close main shutoff valve *(p. 9)*
	Turn off power to affected circuit *(p. 137)* or to entire house *(p. 9)*
	Pierce ceiling to release trapped water *(p. 11)*
	Repair source of leak, let ceiling dry, and patch holes in ceiling *(drywall, p. 12; plaster, p. 30)*
Wall damaged by water	Turn off power to affected circuit *(p. 137)* or to entire house *(p. 9)*
	If wall is hollow, cut ventilation holes to dry wall *(p. 10)*
	If wall contains insulation, break out water-damaged area and cut away wet insulation *(p. 10)*
	Repair source of water leak, let wall dry, and patch wall *(drywall, p. 12; plaster, p. 30)*
Paint or solvent on fire	Use fire extinguisher rated for class B fires *(p. 11)*
	If fire spreads, leave house and call fire department
Walls and ceilings damaged by smoke	Wash with solution of trisodium phosphate and water and clean rags *(p. 11)*
Wet paint spilled on floor	If a small amount of paint is spilled, wipe floor immediately with a rag moistened with water (latex paint) or the appropriate solvent (oil-base paint)
	If a large amount is spilled, scoop it into a dustpan with a putty knife; wipe floor as above
	Clean paint out of crevices with a toothbrush moistened with water or the appropriate solvent
Dried paint on floor	Scrape off paint with a putty knife or razor blade, taking care not to mar the floor
	Rub off remaining paint flecks with fine steel wool moistened with turpentine; carefully use a pointed implement to scrape paint out of crevices
	Wipe floor with a rag moistened with turpentine; wash floor with a mild detergent-and-water solution
Dizziness, nausea, blurred vision when working with paint, solvent or cleaner	Leave room immediately to get fresh air; have someone else cover solvents and ventilate room
	Read instructions on container label and consult a physician if necessary
Paint, solvent or cleaner swallowed	Call local poison center, emergency room or physician immediately
	Follow emergency instructions on the container label; bring the container with you to the hospital
	If the container is not available or has no label, do not induce vomiting

TURNING OFF ELECTRICITY AND WATER

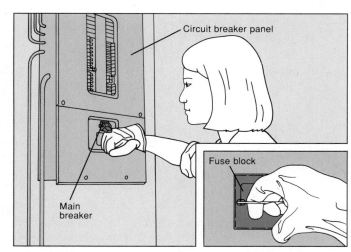

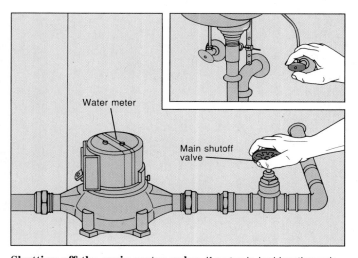

Disconnecting electrical power at the service panel. Stand on a dry board if the floor is wet. Wearing a heavy, dry glove, use the back of one hand to flip off the main breaker *(above)*; any shock will jerk your hand away from the panel. Pull out a main fuse block by gripping its metal handle *(inset)*. If the service panel has a shutoff lever, shift it to the OFF position.

Shutting off the main water valve. If water is leaking through the wall or ceiling from a plumbing fixture, close its shutoff valve *(inset)*. If water is leaking from an undetermined source, turn off the house water supply at the main shutoff valve *(above)*, usually located near the water meter or where the main water supply pipe enters the house.

VENTILATING A WATER-DAMAGED WALL

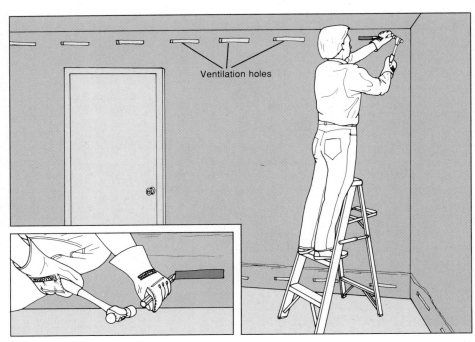

Ventilation holes

Opening the wall for ventilation. If a section of drywall has been damaged by moisture, cut vents through the top and bottom of the wall to allow air circulation behind it. Turn off power at the service panel *(page 9)*. Remove the baseboard *(page 58)* and locate the studs *(page 136)*. Cut a 1-by-6-inch hole 3 inches from the floor between each pair of studs; if a utility knife doesn't cut the drywall easily, use a cold chisel and ball-peen hammer *(inset)*. Stand on a stepladder and cut similar holes 4 to 6 inches from the ceiling *(left)*. To speed drying, open windows in the room and turn on fans, or use a dehumidifier and portable electric heaters. Determine whether the wall is dry by drilling small holes through it at several locations—the drywall dust should be chalky and powdery. After the source of the leak is repaired and the wall has dried completely (this may take several weeks), patch the drywall *(page 12)*.

REMOVING SODDEN DRYWALL AND INSULATION

Scored line
Insulation

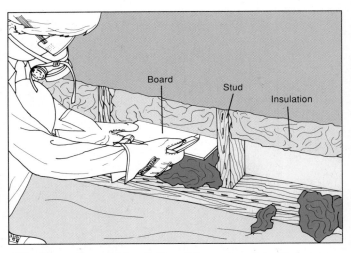

Board
Stud
Insulation

1 **Breaking away damaged drywall.** Turn off power at the service panel *(page 9)*. Pry off the baseboard *(page 58)* and protect the floor with a drop cloth. Using a utility knife and straightedge, score the wall horizontally about 4 inches above the water-damaged area. Break out the damaged drywall with a mallet *(above)*. If the wall doesn't contain insulation, clean out water and dirt in the wall cavity and allow it to dry completely as in the step above, then patch the drywall *(page 12)*. To remove wet insulation, go to step 2.

2 **Removing wet insulation.** If the wall contains fiberglass insulation, wear a respirator, work gloves, long sleeves and safety goggles. Cut away the plastic, foil or paper vapor barrier 3 inches below the drywall edge—the new vapor barrier will overlap it. Compress each batt of insulation with a board, slice through it with a utility knife *(above)* and discard it in a plastic garbage bag. Cut away plastic foam insulation the same way. When the wall is dry *(step above)*, cut and install new insulation *(page 139)*, then patch the drywall *(page 12)*.

PIERCING A WATER-LADEN CEILING

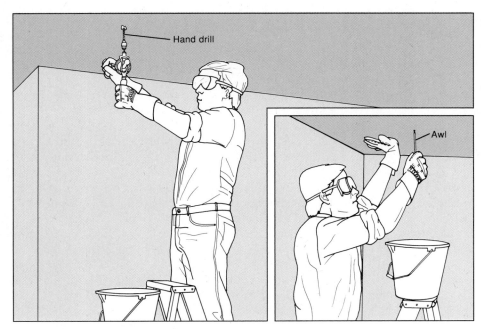

Puncturing a ceiling. Turn off the power *(page 9)*; if water is flowing from a leaking pipe, also close the main shutoff valve *(page 9)*. Wear safety goggles and position a stepladder under the wet ceiling with a bucket on it to catch drips. To release water collected above a drywall ceiling, puncture it with an awl or an ice pick *(inset)*; twist the tool to enlarge the hole. Pierce a plaster ceiling with a battery-operated drill, or a hand drill with a 3/8-inch bit *(left)*. **Caution:** To avoid the risk of electric shock, do not use a power drill. Make more than one hole if necessary to release all the water. Dry the ceiling as described on page 10, and patch the holes *(drywall, page 12; plaster, page 30)*.

DEALING WITH FIRE AND SMOKE

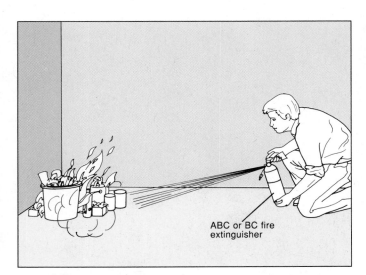

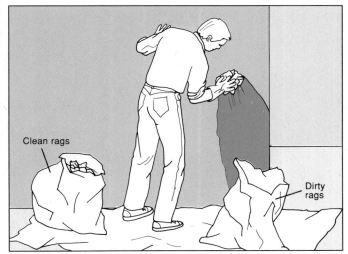

Extinguishing a fire. First have someone call the fire department. If flames or smoke come from the walls or ceiling, leave the house to call for help. To snuff a small fire in paints, solvents or trash, use a dry-chemical fire extinguisher rated ABC or BC. Stand near an exit, 6 to 10 feet from the fire. Holding the extinguisher upright, pull the lock pin out of the handle and aim the nozzle at the base of the flames. Squeeze the handle and spray in a quick side-to-side motion *(above)* until the fire is completely out. Watch for "flashback," or rekindling. If the fire spreads, leave the house.

Washing a smoke-damaged wall. Get a large bag of clean, absorbent cotton rags, which can be purchased in bulk from a textile company (look in the yellow pages under "wiping cloths"). Wearing rubber gloves, soak the rags in a solution of trisodium phosphate and warm water, mixed according to label directions. Wring the rags gently and place them in a large plastic bag. Using one rag at a time, wash the wall from the bottom up in small sections *(above)*, discarding each rag in a second trash bag as it picks up soot. When the wall is clean, rinse and dry it.

DRYWALL

Strong, cheap and easy to install, gypsum drywall panels contributed greatly to the American housing boom of the 1940s and '50s, supplanting labor-intensive plaster for walls and ceilings. Today, drywall is still the material of choice for sheathing home interiors. A standard drywall panel measures 4 by 8 feet and is 1/2 inch thick, though 12-foot panels and other thicknesses are made. Drywall has a core of gypsum—the same mineral from which plaster is made—and a paper cover. The off-white face is designed to accept paints and wall coverings. While there is a broad range of special-purpose drywall, water-resistant drywall in the bathroom is likely to be the only variation found in your home.

A drywall panel is fastened to studs or joists with drywall screws or nails—and possibly an adhesive. In older homes, the panels most likely run vertically, ceiling to floor, but it is now common to hang panels horizontally, reducing the number of joints. Joints between panels and at inside corners are usually sealed with paper tape embedded in joint compound, a plaster-like finishing coat. Adhesive fiberglass-mesh tape is also used, but it is expensive and harder to cover; it works best for reinforcing repairs on flat surfaces. Outside corners are protected by a metal corner bead, screwed or nailed in place and covered with joint compound.

The unique construction of drywall ceilings and walls leaves them prey to certain typical defects. Nail heads may pop out over time. A joint may ridge, or protrude, as the stud behind it twists. A joint installed at the corner of a door or window frame will crack and shift eventually as the house framing moves. And moisture, a wall's greatest enemy, causes deterioration of drywall.

Fortunately, drywall is as easy to fix as it is to install; the tools needed for repairs in this chapter are pictured at right. Small defects can be filled with spackling compound *(page 15)* and large holes patched with drywall *(page 24)*. You can even remove and replace entire panels with minimal damage to the surrounding wall. The Troubleshooting Guide on page 14 lists drywall ailments, along with procedures for correcting them. Remember that drywall-sheathed walls and ceilings, being hollow, often conceal pipes, wires, vents and insulation. Careful "exploratory surgery" can save damage to your home's systems. Refer to the Tools and Techniques chapter *(page 132)* for information before you begin work.

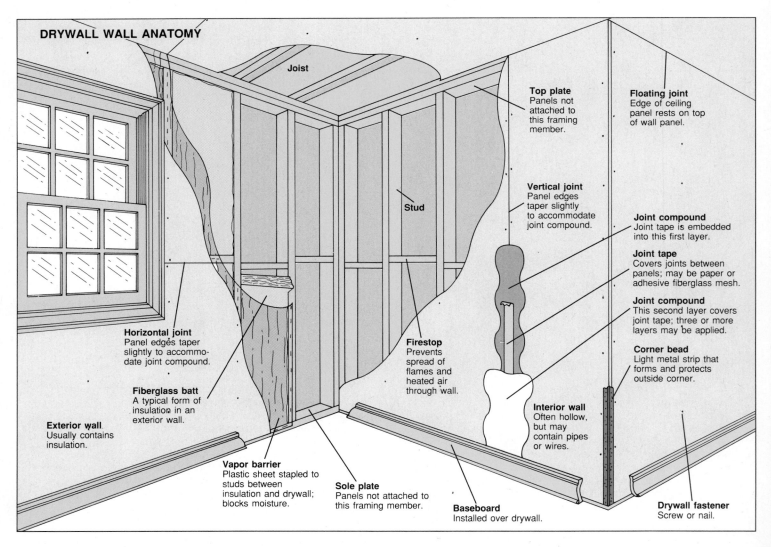

DRYWALL WALL ANATOMY

Joist

Top plate
Panels not attached to this framing member.

Floating joint
Edge of ceiling panel rests on top of wall panel.

Vertical joint
Panel edges taper slightly to accommodate joint compound.

Stud

Joint compound
Joint tape is embedded into this first layer.

Joint tape
Covers joints between panels; may be paper or adhesive fiberglass mesh.

Joint compound
This second layer covers joint tape; three or more layers may be applied.

Horizontal joint
Panel edges taper slightly to accommodate joint compound.

Firestop
Prevents spread of flames and heated air through wall.

Corner bead
Light metal strip that forms and protects outside corner.

Fiberglass batt
A typical form of insulation in an exterior wall.

Interior wall
Often hollow, but may contain pipes or wires.

Exterior wall
Usually contains insulation.

Vapor barrier
Plastic sheet stapled to studs between insulation and drywall; blocks moisture.

Sole plate
Panels not attached to this framing member.

Baseboard
Installed over drywall.

Drywall fastener
Screw or nail.

TOOLS

DRYWALL TOOLS

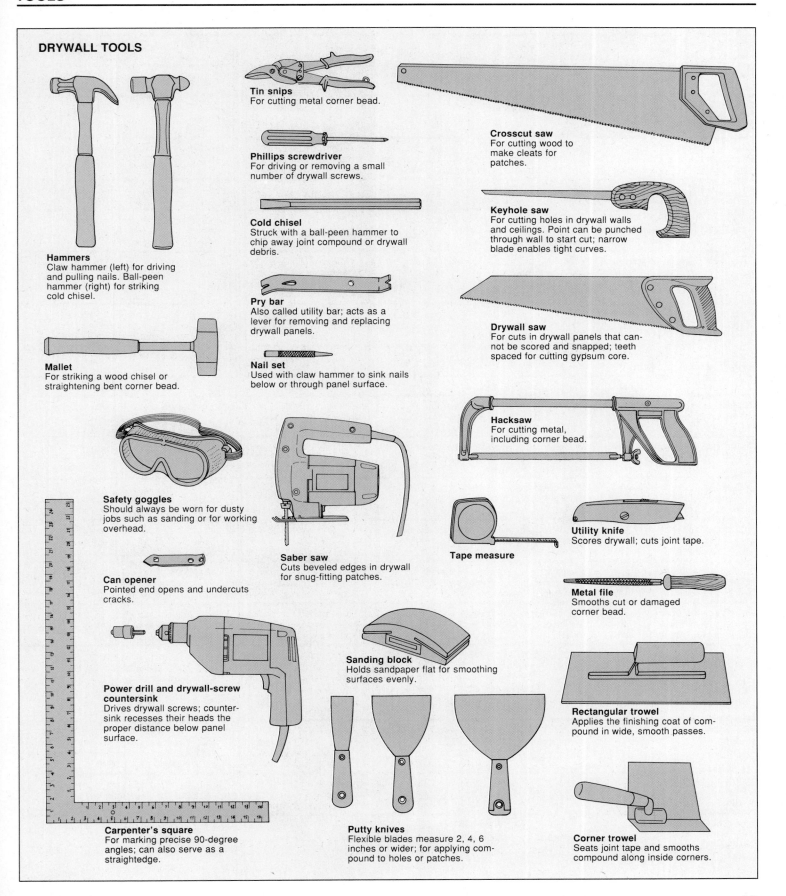

Hammers
Claw hammer (left) for driving and pulling nails. Ball-peen hammer (right) for striking cold chisel.

Mallet
For striking a wood chisel or straightening bent corner bead.

Safety goggles
Should always be worn for dusty jobs such as sanding or for working overhead.

Can opener
Pointed end opens and undercuts cracks.

Power drill and drywall-screw countersink
Drives drywall screws; countersink recesses their heads the proper distance below panel surface.

Carpenter's square
For marking precise 90-degree angles; can also serve as a straightedge.

Tin snips
For cutting metal corner bead.

Phillips screwdriver
For driving or removing a small number of drywall screws.

Cold chisel
Struck with a ball-peen hammer to chip away joint compound or drywall debris.

Pry bar
Also called utility bar; acts as a lever for removing and replacing drywall panels.

Nail set
Used with claw hammer to sink nails below or through panel surface.

Saber saw
Cuts beveled edges in drywall for snug-fitting patches.

Sanding block
Holds sandpaper flat for smoothing surfaces evenly.

Putty knives
Flexible blades measure 2, 4, 6 inches or wider; for applying compound to holes or patches.

Crosscut saw
For cutting wood to make cleats for patches.

Keyhole saw
For cutting holes in drywall walls and ceilings. Point can be punched through wall to start cut; narrow blade enables tight curves.

Drywall saw
For cuts in drywall panels that cannot be scored and snapped; teeth spaced for cutting gypsum core.

Hacksaw
For cutting metal, including corner bead.

Tape measure

Utility knife
Scores drywall; cuts joint tape.

Metal file
Smooths cut or damaged corner bead.

Rectangular trowel
Applies the finishing coat of compound in wide, smooth passes.

Corner trowel
Seats joint tape and smooths compound along inside corners.

TROUBLESHOOTING GUIDE

SYMPTOM	POSSIBLE CAUSE	PROCEDURE
Small hole	Hanger or fastener removed from wall; exploratory hole drilled for finding a stud	Push spackling compound into hole with finger □○
Nick, dent or gouge	Normal wear and tear; blow by a sharp object	Trim edges and fill with spackling compound (p. 15) □○
Popped nail	Settlement of house foundation; fluctuations in temperature or humidity; continual vibration	Reinforce panel with drywall screws and reseat popped nail (p. 16) □○
Narrow crack radiating from door or window frame	Location of a drywall joint at the corner of a door or window; structural movement of house caused by seasonal changes	Reinforce crack with fiber-mesh joint tape and fill with spackling compound (p. 17) □○
Narrow crack at an inside corner	Settlement of house foundation; joint tape poorly applied or missing	Remove damaged joint tape if necessary (p. 19) ▣○ and fill corner (p. 17) □○
Hole through drywall panel, less than 6 inches wide	Blow by a heavy object; rodent activity; removal of an electrical fixture; access hole cut through panel	Install wire-mesh backing and fill hole with spackling compound (p. 18) ▣○
Joint tape peeling, blistering or wrinkling	Shifting of drywall panel joints caused by settlement of house foundation; fluctuations in temperature or humidity; constant moisture or water damage	Remove damaged area of joint tape and repair joint (p. 19) ▣○ or retape entire joint if necessary (p. 140) ▣◗
Hairline crack along edge of joint tape	Shrinkage of joint tape or surface of paint; shifting of drywall panel joint	Fill crack with spackling compound or joint compound and lightly sand smooth; if crack recurs, remove joint tape and repair joint (p. 19) ▣○ or retape entire joint if necessary (p. 140) ▣◗
Corner bead exposed or slightly dented	Normal wear and tear	Repair corner bead (p. 20) □○
Corner bead bent or broken	Blow by a heavy object	Replace damaged section of corner bead (p. 21) ▣◗
Ridging (edges of panels warp outward, raising a ridge along joint)	Shifting or shrinkage of house framing; fluctuations in temperature or humidity	Allow ridging to develop fully—usually 6 months—then hide ridges with joint compound (p. 23) ▣◗
Hole through drywall panel, 6 to 12 inches wide	Blow by a heavy object; removal of an electrical fixture or a recessed cabinet; access hole cut through wall	Cut and install a drywall patch and backing (p. 24) ▣◗
Hole through drywall panel, more than 12 inches wide; stud or joist may be exposed	Recessed cabinet removed from wall; access hole cut through wall; remodeling	Install a drywall patch stud to stud (p. 25) ▣◗
Wall bows outward, may give when pushed	Studs warped or twisted; drywall panel warped by constant moisture or water damage; drywall nails or screws loose	Reseat drywall nails or screws and install supplementary screws (p. 16) □○; if drywall panel is warped, or you suspect a problem in wall framing, remove and replace panel (p. 28) ■◗
Ceiling sags, may give when pushed	Drywall panel warped by constant moisture or water damage; drywall nails or screws loose; joists bowed, twisted or failing	Reseat drywall nails or screws and install supplementary screws (p. 16) □○; if drywall panel is warped, or you suspect a problem in ceiling framing, remove and replace panel (p. 28) ■◗
Wall or ceiling spongy to touch; gypsum core swollen, crumbling or powdery	Constant moisture, severe water damage or flooding; fire damage or continual excessive heat	If damaged area is less than half a panel, cut away damage and install a drywall patch stud to stud (p. 25) ▣◗; if more than half a panel, remove and replace entire panel (p. 28) ■◗
Moisture on wall or ceiling surface	Water leaking from behind wall or ceiling; normal condensation formed in steamy environment such as bathroom, kitchen or laundry room; condensation on an exterior wall or ceiling caused by insufficient insulation or torn vapor barrier	Check for external source of problem, such as a leak from plumbing or roof; on an exterior wall or ceiling, cut an access hole (p. 139) ▣◗ to inspect insulation and vapor barrier; if damaged or missing, remove drywall panels (p. 28) ■◗ and repair or install insulation or vapor barrier (p. 8; p. 139) ▣◗
Mildew on drywall wall or ceiling	Constant high humidity; area contaminated with mildew	Wash away mildew with solution of 1 cup chlorine bleach in 1/2 gallon water; strip paint (p. 57) ▣◗ or remove wallpaper (p. 100) ■◗ if mildew has grown underneath them; if mildew has invaded surface paper of panel, remove and replace panel (p. 28) ■◗
Stain in surface paper of drywall panel	Leakage of rusty or dirty water; new drywall surface not painted immediately	If the wall is painted, wash it (p. 74) □○, then apply a sealant primer (p. 75) □○ and opaque paint; if the wall is unpainted, apply a sealant primer (p. 75) □○ and opaque paint

DEGREE OF DIFFICULTY: □ Easy ▣ Moderate ■ Complex

ESTIMATED TIME: ○ Less than 1 hour ◗ 1 to 3 hours ● Over 3 hours *(Does not include drying time)*

REPAIRING NICKS, DENTS, GOUGES OR SMALL PUNCTURES

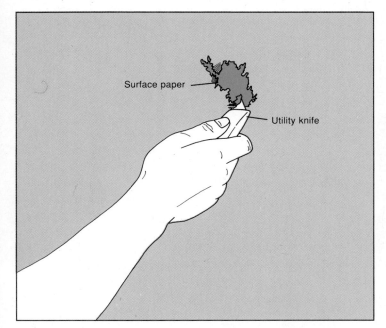

1 **Cutting away frayed surface paper.** Use a utility knife to trim off any loose, frayed or bunched paper around the damaged area of drywall *(above)*. Keep your free hand away from the blade or, if you must use both hands, wear work gloves for protection.

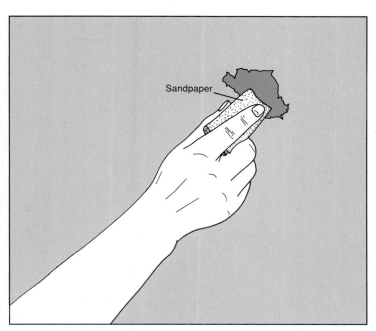

2 **Roughening the damaged surface.** To ensure a firm grip for the filler, roughen the inside and edges of the damaged drywall with coarse sandpaper *(above)*. Any surface paper in the damaged area should be well scuffed. Brush away loose particles.

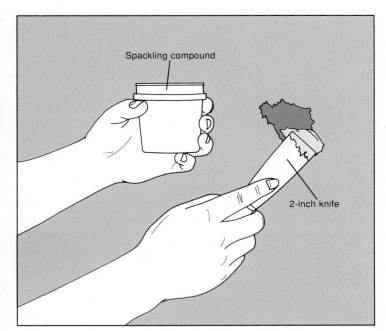

3 **Filling the damaged area.** Dampen the sanded area with a moist sponge to help limit shrinkage of the patching material. Spackling compound, a good filler for minor repairs, shrinks very little and is available premixed in small tubs; drywall joint compound is excellent for shallow defects. Pack the filler into the damaged area with a flexible 2-inch knife *(above)*, working from the center to the outside edges, until the patch is flush with the undamaged surface. Then sweep the knife out across the undamaged surface in broad, smooth passes, scraping off excess compound.

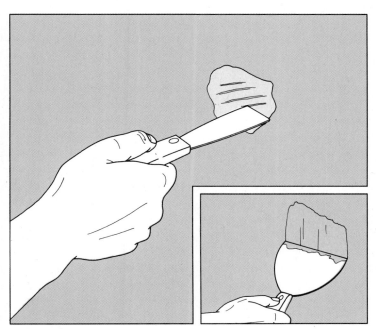

4 **Finishing the surface.** Most fillers shrink as they dry, leaving cracks or depressions that require a second coat. To help this next application adhere, lightly score the surface of the first coat before it dries, using the tip of the knife blade *(above)*. Let the repair dry overnight. Apply a second coat, using a putty knife with a blade wide enough to cover the repair in one pass *(inset)*. Once the final coat is dry, smooth the patch with medium-grit sandpaper on a sanding block and brush off the dust. Seal the repair with primer.

RESEATING POPPED NAILS

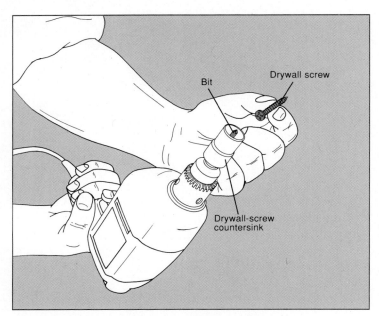

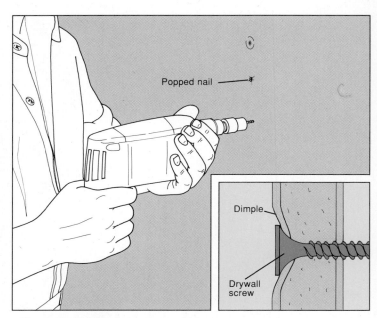

1 **Loading a drywall-screw countersink on a power drill.**
Over time, the head of a drywall nail may pop through the wall surface; install drywall screws to support the area around the popped nail. The screws may be driven by hand with a Phillips screwdriver, but a drywall-screw countersink fitted to a power drill is faster and neater. Load the countersink into the drill chuck like a normal drill bit, making sure that it is centered and held securely. Seat the head of a drywall screw on the magnetic head of the bit *(above)*.

2 **Driving screws into the drywall.** If the popped nail is in a joist, determine the direction in which it runs *(page 136)*; a stud, shown here, is always vertical. Put a drywall screw on the countersink bit and push the screw tip straight into the drywall about 2 inches above, then below, the popped nail *(above)*. Put pressure on the drill as you squeeze the trigger, guiding the countersink with one hand until the drill starts. Stop the drill when the countersink hits the wall and the bit starts chattering, indicating that the screw head is countersunk—or dimpled—below the drywall surface *(inset)*.

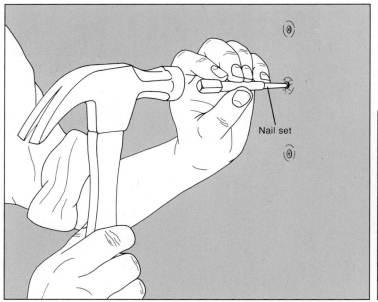

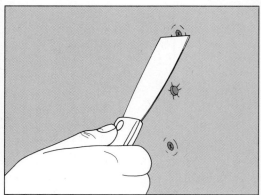

3 **Hiding the popped nail.** If the head of the popped nail protrudes far enough, you may pull it out with pliers and replace it with a drywall screw; however, taking out the nail can damage the drywall. In most cases, a better option is to drive the popped nail back in using a nail set and hammer *(above, left)*, sinking the nail about 1/16 inch below the drywall surface to prevent it from popping again. To check that the nail and screw heads are countersunk properly, run the blade of a putty knife over them *(above, right)*; a clicking sound indicates that they need to be driven in farther. Cover the nail and the screws with joint compound *(page 15)*.

REPAIRING CRACKS

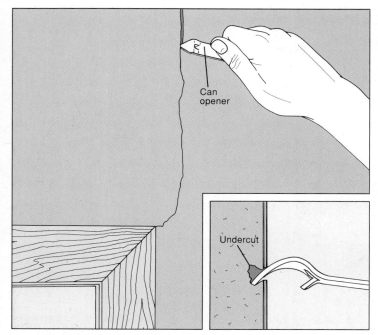

1 Preparing the crack. Slice away any frayed surface paper along the edges of the crack with a utility knife. Although it is claimed to be unnecessary for vinyl-based spackling compounds, ensure a secure hold for the repair by using the pointed end of a can opener to scrape along the crack *(above)*, deepening it slightly and undercutting the edges *(inset)*. Brush out loose particles and, to give hairline cracks an even firmer grip, brush in cut shellac.

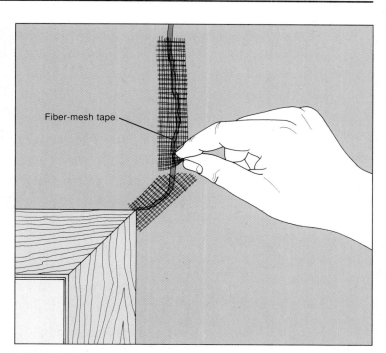

2 Taping the crack. If the crack opens and closes, or is more than 1/4 inch wide, taping it adds support to the repair. Paper tape may be used *(page 19)*, especially at inside corners, but adhesive fiber-mesh tape is stronger and more flexible. Use scissors to cut a strip of tape to cover the entire crack. If the crack zigzags like the one shown here, cut a separate strip for each segment. Press each strip firmly over the crack without overlapping their ends *(above)*.

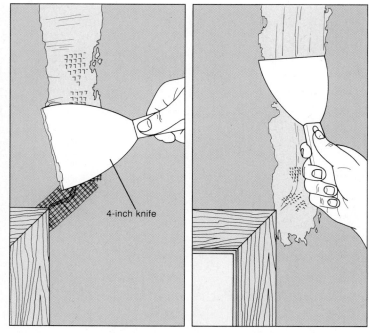

3 Filling the crack. To limit shrinkage of the compound to be used as filler, dampen the inside edges of the crack with water from a spray bottle. Drawing a flexible 4-inch knife across the crack *(above, left)* and then along it *(above, right)*, pack in spackling or joint compound, squeezing it through the mesh until the crack is filled and the surface is flush with the wall. Scrape off excess compound and let the patch dry 24 hours.

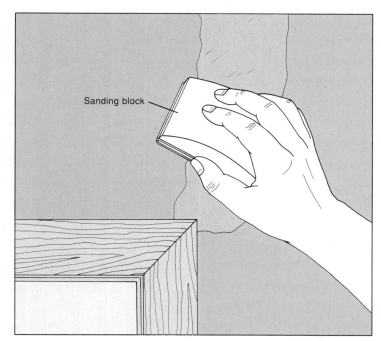

4 Smoothing the patch. Smooth the surface with medium-grit sandpaper on a sanding block, but don't sand into the tape. Brush away loose particles, dampen the patch and apply a thin layer of compound, feathering the edges about 3 or 4 inches *(page 140)*. Let the patch dry 24 hours and, if necessary, repeat this step. Once the final layer of compound is dry, sand again. Brush away dust and seal the patch with primer.

FIXING SMALL HOLES

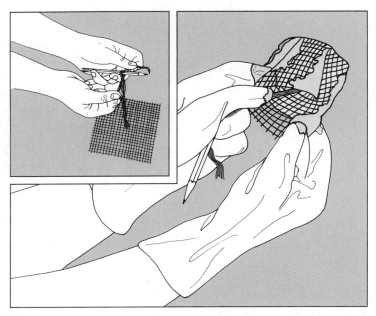

1 **Installing a backing.** Pull out loose pieces of drywall and cut away torn surface paper with a utility knife *(page 15)*. Roughen the edges of the hole with coarse sandpaper and brush away the dust. Using 1/4-inch wire mesh or heavy window screening, cut a backing about 2 inches larger than the hole. Loop a string through the center of the mesh and knot a pencil to the other end, 4 to 6 inches away *(inset)*. Wearing rubber gloves, coat the edges of the mesh backing with spackling or joint compound, roll the backing and work it into the hole, maintaining a grip on the pencil *(above)*.

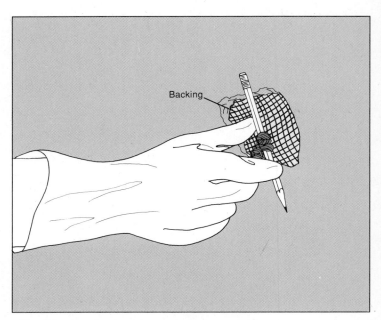

2 **Bracing the backing.** Holding the pencil to keep from losing the backing, reach into the hole to dampen the edges of the drywall with water, and then coat them with compound. Tug on the string to pull the backing flat against the hole, forcing compound through the mesh to secure it. Wrap the string around the pencil to take up the slack, then twist the pencil against the wall to brace the backing firmly in place *(above)*, taking care not to pull it out through the hole.

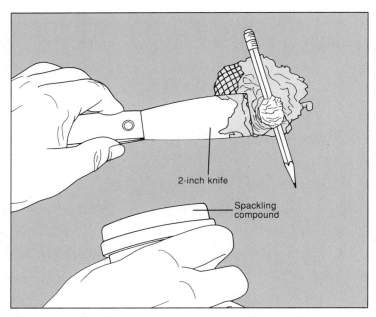

3 **Applying the first coat of compound.** Dampen the hole with a spray bottle of water. Using a flexible 2-inch knife, gently push spackling or joint compound around the edges of the hole and into the mesh of the backing to give a firm grip to the repair. Avoid covering the pencil or the string. This first coat should just barely cover the mesh; too much compound applied at once will sag or fall out, especially in a ceiling. Allow 24 hours for the compound to dry.

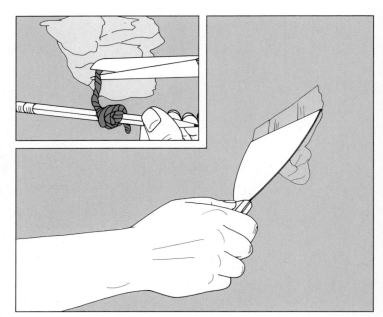

4 **Finishing the repair.** Use scissors to cut the string as close to the backing as possible *(inset)* and remove the pencil. Dampen the patch and fill it with compound until its surface is flush with the wall; use a knife wide enough to cover the patch in one pass *(above)*. Scrape off excess compound and let the patch dry 24 hours. Smooth the patch with medium-grit sandpaper on a sanding block and brush away the dust. Apply another coat if necessary, dampening before application and smoothing after the compound is dry. Seal the repair with primer.

REPAIRING FAILING JOINTS

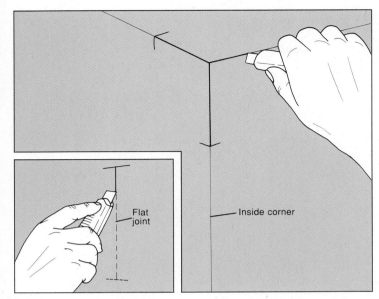

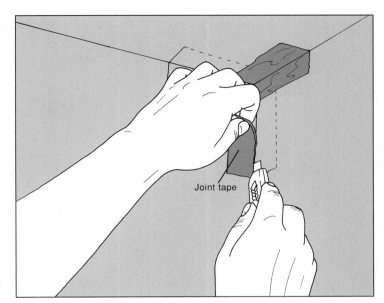

1 Scoring the damaged tape. A failing joint between drywall panels may occur at an inside corner: the meeting of two walls, a wall and a ceiling, or two walls and a ceiling as shown here. It may also be found at a flat joint on a ceiling or a wall as pictured in the inset. The repair is similar for each. Score through the damaged length of tape along its center *(above and inset)* and cut across it at both ends, using a straightedge as a scoring guide if needed. At the junction of two walls and a ceiling, cut through the tape at all three joints.

2 Stripping off the damaged tape. Use a utility knife to pry up a corner of the damaged tape at one cut end. Strip off the tape carefully *(above)*, working ahead with the utility knife to free up problem spots and avoiding tears in the drywall surface paper. Rarely will the damaged tape strip off easily in one piece; continue prying and tugging until it is all removed, keeping your free hand safely behind the cutting action. Sand away remaining joint compound to expose the drywall surface paper and smooth rough edges; brush off dust.

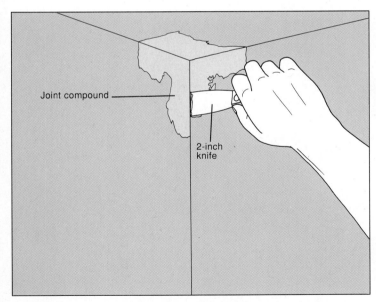

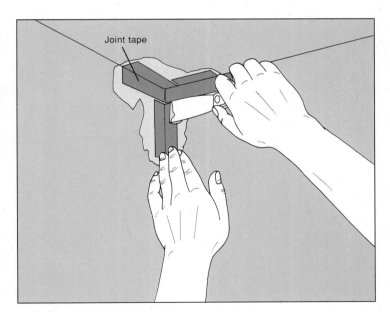

3 Applying a thin bed of compound. Dampen the surface and fill in any gaps between drywall panels with joint compound. To tape an inside corner joint, use a flexible 2-inch knife to cover the joint with a thin bed of compound *(above)*, working only on a length that can be comfortably taped over before the compound dries. Apply a 2- to 3-inch width of compound on one wall at a time; push compound into the corner and then pull back from the corner across the wall. For a flat surface, follow the steps for taping and feathering on page 140.

4 Positioning the tape. For a joint at an inside corner, use paper tape scored to fold easily down the center. For a flat joint, use paper tape *(page 140)* or fiber-mesh tape *(page 17)*. Tear off enough lengths of paper tape to cover the joints without overlapping their ends. Crease a length of tape and use a flexible 2-inch knife to sink the tape into the compound, forcing the crease into the corner *(above)*. Work along the tape one side at a time, starting with the ceiling joints. Use a putty knife to smooth out ripples or puckers in the tape as it swells with compound. If necessary, lift the tape out of the compound and resink it, wetting the knife first for added moisture.

REPAIRING FAILING JOINTS (continued)

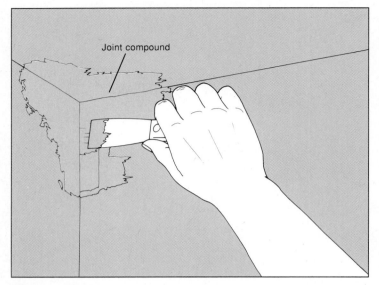

Joint compound

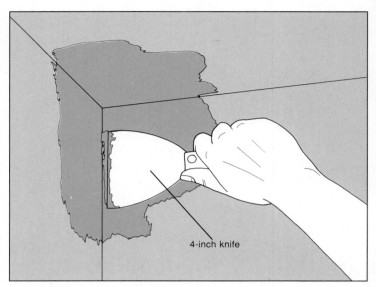

4-inch knife

5 **Embedding the tape.** Cover the tape with a thin coat of compound; at an inside corner *(above)*, work perpendicular to the joint, one side at a time, using a flexible 2-inch knife. Smooth the joint with a wetted corner trowel if desired. Scrape off excess compound and allow 24 hours for the patch to dry thoroughly.

6 **Applying the finishing coats of compound.** Use medium-grit sandpaper on a sanding block to smooth the repair surface; brush clean and dampen. Cover with a thin finishing coat of compound. At an inside corner, apply a 3- to 4-inch width on each surface using a flexible 4-inch knife *(above)*, smoothing with a corner trowel if desired. Feather the edges *(page 140)* and let the compound dry 24 hours. Repeat this step with a flexible 6-inch knife. Apply primer.

MINOR REPAIR TO AN OUTSIDE CORNER

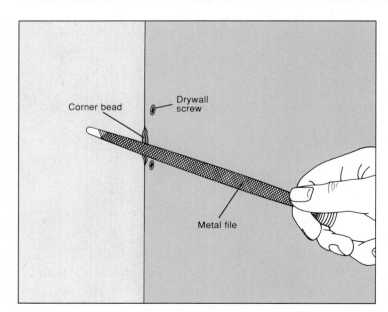

Corner bead

Drywall screw

Metal file

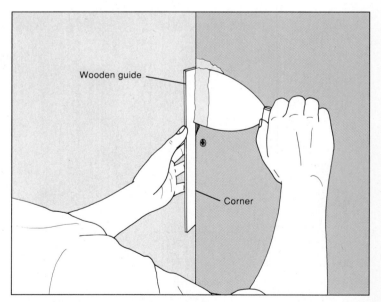

Wooden guide

Corner

1 **Filing the damaged corner bead.** Use a putty knife to chip away loose compound covering the corner bead. If necessary, reseat the corner bead by driving drywall screws or nails through the flange into the corner studs, dimpling the surface slightly *(page 16)*. Use a metal file to flatten bends in the bead that protrude beyond the corner *(above)*. Run the blade of a putty knife across the surface on each side of the corner; jumps indicate that either the nailheads must be driven in farther or the corner bead needs more filing.

2 **Rebuilding the corner.** Roughen the damaged surface on each side of the corner with coarse sandpaper; brush clean and dampen. Cover nails and fill in the damaged surface on each side of the corner with joint compound. Use a flat piece of wood as a guide for rebuilding the corner, holding it against one side of the corner as you apply joint compound to the other *(above)*. Scrape off excess compound and let dry 24 hours. Repeat this step as required, using medium-grit sandpaper on a sanding block to smooth the patch after each coat. Seal the patch with primer.

REPLACING A SECTION OF CORNER BEAD

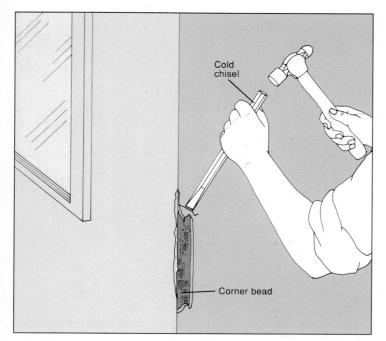

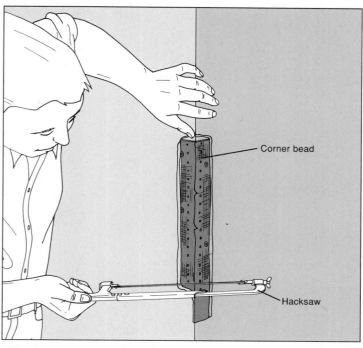

1 Exposing the corner bead flange. Chip away the compound covering the corner bead flanges along the damaged corner by tapping on a cold chisel with a ball-peen hammer *(above)*. Work from the corner bead out about 3 inches on each side, exposing the flanges along the length of the corner a little above and below the damaged area. Take care not to damage the drywall surface beyond the edges of the corner bead.

2 Cutting out the damaged corner bead. Using a hacksaw, cut through the corner bead a few inches above and below the damaged area *(above)*. Hold the saw perpendicular to the corner and, in straight, smooth strokes, make a clean break across the bead to the outside edges of the flange. You will also have to saw through the drywall and into the framing beneath the corner bead.

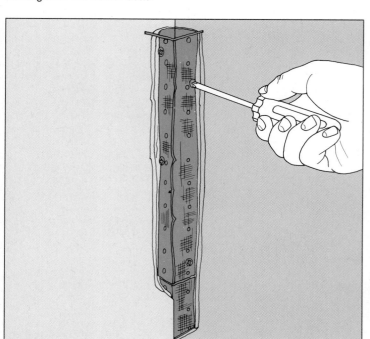

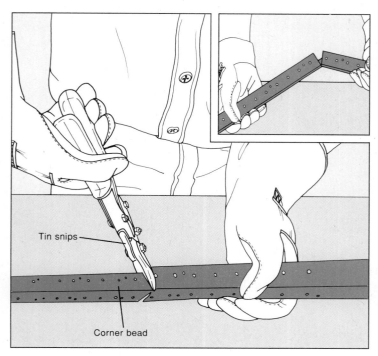

3 Removing the damaged section. Remove the fasteners holding the damaged corner bead section in place, using a Phillips screwdriver for drywall screws *(above)* and a pry bar or claw hammer for drywall nails. Unseat and lift out the damaged corner bead, wearing work gloves to protect your hands from sharp metal edges. Roughen the edges of the exposed drywall surface using coarse sandpaper and brush away loose particles.

4 Cutting and snapping corner bead. Mark off a length of new corner bead slightly shorter than the break in the corner; a small gap between ends is easier to conceal than a ridge caused by overlapping them. Cut through each flange using tin snips *(above)*, then bend the corner bead back and forth to snap it cleanly *(inset)*. Smooth rough edges with a metal file.

REPLACING A SECTION OF CORNER BEAD (continued)

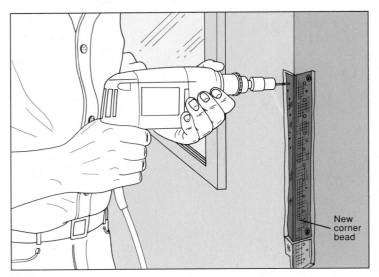

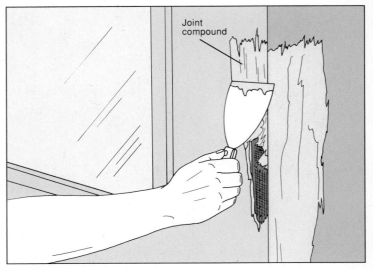

5 **Installing the new section of corner bead.** Seat the new section against the corner, its ends aligned with but not overlapping the undamaged corner bead. Install a pair of drywall screws or nails through the flanges at each end *(above)*, driving them into the metal, not the holes. Recess the heads of the fasteners slightly. If necessary, secure the cut ends of the undamaged corner bead the same way. Draw the blade of a putty knife across the corner bead to check that the heads are recessed; if not, drive them farther.

6 **Finishing the corner.** Using a flexible 4-inch knife, apply a 4- to 6-inch-wide layer of joint compound over each side of the corner with vertical strokes, using the edge of the corner bead to guide the knife *(above)*. Scrape off excess compound and let the patch dry 24 hours. To complete the repair, apply thin finishing passes of compound with flexible 6- and 10-inch knives, following the technique for feathering a joint *(page 140)*. Seal the repair with primer.

REPLACING AN ENTIRE CORNER BEAD

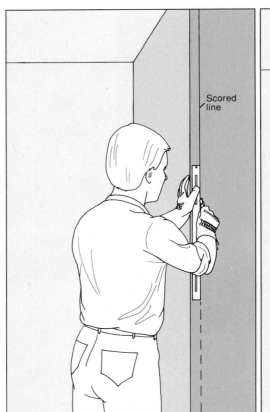

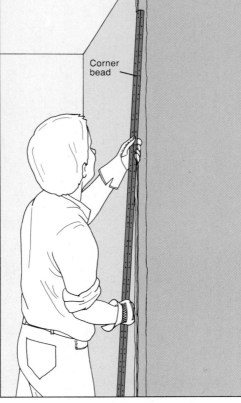

Replacing a full length of corner bead. Remove any molding or trim that covers the damaged corner *(page 58)*. With a straight-edge as a guide, use a utility knife to score a shallow vertical line about 3 inches from the corner on each wall *(far left)*, to prevent damage to the drywall surface beyond the edges of the corner bead. Keep your free hand away from the blade or wear work gloves for protection. Follow steps 1 and 3 on page 21 to expose the corner bead flanges along the entire length of the corner and to remove the fasteners. Lift off the corner bead, then sand the rough edges of the repair surface and brush away the dust. Fit the corner with a full length of corner bead, cutting it to size *(page 21, step 4)* if necessary. Press the new corner bead onto the corner *(near left)*, and follow step 5 *(above)* to drive drywall screws or nails opposite one another every 6 inches along the flanges, leaving about 8 inches free at both ends. Do not fasten the corner bead to either the top plate at the ceiling or the sole plate along the floor. Finish the corner as in step 6 *(above)*, applying successively wider layers of joint compound. Seal the repair with primer.

HIDING RIDGES

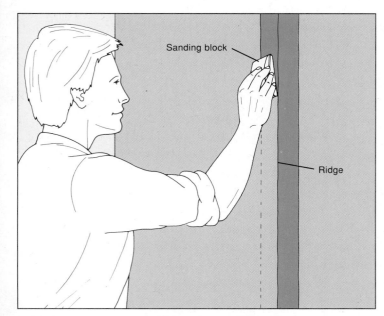

1 **Sanding to expose the joint tape.** With medium-grit sandpaper on a sanding block, sand away the joint compound along each side of the ridge to expose the joint tape. Work slowly and gently to avoid scuffing either the tape or the drywall surface paper; cut away any lifted surface paper with a utility knife *(page 15)*. Brush the surface clear of dust and particles.

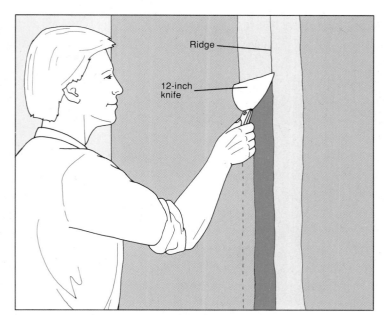

2 **Building up compound along the ridge.** To camouflage the ridge, fill the flat areas on each side of it with wide layers of joint compound. Use a spray bottle of water to dampen the wall along one side of the ridge, but not enough to loosen or lift the joint tape. Using a flexible 12-inch knife, spread a wide, thin layer of joint compound down along the ridge. Rest one end of the knife blade on the crown of the ridge, so that the compound tapers in thickness from the ridge outward.

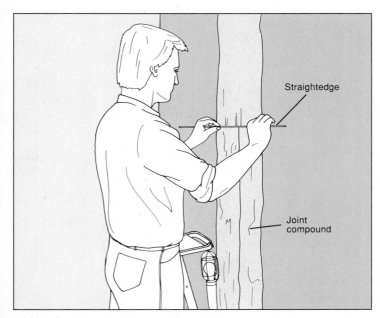

3 **Checking the level of the compound.** To help you see depressions requiring more filler, shine a bright light on the wall and hold a rigid straightedge horizontally across the compound, resting one end on the crown of the ridge and the other end against the drywall surface. If light shows between the straightedge and the wall, add more compound; if the straightedge sinks into the filler, scrape off some compound. Repeat this step at intervals along the ridge or, alternatively, wet the straightedge and glide it slowly down the ridge to smooth the surface of the compound.

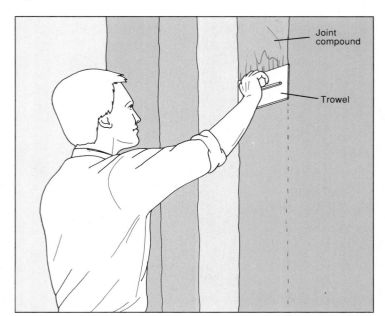

4 **Disguising the buildup.** Smooth the compound with a wet trowel *(above)* or a flexible 12-inch knife and feather the edges *(page 140)*. Repeat steps 2 and 3 along the other side of the ridge and let the compound dry 24 hours. With medium-grit sandpaper on a sanding block, smooth the repair surface and brush away dust. Apply successive thin layers of compound along the edges of the repair, overlapping the previous passes slightly, until the wall appears flat. Finally, cover the entire repair surface with a thin film of joint compound, feather the edges, and let dry 24 hours. Sand again with medium-grit sandpaper, brush away dust and seal with primer.

REPAIRING A MEDIUM-SIZE HOLE

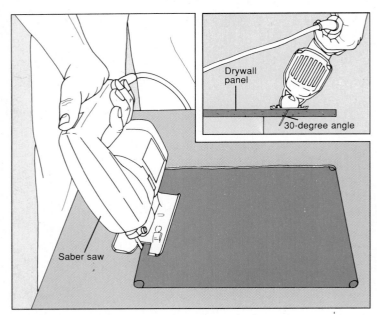

1 **Cutting a drywall patch.** From a drywall panel of the same type and thickness as the damaged drywall, cut a rectangular patch 4 to 6 inches longer and wider than the hole *(above)*. Use a saber saw set at a 30-degree angle to provide a better fit for the patch *(inset)*. With the front surface of the drywall facing up, cut out the patch in a counterclockwise direction, keeping the saw support plate flat against the surface, so that each edge of the patch is beveled identically. A hole drilled at each corner will help you turn the saw blade.

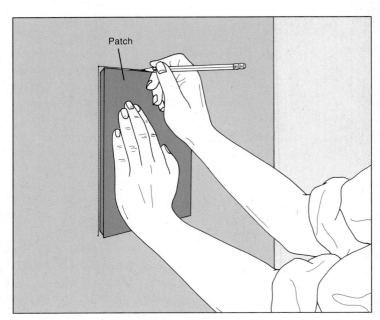

2 **Tracing the patch.** Sand rough edges on the patch using coarse sandpaper on a sanding block. Hold the patch securely over the hole, face out, and trace it with a pencil *(above)*. Keep the pencil at a 90-degree angle to the front of the patch, marking the outside edge of the bevel—not the inside edge. It might seem less difficult to trace if the patch is turned over, but the resulting outline will not be the same.

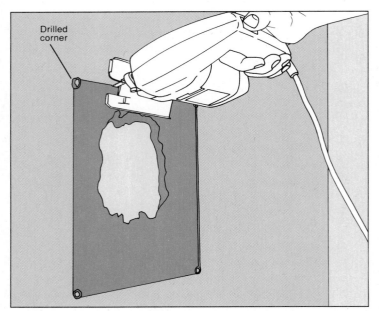

3 **Cutting the opening for the patch.** Drill a large hole in the wall just inside each corner of the penciled outline; check first inside the hole to make sure there are no obstructions *(page 134)*. Cut the opening for the patch with the saber saw set at the same 30-degree bevel used to cut the patch. Cut along the penciled outline of the patch in a counterclockwise direction *(above)*, turning the saw blade at the drilled corners and keeping the saw support plate flat against the surface, beveling each edge identically. Sand the edges with coarse sandpaper on a sanding block. Use a utility knife to cut away frayed surface paper.

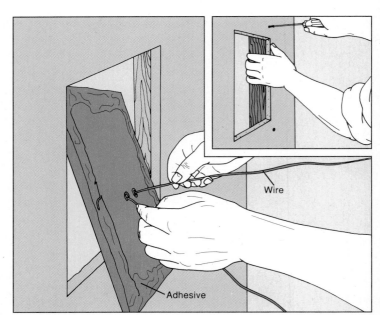

4 **Installing a backing for the patch.** Cut a section of drywall 2 to 4 inches larger than the patch. Drill two holes through the center and loop a heavy wire through them. Apply drywall adhesive around the front edges of the backing and the back edges of the opening. Angle the backing in through the opening *(above)* and pull on the wire to seat it against the wall for a minute—until the adhesive begins to set. Remove the wire and let the adhesive set 24 hours. To install cleats instead *(inset)*, saw two lengths of scrap wood 4 to 6 inches longer than the opening. Hold each against the back of the hole with half its face showing and screw it in place through the wall.

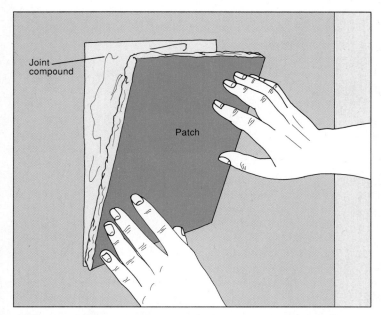

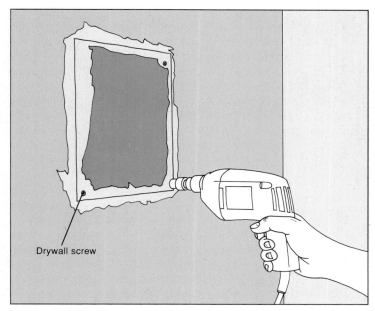

5 **Installing the patch.** Dampen the edges of both the opening and the patch; scuff the front of a solid backing with coarse sandpaper and dampen it as well. Using a putty knife, butter the edges of the patch with joint compound; also thinly coat the front of the backing and the back of the patch with compound or adhesive. Set the bottom edge of the patch in the opening *(above)* and press it firmly against the backing or cleats until it is flush with the wall. Scrape off excess compound that oozes out at the edges of the patch with the putty knife.

6 **Fastening the patch to the backing.** Drive drywall screws *(page 16)* through the patch into the backing or cleats at each corner *(above)*. Cover the heads with joint compound; finish the edges of the patch with joint tape *(page 19)*. Feather compound over the joint tape *(page 140)* until the surface is smooth, allowing 24 hours between coats. Smooth the repair with medium-grit sandpaper on a sanding block, brush away dust and seal the surface with primer.

REPAIRING A LARGE HOLE

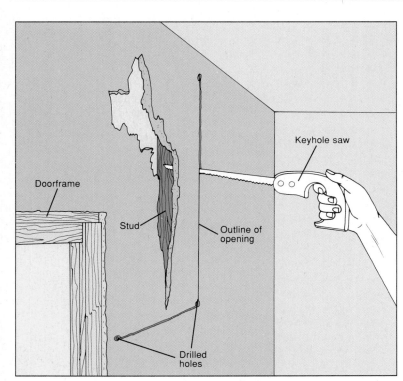

1 **Cutting away the damaged drywall.** Locate the position of the nearest stud or joist on each side of the hole *(page 136)*. Using a pencil and a carpenter's square, mark the opening to be cut in the wall around the hole: along the inside edges of the two studs or joists on each side of the hole, and across the wall between them. Make sure the corners of the opening are marked at a precise 90-degree angle. If the hole is very near an inside corner, draw to the end of the panel to avoid an extra joint. Remove wood trim *(page 58)* on the damaged drywall inside the marked-off area. If there are electrical fixtures or outlets, turn off power *(page 137)* and remove cover plates *(page 138)*. Drill a hole at each corner of the marked-off area and cut out the opening with a keyhole saw *(left)*; if there are obstructions within the wall *(page 134)*, use a utility knife. If the damage extends over the nearest stud, or if the nearest stud is at the corner of a door or window, as shown at left, cut the opening past it to the next stud.

REPAIRING A LARGE HOLE (continued)

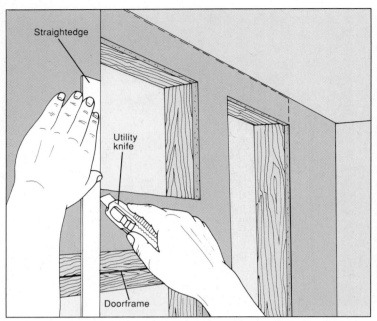
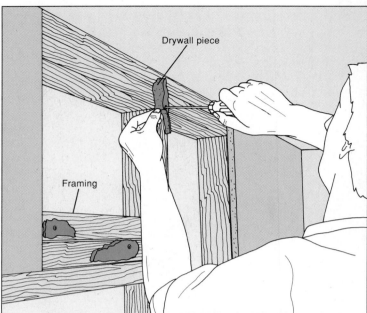

2 **Removing drywall over framing.** To remove supported drywall, cut through it with a utility knife, using a straightedge as a guide *(above, left)*. Take out the fasteners, using a Phillips screwdriver for drywall screws *(above, right)* or a claw hammer to pull out drywall nails; a cold chisel and mallet may be necessary to chip off the drywall if it was mounted with an adhesive. Cut away joint tape and torn surface paper with a utility knife *(page 19)*. At an inside corner, pull out pieces of drywall wedged in the butted joint. Sand uneven edges around the opening with coarse sandpaper on a sanding block and brush away debris, making sure the exposed framing is clear.

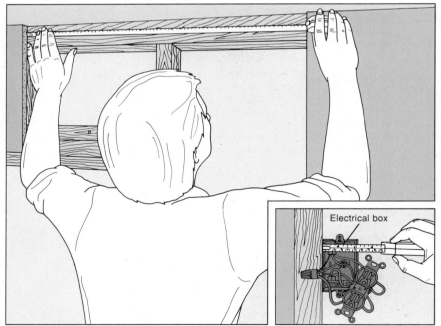
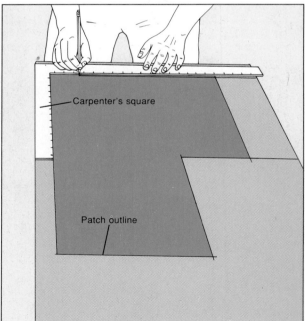

3 **Measuring the opening and marking the patch.** Measure the opening *(above, left)* as well as the size and position of any electrical boxes *(inset)*, or door or window frames, within the opening. Transfer the measurements—minus 1/4 inch so that the patch will fit—to a drywall panel of the same type and thickness as the damaged drywall. Mark with a carpenter's square *(above, right)* to ensure that the corners are drawn at a 90-degree angle. Do not mark the tapered edge of the drywall unless that edge of the opening is at a joint—an inside corner, for example.

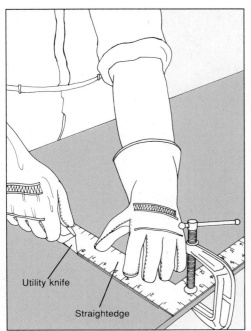

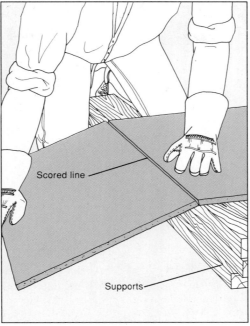

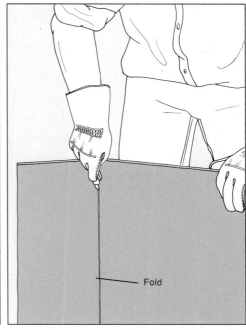

Utility knife

Straightedge

Scored line

Supports

Fold

4 **Scoring, snapping and cutting the patch.** Straight cuts across a drywall panel can be made quickly and easily without a drywall saw. Using a utility knife, score the drywall panel along a straightedge, clamped to the panel for stability *(above, left)*; wear work gloves to protect fingers from the sharp blade. Lift the panel onto straight boards or a table, positioning the scored line along one edge. With a sharp push, snap a clean break in the drywall panel along the scored line *(above, center)*. Carefully stand the panel on its side with the break vertical; bending the panel slightly at the break, cut through the fold in the back paper with the utility knife *(above, right)*. Repeat this step for any other straight cuts.

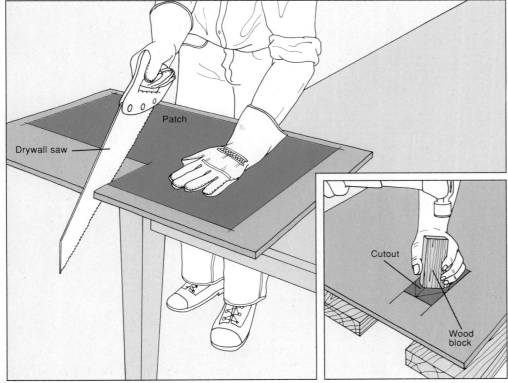

Drywall saw

Patch

Cutout

Wood block

5 **Cutting for openings and fixtures.** To make a straight-edged cutaway in the drywall panel for an opening such as a doorframe, raise the panel onto a support and use a drywall saw to cut the shorter edge *(left)*. Then score, snap and cut the longer edge as in step 4, above. To make a cutout for an electrical fixture, use the utility knife and straightedge to score the drywall panel along the penciled outline, then score an X from corner to corner through its center. Support the patch on wood blocks and, holding a short wood block against the center of the scored X, punch out the cutout with a sharp blow from a hammer *(inset)*. A keyhole saw may be used instead to cut the opening. For a curve or cutaway in the drywall around an opening such as an arch, use a pencil to trace the exact location and length of the edge on the back of the panel or on a sheet of cardboard the same size and shape. Cut curved or round patches with either a saber saw or keyhole saw.

REPAIRING A LARGE HOLE (continued)

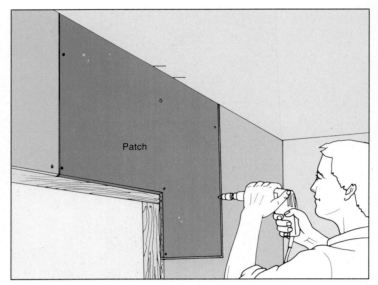

6 **Adding cleats.** To support the patch with drywall fasteners, add 2-by-4 cleats to the studs or joists along the edges of the opening, cutting them 2 to 3 inches longer than the opening. Position each cleat flush against the stud or joist with the narrower surface to the front. Hammer 3-inch wood nails through the cleat into the stud or joist every 4 to 6 inches along its length *(above)*. Before positioning the patch, mark the position of any exposed stud or joist on the undamaged drywall surface around the opening.

7 **Installing the patch.** Fit the patch in the opening, seating it against the cleats and flush with the wall surface. Drive drywall screws *(page 16)* through the patch about every 6 inches *(above)* into each cleat, stud or joist, starting at the middle and working to the edges. Do not install fasteners in a top plate or a sole plate *(page 12)*. Finish the repair following step 6 for a medium-size hole *(page 25)*.

REMOVING AND INSTALLING A DRYWALL PANEL

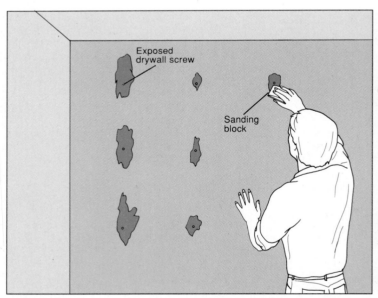

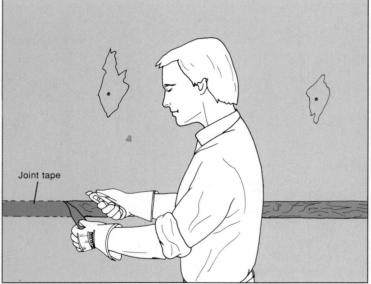

1 **Finding the edges of the drywall panel.** Locate the stud or joist *(page 136)* closest to the damaged area of the drywall panel. Sand along the stud or joist with medium-grit sandpaper on a sanding block *(above, left)* until you expose a drywall fastener; dig out the compound covering it with a utility knife or the blade of a putty knife. Continue in both directions along the stud or joist at 8-inch intervals, the usual spacing for fasteners, until you find the top and bottom of the panel—indicated by the uncovering of joint tape. Repeat this procedure on succeeding studs or joists to each side of the damaged area until you find the other two edges of the panel; note that a standard panel measures 4 by 8 feet, and may be installed horizontally, as shown here, or vertically. Strip off the joint tape *(page 19)* around the edges of the panel *(above, right)*.

REMOVING AND INSTALLING A DRYWALL PANEL (continued)

Drywall screw

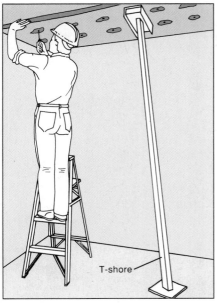

T-shore

Pry bar

2 Removing the drywall fasteners. Either screws or nails may have been used to support the drywall panel. Use a Phillips screwdriver to take out screws *(above, left)*; nails are difficult to pull out—hammer them through using a nail set. Work from the edges of the panel toward the center, making sure to leave enough fasteners in the panel to support it until someone is on hand to help take it down. For bracing a ceiling panel, use a T-shore *(above, right)* about 2 inches longer than the height of the ceiling, made from 2-by-4s nailed together; cardboard, carpet or a towel wrapped around the top protects a drywall panel that is to be reused.

3 Unseating the panel. With a helper nearby, use a pry bar to lever the drywall panel away from the wall. Dig the pry bar under the panel and work it along the edge, wedging it between the panel and a stud or joist behind it to pry away the panel. Continue along the edge of the panel until it can be securely held by hand without pinching any fingers. You may find that the panel was glued in place; in this case, cut the panel into pieces with a utility knife.

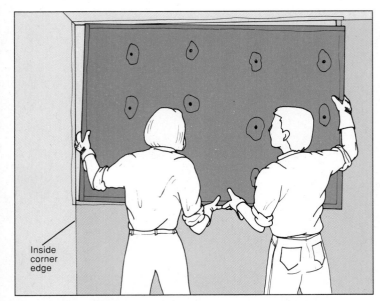

Inside corner edge

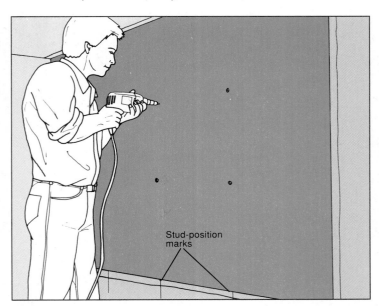

Stud-position marks

4 Pulling off the old panel. With a firm grip on the drywall panel, pull it away from the studs or joists behind it, jimmying it back and forth if necessary to free it. A panel at an inside corner requires careful attention: On a wall *(above)* lift out the edge farthest from the corner, then slide out the corner edge before lowering the panel; for a ceiling panel, pull down the edge farthest from the corner and slip out the edge resting on the top of the wall panel. Clean any nails or drywall particles from the studs or joists and mark their positions on the wall or ceiling. Rasp uneven edges around the opening with coarse sandpaper on a sanding block.

5 Installing a new panel. Replace the drywall panel with one of the same type and thickness. With a helper, fit the panel into position. At an inside corner, slide butted or floating edges of the panel into place first, then work along the other edges to press the panel firmly against the studs or joists. Starting at the center of the panel, install fasteners *(page 16)*. Center fasteners along the studs or joists *(above)*, every 12 inches for screws in a wall panel and every 8 inches for a ceiling panel or for nails. Leave 8 inches free at the top of a wall or the corner edge of a ceiling, and 1/2 inch at the bottom of a wall. Tape and cover joints *(page 140)* and apply primer.

PLASTER

The standard of interior construction for centuries, plaster walls have gone the way of the horse and buggy—and skilled plasterers have become as scarce as buggy-whip makers. But you can make sturdy, good-looking repairs to your plaster walls and ceilings without a plasterer's expertise by using modern patching materials and the techniques in this chapter.

Understanding the construction of your plaster walls and ceilings will help you diagnose their ills and select the correct repair procedures. If your house was built before 1930, its walls and ceilings probably resemble those pictured in the cut-away anatomy below. A grillwork of wood strips called lath is covered with a base coat of mortar and a scratch coat and finish coat of plaster. Wood lath, pieces of rough-sawn wood 1 1/2 inches by 1/4 inch and 48 inches long, is nailed horizontally onto the studs or ceiling joists—or in some cases onto furring strips—in staggered groups of six to ten. The base mortar oozes into spaces between the lath strips and hardens to form hooks called keys, which grip the lath. On masonry party walls, the base mortar was often applied directly to the brick or concrete surface.

After 1930, wood lath was superseded by gypsum-board lath in new home construction. Resembling drywall, gypsum-board lath is chemically treated to provide an adhesive surface for the plaster, and may be perforated with small holes to provide a grip for the plaster keys. The use of gypsum-board lath makes a coat of base mortar unnecessary.

Although not as common, metal lath was also used in some houses; it is most often seen as reinforcement at inside corners. Metal lath is of two types: expanded-metal or diamond-mesh lath, and a lighter, more flexible woven-wire mesh.

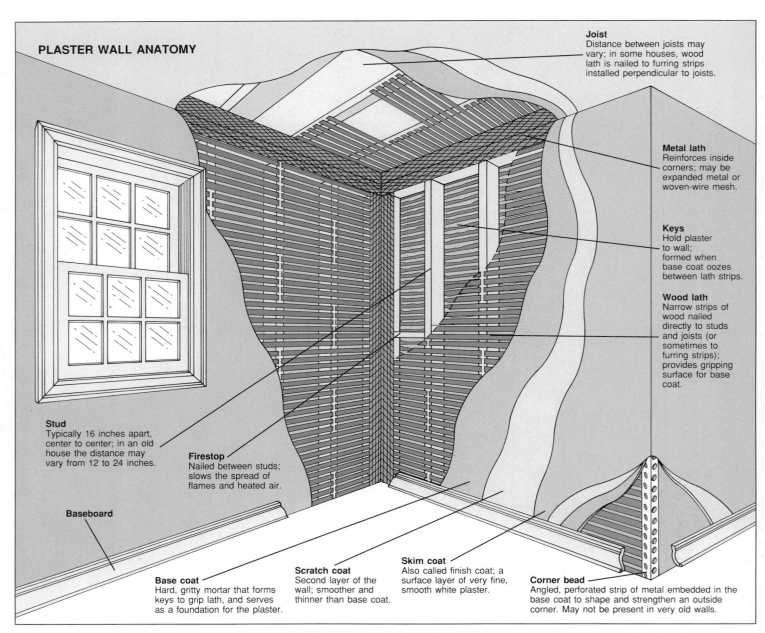

PLASTER WALL ANATOMY

Joist
Distance between joists may vary; in some houses, wood lath is nailed to furring strips installed perpendicular to joists.

Metal lath
Reinforces inside corners; may be expanded metal or woven-wire mesh.

Keys
Hold plaster to wall; formed when base coat oozes between lath strips.

Wood lath
Narrow strips of wood nailed directly to studs and joists (or sometimes to furring strips); provides gripping surface for base coat.

Stud
Typically 16 inches apart, center to center; in an old house the distance may vary from 12 to 24 inches.

Firestop
Nailed between studs; slows the spread of flames and heated air.

Baseboard

Base coat
Hard, gritty mortar that forms keys to grip lath, and serves as a foundation for the plaster.

Scratch coat
Second layer of the wall; smoother and thinner than base coat.

Skim coat
Also called finish coat; a surface layer of very fine, smooth white plaster.

Corner bead
Angled, perforated strip of metal embedded in the base coat to shape and strengthen an outside corner. May not be present in very old walls.

Metal lath makes an ideal reinforcement for patching weak or damaged wood lath.

Even the most carefully maintained plaster walls suffer from the normal settling of the house foundation and changing temperatures and humidity. As wood lath dries with age, the plaster keys may crack or break, causing a wall or ceiling to bulge. Other bulges may be caused by swelling due to water leaks and dampness. Plaster around an old staircase is vulnerable to damage caused by years of pounding, and door and window frames suffer recurring cracks caused by seasonal cycles of heat and cold, dryness and dampness. The Troubleshooting Guide on page 32 lists typical plaster defects and directs you to the procedures for correcting them.

Plaster walls and ceilings are rarely patched using old-fashioned plastering techniques. Large holes are usually filled with drywall rather than plaster, and damaged wood lath is reinforced with wire mesh or replaced with gypsum-board lath. Paper joint tape or fiber-mesh tape, designed for joining drywall panels, can help reinforce cracks and the edges of large patches. Modern plaster-patching compounds are specially formulated for ease of application; several are listed in the chart on page 33.

The tools pictured below will handle most plaster-repair tasks. Specialized plastering tools are rarely necessary, although a hawk and a rectangular trowel can be convenient for filling large areas with patching compound.

Plaster dust is extremely messy, and can be dangerous if it gets into eyes or lungs. When tearing down plaster, protect floors and furniture with dropcloths (page 141). Wear a respirator, goggles and, when working on the ceiling, a hard hat.

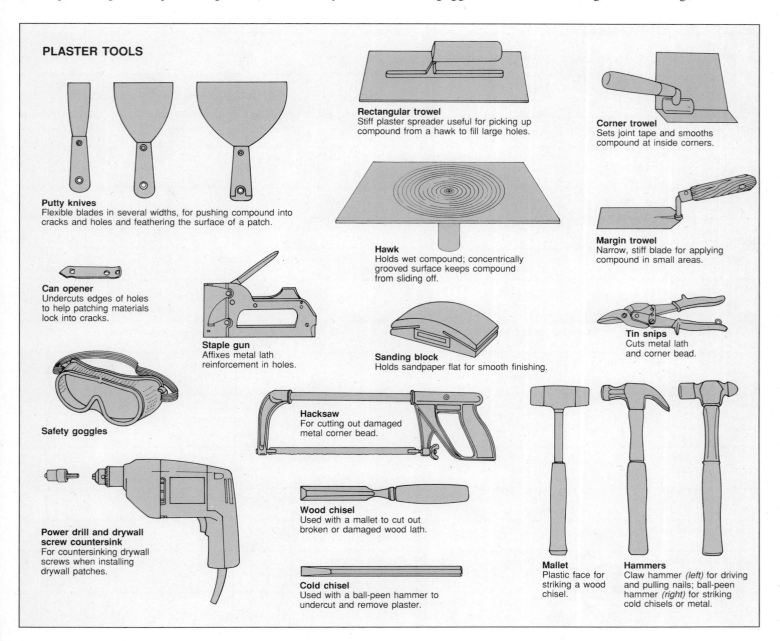

PLASTER TOOLS

Putty knives
Flexible blades in several widths, for pushing compound into cracks and holes and feathering the surface of a patch.

Can opener
Undercuts edges of holes to help patching materials lock into cracks.

Safety goggles

Power drill and drywall screw countersink
For countersinking drywall screws when installing drywall patches.

Staple gun
Affixes metal lath reinforcement in holes.

Rectangular trowel
Stiff plaster spreader useful for picking up compound from a hawk to fill large holes.

Hawk
Holds wet compound; concentrically grooved surface keeps compound from sliding off.

Sanding block
Holds sandpaper flat for smooth finishing.

Hacksaw
For cutting out damaged metal corner bead.

Wood chisel
Used with a mallet to cut out broken or damaged wood lath.

Cold chisel
Used with a ball-peen hammer to undercut and remove plaster.

Corner trowel
Sets joint tape and smooths compound at inside corners.

Margin trowel
Narrow, stiff blade for applying compound in small areas.

Tin snips
Cuts metal lath and corner bead.

Mallet
Plastic face for striking a wood chisel.

Hammers
Claw hammer (left) for driving and pulling nails; ball-peen hammer (right) for striking cold chisels or metal.

TROUBLESHOOTING GUIDE

SYMPTOM	POSSIBLE CAUSE	PROCEDURE
Alligatoring (a network of shallow cracks in surface of plaster)	Plaster improperly mixed or applied; poor bond between plaster and base coat; fluctuations in temperature or humidity	Sand and fill cracks (p. 34) □○, or cover with textured plaster (p. 45) ▣●
Hairline crack, stable, less than 1/4 inch wide	Settlement of house foundation; permanent shrinkage of house framing or lath	Fill crack with spackling compound (p. 34) □○
Hairline crack that opens and closes, or shifts, less than 1/4 inch wide	Structural movement of house caused by seasonal changes; removal of a bearing wall	On wall or ceiling, apply fiber-mesh tape (p. 35) □○; at inside corner, apply paper tape (p. 37) □○
Crack, stable, 1/4 inch to 1 inch wide	Same as stable hairline crack; may involve deterioration of plaster	On wall or ceiling, undercut edges and fill with spackling compound (p. 35) □○; at inside corner, apply paper tape (p. 37) □○
Crack that opens and closes, or shifts, 1/4 inch to 1 inch wide	Same as hairline crack; may involve deterioration of plaster	On wall or ceiling, undercut edges and fill with spackling compound (p. 35) □○, then apply fiber-mesh tape (p. 35) □○; at inside corner, apply paper tape (p. 37) □○
Crack along baseboard, 1/4 inch to 1 inch wide	Same as stable crack; often caused by settlement of a stairway	Fill with spackling compound (p. 37) □○
Hole less than 1 inch wide; small nick, dent or gouge	Hanger or fastener removed from wall; normal wear and tear	Fill with spackling compound (p. 33) □○
Hole 1 inch to 10 inches wide, lath intact	Doorknob hits wall; shelf or cabinet fallen or pulled from wall	On wall or ceiling, undercut edges, fill with spackling compound (p. 35) □○; at inside corner, install expanded-metal reinforcement (p. 43) ▣○
Hole 1 inch to 10 inches wide, no lath backing	Removal of electrical box; rodent activity	On wall or ceiling, install wire-mesh backing and fill with spackling compound (p. 38) ▣●; at inside corner, install expanded-metal reinforcement (p. 43) ▣●
Hole more than 10 inches wide, lath intact	Deteriorated plaster fallen or removed	Install a drywall patch (p. 40) ▣●, or fill with patching compound (p. 42) ▣●
Hole more than 10 inches wide, lath broken or missing	Access hole made for work within wall; recessed cabinet removed from wall; remodeling	Install drywall patch and fill with patching compound (p. 42) ▣●, or install a drywall patch (p. 40) ▣●
Corner bead exposed or slightly dented	Normal wear and tear	Repair corner bead (p. 44) □○
Corner bead severely bent or broken	Accident; remodeling	Replace damaged section of corner bead (p. 44) ▣●
Outside corner damaged; no corner bead	Normal wear and tear; accident; remodeling	Rebuild plaster around corner (p. 43) □○
Outside corner badly damaged; corner studs cracked or misaligned	Accident; remodeling	Call for service
Wall bulges, gives when pushed; plaster surface sound	Plaster keys broken or lath detached from studs	Wall may last several years in this condition but will eventually need to be replaced; call a professional for assessment
Wall bulges; plaster surface cracked or pieces falling from wall	Plaster keys broken or lath detached from studs; plaster deteriorated	Wall should be replaced immediately; call for service
Ceiling sags, gives when pushed; plaster surface may appear sound or may be cracked or falling	Plaster keys broken or lath detached from studs; structural weakness in joists; plaster deteriorated	A dangerous condition; ceiling should be replaced immediately; call for service
Plaster surface soft, crumbling, powdery	Extreme humidity; water leaks behind wall; moisture seeps through masonry-backed wall	Repair the cause of moisture and allow wall to dry; scrape away loose plaster; repair surface according to extent of damage
Plaster surface uneven or unsightly; plaster sound	Plaster improperly mixed or applied; old patches poorly finished	Apply a textured plaster finish to entire wall or ceiling (p. 45) ▣●
Textured plaster surface damaged or uneven	Old patches poorly finished; textured surface removed for patching	Rebuild a matching textured surface in damaged area (p. 45) ▣●
Mildew on plaster wall or ceiling	High humidity; area contaminated with mildew	Wash away mildew with solution of 1 cup chlorine bleach in 1/2 gallon water □○; strip paint (p. 57) or remove wallpaper (p. 100) if necessary

DEGREE OF DIFFICULTY: □ Easy ▣ Moderate ■ Complex
ESTIMATED TIME: ○ Less than 1 hour ◔ 1 to 3 hours ● Over 3 hours *(Does not include drying time)*

PATCHING COMPOUNDS

COMPOUND	COMPOSITION	CHARACTERISTICS	SETTING TIME	RECOMMENDED USES
Base mortar	Gypsum plaster with mica, perlite and sometimes sand; in old walls, may contain horsehair.	Sets hard; rough and gritty; can't be smoothed.	24 hours.	An original base coat; not recommended for repairs.
Perlite plaster	Base mortar with a large proportion of perlite—expanded volcanic glass—for light weight.	Sets hard; rough and gritty; can't be applied in thin coats.	24 hours.	Over masonry and wood, metal or gypsum lath; as a first layer in large, deep holes.
Patching compound	Gypsum plaster with a vinyl additive for cohesiveness and strength.	Stronger than joint compound or spackling compound; less prone to shrinkage.	3 hours.	As a filler for broad cracks and deep holes. Not a finish coat.
Rapid-setting patching compound	Gypsum plaster with lime, a vinyl binder and calcium sulfate. Available ready-mixed.	Sets hard; shrinkage minimal; can be difficult to sand.	25 to 90 minutes.	For broad cracks and deep holes; installing new corner bead. Not a finish coat.
Finishing plaster	Gypsum plaster with large proportion of lime.	Smooth and fine; requires skill to apply over large area.	24 hours.	An original finish coat; difficult to use for repairs.
Spackling compound	Vinyl latex with calcium carbonate, or acrylic latex. Available ready-mixed.	Smooth buttery consistency; good adhesion.	8 to 24 hours.	For small holes and narrow cracks; as a finishing coat over patching compound.
Vinyl spackling compound	Gypsum plaster with silicone in a vinyl latex base. Available ready-mixed.	Sets hard; good adhesion; shrinkage minimal.	24 hours.	For small holes, narrow cracks, any spot repairs.
Joint compound	Gypsum plaster or vinyl latex base with a retardant to slow setting. Available ready-mixed.	Good only in very thin coats; very spreadable and sandable; water-soluble after drying.	Depends on manufacturer's formulations; typically 12 to 24 hours.	Very narrow cracks; best as a finish coat over other fillers and for taping joints.
Plaster of paris	Almost pure gypsum plaster; may contain a retardant to slow setting.	Dries smooth, snow-white, sandable; shrinkage minimal.	2 to 15 minutes; cold water or vinegar retards setting.	Repairing ornamental plaster moldings.

The chart above lists nine gypsum-plaster compounds, along with their composition, characteristics, setting times and recommended uses. Setting times can vary greatly, depending on temperature, humidity and thickness of application. Some materials, such as spackling compound, are sold premixed in small quantities; others, such as base mortar, are available only dry and in bulk. Always follow the package instructions for mixing and applying the compound. Use clean water, and make no more than you plan to use in the time it takes to set. Wash containers, utensils and tools while the compound is still wet; compounds made for permanent repairs can set permanently on tools.

REPAIRING MINOR HOLES

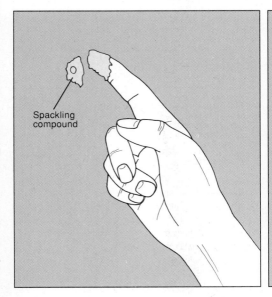

Spackling compound

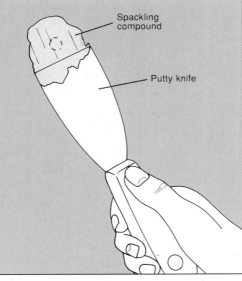

Spackling compound

Putty knife

Filling nail holes and small dents. Nail holes, nicks, dents and gouges may be filled with spackling compound applied with a small putty knife or even a finger, as shown. Wipe or blow dust and loose plaster out of a hole; roughen a depression with sandpaper. Dampen the spot with a moist sponge to keep the spackling compound from drying out too fast. Push spackling compound into a small hole with your fingertip *(far left)*; use a small putty knife to spread spackling compound over a dent *(near left)*, filling it flush with the wall. Allow the spackling compound to dry until your fingernail can no longer dent it—usually several hours—then smooth the patch with fine sandpaper, wipe it clean and prime it before painting.

SMOOTHING AN ALLIGATORED SURFACE

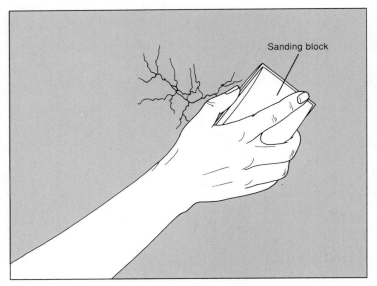

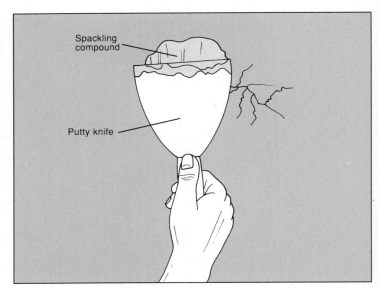

1 **Sanding alligator cracks.** Alligatoring, a network of shallow fissures, is caused by shrinkage in the top coat of plaster. To refinish an alligatored wall, first degrease it with a strong detergent solution, then rinse and dry it thoroughly. Fit a padded sanding block with medium-grit sandpaper and rub down the cracked area in a circular motion *(above)*, to smooth any high spots. Dust off the plaster powder and dampen the sanded area with a moist sponge.

2 **Filling the surface.** Using a flexible 5-inch putty knife, spread a very thin layer of spackling compound over the alligatored area *(above)*, filling the cracks without building up the wall surface. Allow the spackling compound to dry at least an hour, then lightly sand the patch, smoothing its edges into the undamaged wall area around it. Dust off the patch and apply a coat of primer.

FILLING A HAIRLINE CRACK

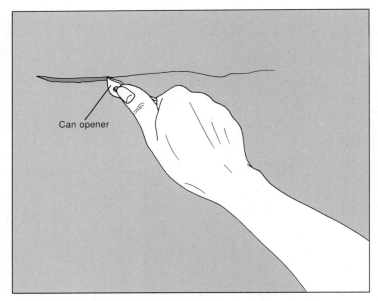

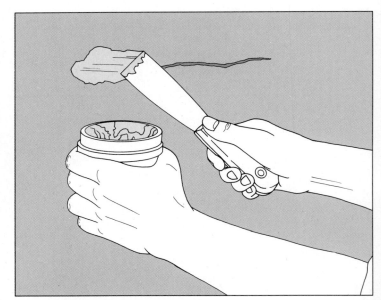

1 **Cleaning the crack.** Very narrow, non-expanding cracks, often caused by permanent settlement of the house framing, may be filled with spackling compound. First open the edges of the crack by lightly drawing the tip of a can opener along it *(above)*, then use an old paintbrush to clear out loose plaster. Moisten the inside of the crack with a dampened paintbrush or sponge.

2 **Filling the crack.** Using a narrow putty knife, press spackling compound into the crack. Stroke the knife across the crack if necessary to fill it, and then along the crack. Allow the spackling compound to set several hours, then lightly sand the area, dust it and apply primer.

PATCHING A RECURRING HAIRLINE CRACK

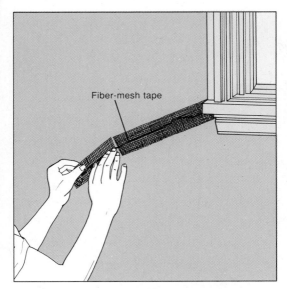

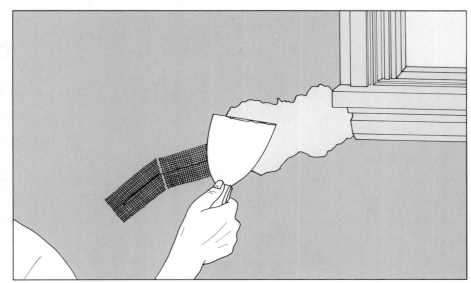

1 **Applying fiber-mesh joint tape.** Flexible and self-adhesive, fiber-mesh tape helps to stabilize repairs made to recurring or shifting cracks. First follow step 1 for filling a hairline crack *(page 34)*. Then press a length of fiber-mesh tape over the entire crack; if the crack is crooked or branched, apply several short lengths without overlapping their ends.

2 **Feathering joint compound over the tape.** Using a flexible 5-inch knife, spread a thin layer of joint compound over the tape, pushing it into the mesh and the crack *(above)*. Allow this layer to dry. Next, using an 8-inch knife, lay a second, wider layer of compound over the first in one smooth motion. Finally, draw the knife along each side of the compound layer, tapering the edges of the patch to the level of the surrounding wall. Let the patch dry. Smooth the patch with a sanding block and medium-grit sandpaper and wipe clean, or wipe it smooth with a damp sponge. Apply primer.

REPAIRING A WIDE CRACK OR SMALL HOLE

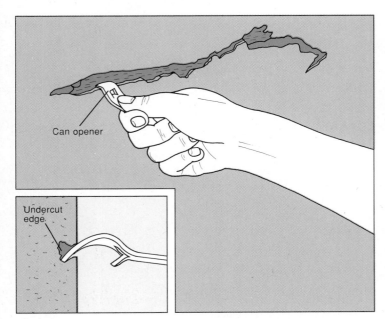

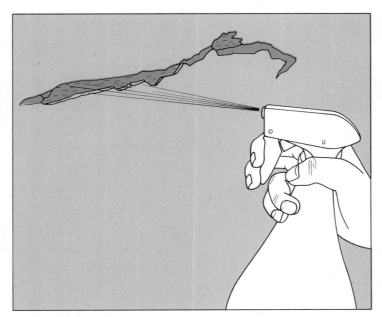

1 **Undercutting the edges of the crack.** To help lock the patching material into the crack, use the tip of a can opener to scrape some of the plaster from behind its edges *(above)*, resulting in an undercut edge that is wider at the base than at the surface *(inset)*.

2 **Moistening the crack.** Brush out dust and loose plaster fragments with an old paintbrush. To dampen a crack with undercut edges, use a spray bottle to direct water inside the crack and behind its edges *(above)*. Lightly moisten the crack without soaking it.

REPAIRING A WIDE CRACK OR SMALL HOLE (continued)

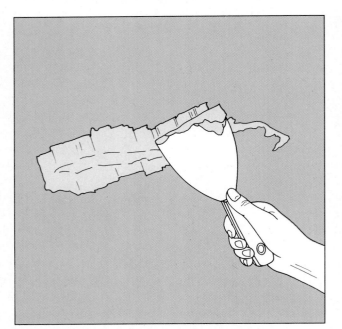

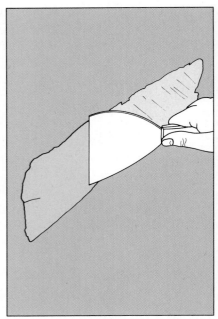

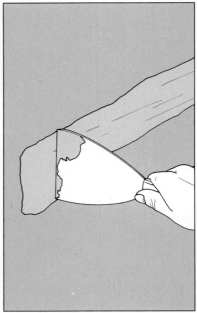

3 **Filling the crack.** Using a flexible 5-inch knife, pack spackling compound into the crack, working it behind the undercut edges *(above)*. Stroke the knife back and forth across the crack until it is completely filled, then draw the knife along the crack to bring its surface flush with the wall. Allow the compound to dry overnight.

4 **Applying a second coat of spackling compound.** As the first coat of spackling compound dries it will shrink, leaving the surface dimpled or cracked. Fill the crack again, passing the knife along its length *(above, left)*, then clean excess spackling compound from the wall by stroking the edge of the knife blade over the patch without flexing the blade *(above, right)*. Allow this coat to dry for several hours.

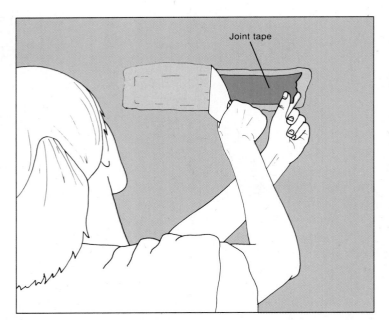

Joint tape

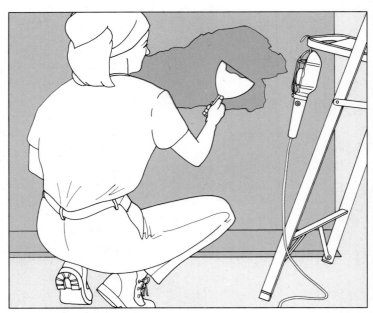

5 **Reinforcing the patch with paper joint tape.** Joint tape can strengthen a patch made in a crumbly or vibration-prone wall. Tear a piece of paper tape to the length of the crack (torn edges are easier to hide than neatly cut edges). With a 5-inch knife, spread a thin layer of joint compound over the crack. Press one end of the tape into the compound at one end of the crack, then run the knife blade along the tape, setting it in the compound *(above)*. If the crack is crooked or branched, apply several lengths of tape without overlapping their ends. Stroke the knife over the tape again to smooth out any bubbles. Allow the compound to dry overnight.

6 **Feathering the patch.** Using a flexible 8-inch knife, spread a thin layer of joint compound over the tape in one smooth motion. Then draw the knife along each side of the compound layer, tapering the edges of the patch to the level of the surrounding wall *(above)*. A utility light shining on the wall at an oblique angle, as shown above, can help define bumps or depressions that need smoothing. Allow the compound to dry overnight. Smooth the patch with medium-grit sandpaper on a sanding block and wipe clean, or wipe it smooth with a damp sponge. Apply primer.

PATCHING AN INSIDE CORNER CRACK

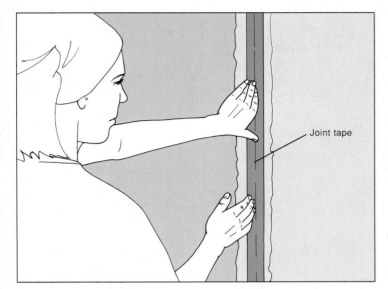

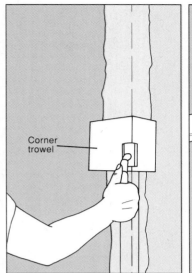

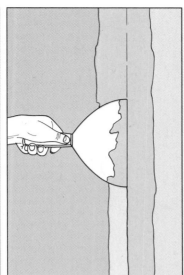

1 **Filling and taping a corner crack.** Undercut, moisten and fill a corner crack as for a wide crack *(pages 35-36, steps 1-4)*, but apply the spackling compound by alternately drawing the knife down one wall, then the other. Because corner cracks tend to shift and reopen, reinforce the patch with paper joint tape, which has a crease line down the center for corner application. Use a flexible 5-inch knife to spread a thin layer of joint compound over the patch, first on one wall, then the other. Tear a piece of joint tape the length of the crack, crease it down the middle and press it into the corner *(above)*. Then run the knife blade over the tape, first along one side of the crease, then the other, to seat the tape in the compound.

2 **Smoothing the repair.** To ensure a perfect corner, especially for large repairs, use a specialized tool called a corner trowel to form the corner angle. Draw the trowel straight down the tape, its blades flat against the walls and its point in the corner *(above, left)*. Next cover the tape with joint compound, using a flexible 8-inch knife to spread a thin layer from the corner out to the wall on each side *(above, right)*, tapering the compound to the level of the wall. Run the cornering trowel along the patch once again to smooth it. Finish the patch as on page 36, step 6.

REPAIRING A CRACK ALONG A BASEBOARD

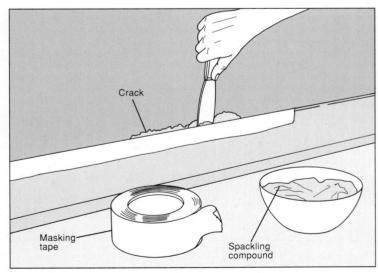

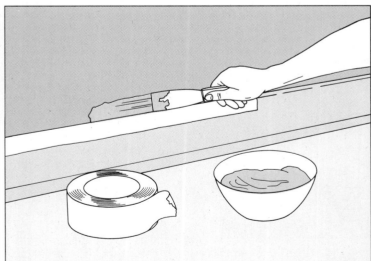

Filling a baseboard crack. Commonly caused by the vibration and settlement of a stairway, a crack along the top edge of a baseboard can usually be repaired without removing the woodwork. Apply a strip of wide masking tape over the edge of the baseboard without covering the wall or the crack. Undercut and moisten the crack *(page 35, bottom)*, then apply the spackling compound with a flexible 2-inch knife in short, upward strokes *(above, left)*. Do not lap spackling compound over the baseboard. Allow the spackling compound to dry overnight, then bring the surface of the patch flush with the wall by applying a second coat of spackling compound along the crack *(above, right)*, using a knife that is wider than the crack. When it is dry, smooth the patch with medium-grit sandpaper on a sanding block.

REINFORCING A SMALL HOLE (Plaster without lath backing)

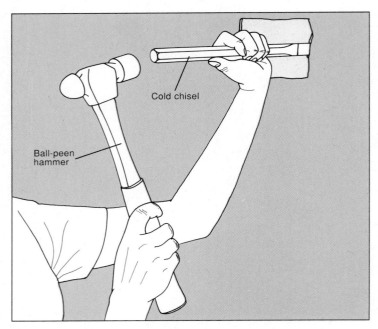

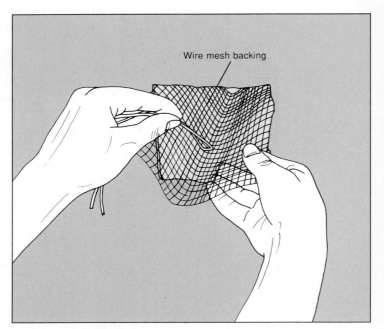

1 Opening and cleaning the hole. A small hole with the lath missing can be patched if a backing—a square of wire mesh in this technique—is first installed to anchor the filler. Score the outline of the hole with a utility knife. Then dislodge loose plaster from the hole and undercut its edges using a sharp cold chisel and a ball-peen hammer *(above)*. Take care not to crack the surrounding wall.

2 Inserting the wire mesh backing. Using tin snips, cut a piece of 1/4-inch wire mesh about 2 inches larger than the hole. Thread a length of heavy string through the center of the mesh and, holding onto the string, bend the mesh backing and slip it through the hole. Tug the string to seat the mesh flat against the back of the hole.

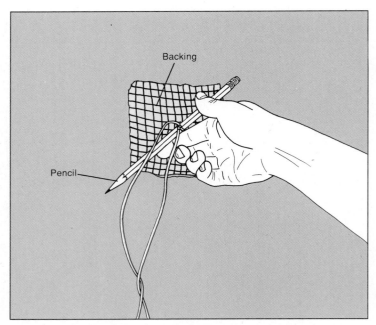

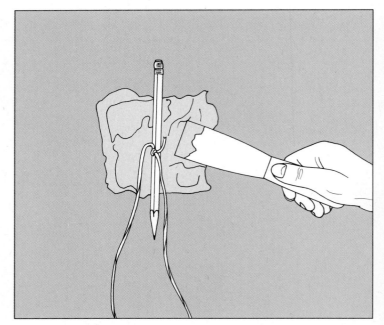

3 Securing the mesh backing to the wall. Choose a pencil or a stick longer than the width of the hole, and tie it loosely to the backing with the string. Twist the pencil against the wall to tighten the string, drawing the backing snug against the hole without pulling it through. The friction of the pencil on the wall will hold the backing in place.

4 Filling the hole. Moisten the edges of the hole using a spray bottle. With a flexible 2-inch knife, pack patching compound behind the undercut edges of the hole without dislodging the mesh backing. Then force a layer of compound into the mesh, but do not attempt to fill the hole level with the wall. Avoid covering the pencil with compound. Allow the first coat of patching compound to dry overnight.

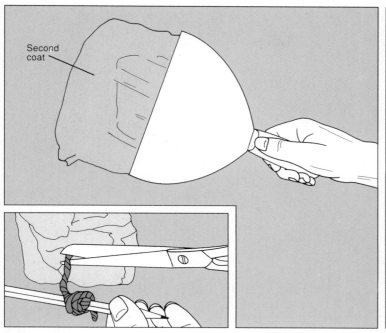

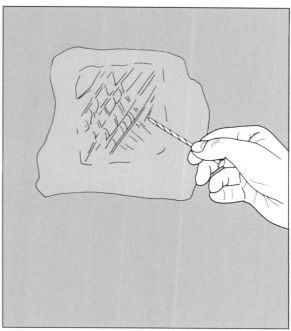

5 **Applying a second coat of patching compound.** When the first coat has dried, snip the string holding the pencil and remove it *(inset)*. Using a larger flexible knife, apply a second coat of patching compound *(above, left)*, working carefully to avoid pushing the patch through the wall. Fill the hole to within 1/4 inch of the wall surface, then lightly scratch the compound with a nail to provide a gripping surface for the final coat *(above, right)*. Let the patch dry overnight. Using a knife wider than the hole, apply joint compound as a final coat, bringing the surface of the patch flush with the wall.

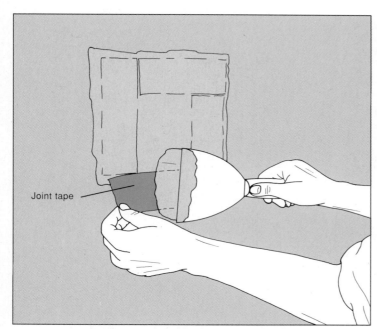

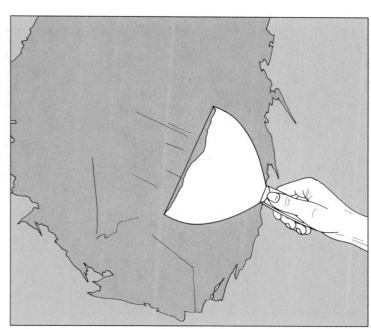

6 **Taping the edges of the hole.** If you do not intend to tape the patch, go to step 7. Use paper joint tape to reinforce a patch made in weak or unstable plaster *(page 36, steps 5 and 6)*. Embed strips of tape around the edges of the hole without overlapping the ends of the strips *(above)*.

7 **Feathering the edges of the patch.** Using a flexible 8-inch knife, stroke the surface of the joint compound from the center of the patch outward, tapering the edges of the patch to the level of the surrounding wall. Allow the patch to dry for 24 hours, then smooth it with medium-grit sandpaper on a sanding block and wipe clean, or smooth with a damp sponge. Apply primer.

PATCHING A LARGE HOLE WITH DRYWALL (Plaster with lath backing)

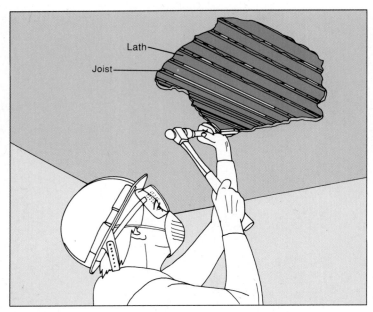

1 **Cutting back the edges of the hole.** When working on the ceiling, as shown here, wear a respirator, goggles and a hard hat. Using a ball-peen hammer and a cold chisel, chip away loose plaster around the edges of the hole *(above)*, stopping when you reach sound plaster securely keyed into the lath. Dig out chunks of plaster left between the lath strips. Then carefully continue cutting back the edges to expose the nearest joist (or furring strip or stud) on each side of the hole—these provide a nailing surface for the drywall patch.

2 **Cutting and fitting the drywall patch.** Measure the hole's greatest width and length, and its shallowest depth. To make the patch, choose a piece of drywall no thicker than the shallowest part of the hole. Score and snap a rectangular piece *(page 27)* just large enough to cover the hole and the joists (or furring strips or studs) on each side of it. Hold the patch over the hole and mark its outline with a pencil *(above)*.

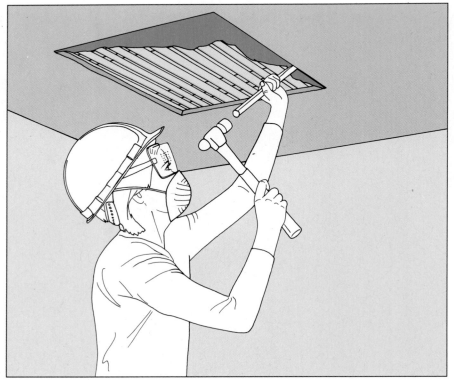

3 **Trimming the hole to fit the patch.** Carefully cut the plaster along the penciled outline, using a ball-peen hammer to strike a sharp cold chisel *(left)*, a brickset or a stiff putty knife. Take care not to damage plaster beyond the outlined area. Pencil the positions of the two exposed joists (or furring strips or studs) on the plaster surrounding the hole; these markings will serve as guidelines for screwing the patch to the joists. Then insert the patch into the hole and check its fit. When it is properly positioned, mark one corner of the patch and the corresponding corner of the hole for reference.

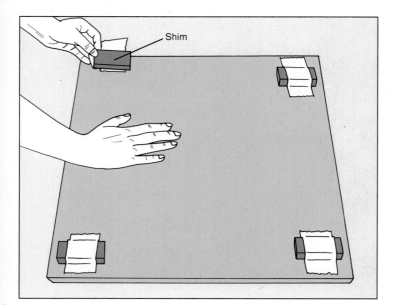

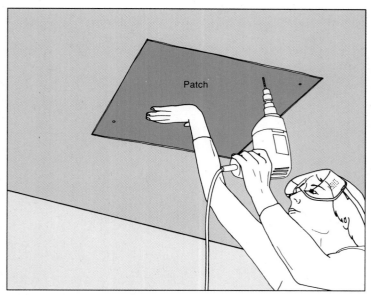

4 **Shimming the patch.** To bring the surface of the patch flush with the surrounding plaster, attach shims—thin scraps of wood or drywall—to its back edges. First measure the thickness of the plaster in several places around the edges of the hole, especially over the joists (or furring strips or studs). These measurements will probably vary one from another—subtract the thickness of the patch from each measurement and cut a shim the thickness of the difference. Tape each shim to its corresponding spot on the back of the patch (above). Check the fit of the shimmed patch and adjust the shims if necessary.

5 **Installing the patch.** Choose drywall screws long enough to penetrate the patch, shims, lath and one inch of the joist (or furring strip or stud). Secure the patch by driving screws through two opposite corners into the joists (above). Continue driving screws at 6-inch intervals around the perimeter of the patch, into the joists wherever possible. Seat all screw heads slightly below the surface of the patch. Fill, tape and feather the edges of the patch as for a wide crack (pages 35-36, steps 2-6), and cover the screw heads (page 33).

REPLACING BROKEN WOOD LATH WITH GYPSUM-BOARD LATH

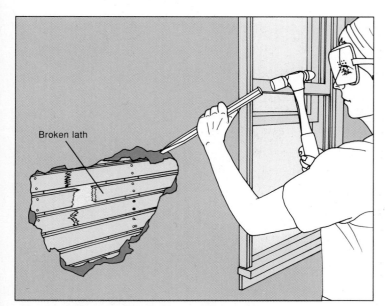

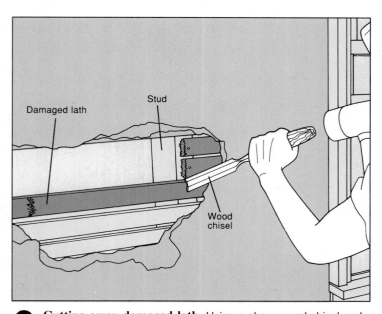

1 **Exposing the broken lath.** Wearing goggles, chip away damaged plaster with a ball-peen hammer and cold chisel, uncovering all the damaged lath and the studs on each side of the damaged area (above). Knock out loose plaster from between the strips of lath. Undercut the edges of the hole with the cold chisel (page 35, bottom, step 1).

2 **Cutting away damaged lath.** Using a sharp wood chisel and the plastic face of a mallet, cut each strip of damaged lath at the center of the stud (above). Hold the chisel at a 90-degree angle to the lath strip, with its beveled side toward the damaged part of the lath, and cut straight through. If the end of the lath strip is nailed to the stud, just pry out the nail to remove the strip. Remove loose nails and bits of broken lath or plaster from the stud.

REPLACING BROKEN WOOD LATH WITH GYPSUM-BOARD LATH (continued)

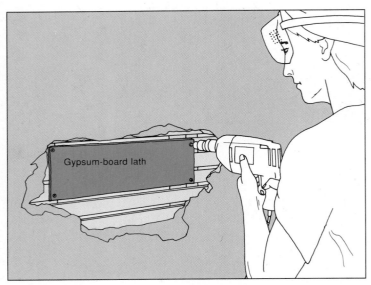

3 **Replacing the wood lath with gypsum-board lath.** Measure the distance between the centers of each of the two exposed studs, and the width of the space left by the removal of the broken lath. Cut a rectangular patch of gypsum-board lath (or 3/8-inch drywall, its surface deeply scratched with a nail to provide a gripping surface for the patching compound) 1/4 inch smaller all around than this measurement. This leaves a 1/4-inch space on the top and bottom for the plaster to key into. Using a power drill fitted with a drywall-screw bit or a Phillips-head bit, secure the patch to the studs with drywall screws at each of its four corners. To fill the hole with patching compound, go to step 4. To install a drywall patch, go to page 40, step 2.

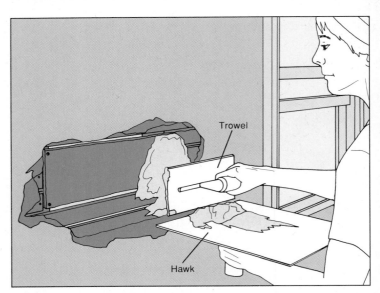

4 **Applying patching compound.** Mix just as much quick-setting patching compound as you will need to fill the hole halfway to the wall surface. Moisten the hole with a spray bottle, including the undercut edges and the lath. Place the plaster compound in the center of the hawk and hold it close to the hole. Tip the hawk toward you slightly and, using the long edge of the trowel, cut a slice of plaster from the hawk, pushing the trowel away from you. With one smooth motion and a quick wrist action, sweep the trowel upward off the hawk and press the compound into the hole *(above)*, pushing it under the edges and between the lath strips. As you cut each slice of plaster compound from the hawk, give the hawk a quarter turn so that the pile of compound remains centered, making the hawk easier to manage.

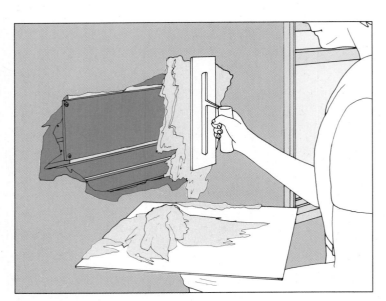

5 **Filling the hole.** Push the trowel toward the edges to pack the undercuts, then fill the spaces between the lath strips. Pass the trowel back and forth over the surface of the compound, taking care not to apply too much pressure if using gypsum-board lath (it snaps easily). This first layer of patching compound should fill a little more than half the depth of the hole. Wipe compound off the wall around the hole with the trowel or a damp sponge. Scratch this first coat with a nail and let it dry overnight. Mix and apply a second layer so that it is almost flush with the wall surface and let it dry overnight.

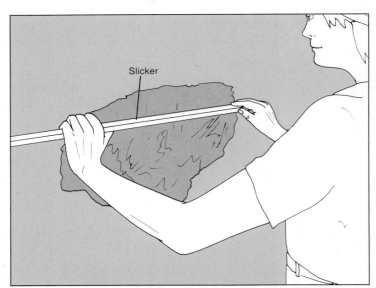

6 **Smoothing the final coat with a slicker.** For the final layer, apply joint compound with a flexible 5-inch knife. Use a plasterer's slicker or a straightedge such as a stiff metal yardstick to remove compound that exceeds the level of the surrounding wall, or to spot low areas that need more compound. Draw the straightedge across the patch *(above)*, and add more compound where necessary. If you have trouble achieving a smooth final coat, let the compound dry overnight, then go over it with a wet paintbrush, blending uneven ridges with smooth strokes. When the final coat is dry, sand the patch with medium-grit sandpaper on a sanding block. Wipe clean and prime.

PATCHING AN INSIDE CORNER

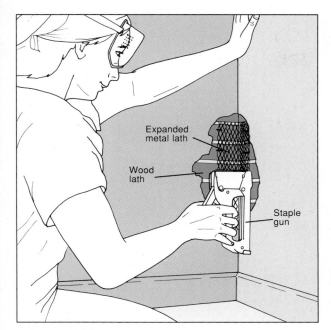

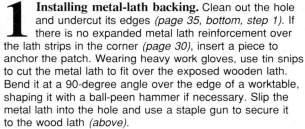

Expanded metal lath

Wood lath

Staple gun

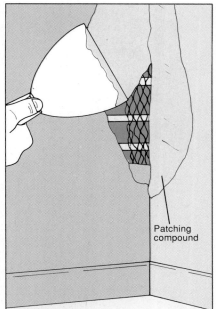

Patching compound

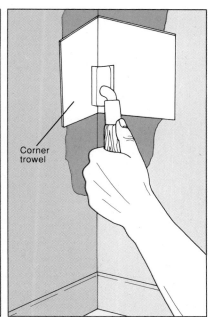

Corner trowel

1 Installing metal-lath backing. Clean out the hole and undercut its edges *(page 35, bottom, step 1)*. If there is no expanded metal lath reinforcement over the lath strips in the corner *(page 30)*, insert a piece to anchor the patch. Wearing heavy work gloves, use tin snips to cut the metal lath to fit over the exposed wooden lath. Bend it at a 90-degree angle over the edge of a worktable, shaping it with a ball-peen hammer if necessary. Slip the metal lath into the hole and use a staple gun to secure it to the wood lath *(above)*.

2 Filling the hole. Moisten the lath and the undercut edges of the hole with a spray bottle of water. Apply the first layer of patching compound with a flexible 5-inch knife, working from the edges to the center *(above, left)*. Press a thin layer of compound behind the undercut edges, through the metal lath and between the wood lath strips. Let the first layer dry overnight. Apply a second layer, filling the hole to within 1/4 inch of the wall surface. Scratch this coat with a nail to provide a grip for the final layer and let it dry overnight. Apply a final layer of joint compound, using a corner trowel to smooth it *(above, right)*. Draw the trowel down firmly and evenly, its point in the corner and its blades flat against the walls. A flexible 3- or 4-inch knife can also be used to apply the final layer of compound. Feather the patch with a flexible 8-inch knife, tapering its edges to the level of the surrounding wall.

PATCHING AN OUTSIDE CORNER

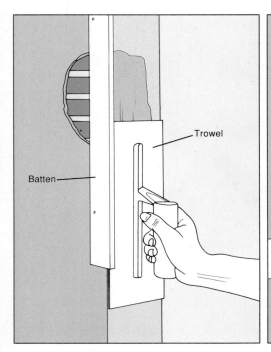

Batten

Trowel

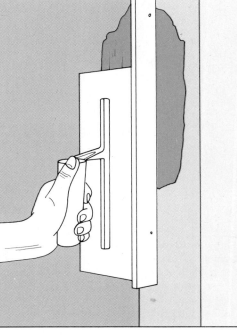

Using a temporary batten as a guide.
Nail a batten—a straight, narrow strip of wood—along the corner to serve as a guide for the trowel. Clean the hole and undercut its edges. Nail the batten into sound plaster along one side of the corner, so that about an inch of its edge protrudes beyond the corner. Moisten the hole with a spray bottle of water and use a flexible 5-inch knife to work a thin first layer of patching compound into the side opposite the batten. Let the compound dry overnight. Apply a second layer with a rectangular trowel *(far left)*. Fill the hole to within 1/4 inch of the wall surface and scratch the compound to provide a gripping surface for the final layer. Allow the compound to dry overnight. Apply joint compound as the final layer, pressing it flush against the batten to mold a straight corner. Allow the third layer to dry overnight, then carefully pull off the batten and nail it to the opposite side of the corner. Repeat the procedure to patch the other side *(near left)*. Remove the batten and smooth the repair with medium-grit sandpaper on a sanding block. Wipe clean and prime.

REPAIRING A CORNER BEAD

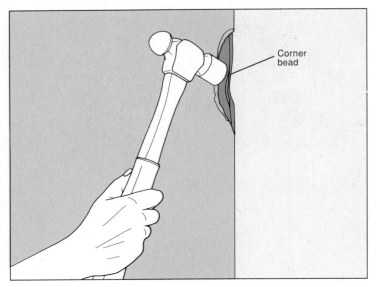

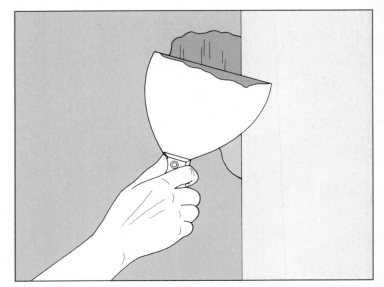

1 **Straightening the corner bead.** Using a ball-peen hammer or a small mallet, lightly tap the dented corner bead to straighten it *(above)*. If vibrations from the hammer blows start to loosen or crack the surrounding plaster, use pliers instead to gently bend the bead back into shape. The flanges may remain slightly deformed, but make the corner edge of the bead as straight as possible.

2 **Covering the corner bead.** On one side of the corner bead, undercut, moisten and fill the damaged plaster as for a wide crack *(pages 35-36, steps 1-3)*. Apply a final layer of joint compound using a knife wider than the damaged area. Draw the knife down the side of the bead with the blade extending past its edge *(above)*, using the edge of the bead as a guide for evenly filling the corner. Repeat this technique on the other side of the corner. Feather the patch by drawing the knife over the compound away from the corner, tapering the edges of the patch to the level of the wall.

REPLACING A DAMAGED SECTION OF CORNER BEAD

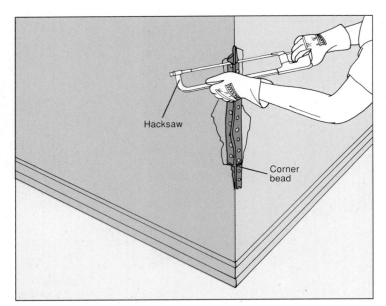

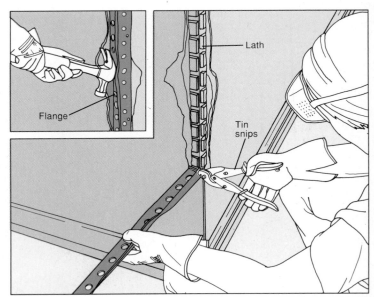

1 **Sawing out the damaged bead.** If damage to the corner bead is too severe to be straightened *(above)*, remove the damaged section. Wearing work gloves, use a hacksaw to cut horizontally through the corner of the bead a few inches above and below the damaged area *(above)*. It is not necessary to cut all the way through the flanges of the bead with the hacksaw.

2 **Snipping the flanges.** If the corner bead is nailed to the lath or studs, use a claw hammer or prybar to pull the nails out of the damaged section *(inset)*. Then use tin snips to cut through the flanges of the bead at a right angle, completing the cuts started with the hacksaw *(above)*. Take care not to deform the ends of the flanges remaining in the wall. Pull the damaged section of corner bead out of the plaster and discard it.

REPLACING A DAMAGED SECTION OF CORNER BEAD (continued)

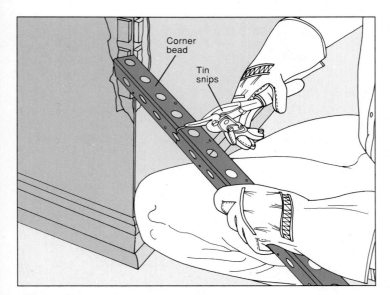

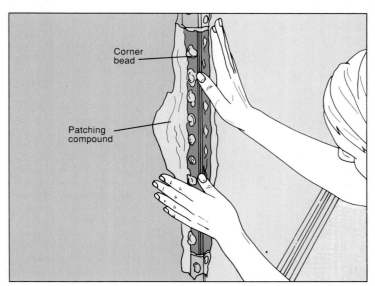

3 **Measuring and cutting a new corner bead.** Measure the space left along the corner, and cut a length of new corner bead 1/8 to 1/4 inch shorter. First set the corner bead on a worktable, flanges down, and cut through the rounded corner of the bead with a hacksaw, at a right angle to the bead. Then snip each flange straight to the cut with tin snips *(above)* to part the bead. Clean the damaged area, undercut its edges and moisten it as for a wide crack *(page 35, bottom, step 1)*.

4 **Installing the new corner bead.** Using a small knife or trowel, cover the exposed lath with a layer of quick-setting patching compound. Press the new section of corner bead into the wet compound, allowing it to ooze through the holes in the bead to form keys. Carefully position the new bead to the same depth as the existing bead, and align their ends perfectly. If the compound keying through the holes of the bead exceeds the level of the wall, smooth it down with a knife. Allow the compound to dry overnight. Finish the corner repair as on page 44, top, step 2.

RESTORING A TEXTURED SURFACE

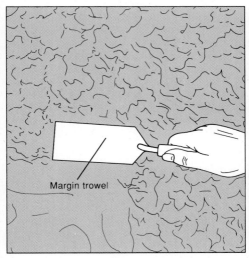

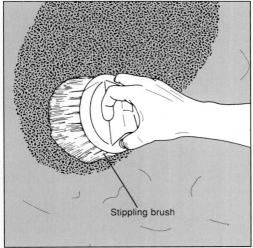

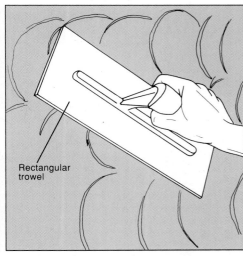

Creating special textures. Finishing a repair in textured plaster takes a light touch and a bit of artistry. To fill nail holes and hairline cracks, a finger is best able to maneuver a bit of spackling compound into tiny crevices *(page 33)*. For larger repairs, a wide range of effects can be created by brushes, sponges, trowels and putty knives. Repair damaged plaster as shown in this chapter, but do not apply joint tape. Reproduce the wall texture in the final layer of joint compound. Experiment before you begin—a scrap of drywall or a thick heavy piece of cardboard makes a good surface on which to practice. A stucco effect

(above, left) can be achieved by dabbing at the wet compound with a small margin trowel, placing the blade flat against the surface and then pulling it away to form peaks. To recreate a stippled effect, use a stippling brush *(above, center)*, a whisk broom, or a wire brush to strike the surface of the wet compound. A rectangular trowel handled with a semicircular motion creates a ridged adobe effect *(above, right)*. If the original plaster texture is worn or covered with heavy layers of paint, soften the peaks of the new texture with fine sandpaper after it dries.

WOOD TRIM AND PANELS

Wood trim is more than just decoration. It seals joints between unlike surfaces such as floor and wall, or panels and ceiling. Baseboards and chair rails protect walls from bumps, the trim around doors and windows hides rough framing, and panels may disguise an unsightly wall.

The anatomy on page 48 presents a fanciful composite of the wood trim and panels that may be found in your home. Wood moldings come in hundreds of profiles. Antique moldings are often made of fine hardwoods such as walnut or cherry, and may have been custom designed and hand-shaped. Modern moldings are made of softwood such as fir or pine, and are mechanically milled by the mile. Some consist of short lengths of wood glued together; these are meant to be painted.

Moldings are installed with finishing nails of various sizes. These narrow nails with small heads can be countersunk with a nail set and camouflaged with filler. Moldings should be nailed through the wall into underlying studs with finishing nails one-third longer than the combined thickness of the molding and wall; the exception is a molding so delicate that a large nail would split the wood.

Where two strips of molding meet at an outside corner, their ends are miter-cut at a 45-degree angle. At an inside corner, one strip is coped (page 60) to fit the contours of the other.

Panels or boards of solid wood are cared for in the same way as fine wood trim. Tongue-and-groove pine boards are commonly installed partway up the wall in a style called wainscoting. More popular are 4-by-8-foot plywood or hardboard panels. They are veneered with real wood or with wood-printed paper or vinyl, and the surface is sealed with a protective layer of plastic. The panels may be installed with panel nails, panel adhesive, or both, to furring or directly to the wall.

How wood is cleaned, stripped and repaired depends on its finish. Wood trim may have a clear finish such as oil, shellac, lacquer, alkyd or polyurethane varnish, or it may be painted. Always test a clear finish in a hidden area first. Alcohol dissolves shellac, lacquer thinner (acetone) dissolves lacquer, and both are softened by water. Varnish and paint are washable and must be removed with paint stripper.

Because wood trim protects the wall, it suffers its share of dents and scratches. Settling of the house framing can work

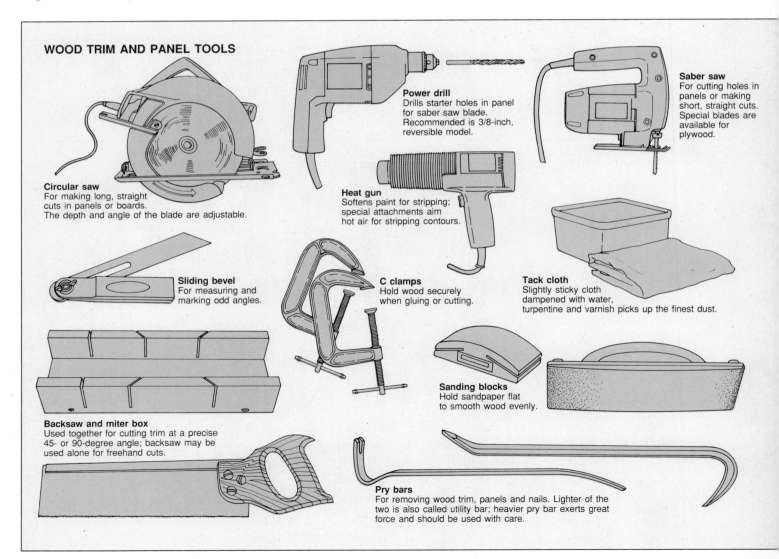

WOOD TRIM AND PANEL TOOLS

Circular saw
For making long, straight cuts in panels or boards. The depth and angle of the blade are adjustable.

Power drill
Drills starter holes in panel for saber saw blade. Recommended is 3/8-inch, reversible model.

Saber saw
For cutting holes in panels or making short, straight cuts. Special blades are available for plywood.

Heat gun
Softens paint for stripping; special attachments aim hot air for stripping contours.

Sliding bevel
For measuring and marking odd angles.

C clamps
Hold wood securely when gluing or cutting.

Tack cloth
Slightly sticky cloth dampened with water, turpentine and varnish picks up the finest dust.

Sanding blocks
Hold sandpaper flat to smooth wood evenly.

Backsaw and miter box
Used together for cutting trim at a precise 45- or 90-degree angle; backsaw may be used alone for freehand cuts.

Pry bars
For removing wood trim, panels and nails. Lighter of the two is also called utility bar; heavier pry bar exerts great force and should be used with care.

trim loose from the walls, causing gaps. Overzealous painters may obliterate its contours with layer after layer of paint. Panels present a different set of problems. They may bow when nails or adhesive let go, or suffer water damage caused by condensation or plumbing problems within the wall.

With few exceptions, wood trim and panels should be repaired in place. If a panel was installed with adhesive, it will be impossible to remove intact. Old wood trim becomes brittle with age and molding is fragile. If a molding breaks, save the pieces, even the splinters. An irreplaceable molding can be reassembled with white glue and carefully clamped until dry.

Consult the Troubleshooting Guide on page 49 for a list of problems affecting wood trim and panels, along with their best solutions. The most tedious—and most rewarding—repair is stripping years of paint off old wood. Only fine hardwoods or mellow old pine deserve the labor it takes to strip down their complicated contours. Before stripping an old painted molding, remove paint from a hidden spot and check whether the wood grain should be highlighted by a clear finish; if not, just partially strip the wood to sharpen its contours, then repaint it.

If you decide to use a chemical stripper, choose a compound containing methylene chloride, and buy the heaviest can—it contains the strongest formulation. Chemical stripper is extremely hazardous. Ventilate the room very well while using it, and extinguish all flames. Wear heavy rubber gloves, long sleeves and safety goggles, and protect the floor and surrounding surfaces (page 141). Allow paint and stripper residue on rags to dry before discarding them in a cool, ventilated place. Other chemicals used when working with wood—panel adhesive, varnish, wood filler—can also be hazardous. Always follow label directions, and consult the Emergency Guide (page 8) and the chapter on paint (page 68) for more information.

Repairs to wood require a variety of cutting and measuring tools, plus other basic tools, pictured below. A tack cloth, for picking up dust, can be made by dampening a square of soft cotton fabric with water, then sprinkling it evenly with a few teaspoons of turpentine and a few teaspoons of varnish. Fold the cloth and wring it, then store it in a sealed container. The cloth can be replenished as needed.

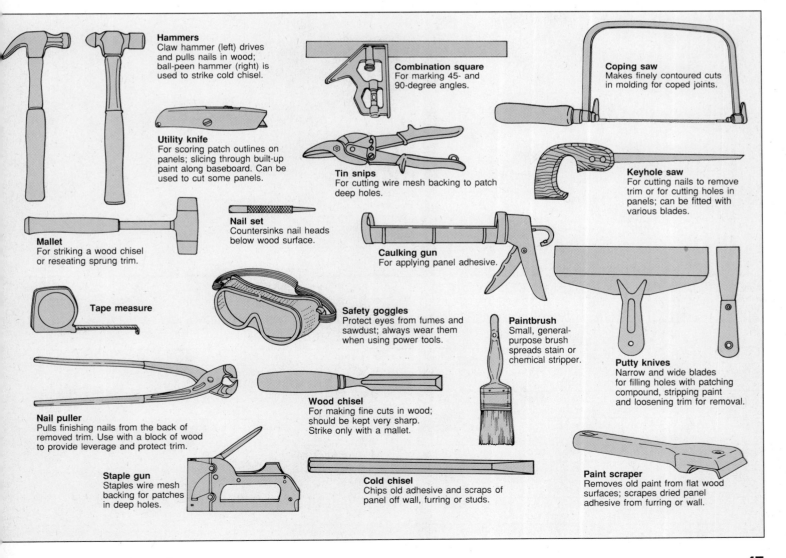

Hammers
Claw hammer (left) drives and pulls nails in wood; ball-peen hammer (right) is used to strike cold chisel.

Utility knife
For scoring patch outlines on panels; slicing through built-up paint along baseboard. Can be used to cut some panels.

Mallet
For striking a wood chisel or reseating sprung trim.

Nail set
Countersinks nail heads below wood surface.

Tape measure

Nail puller
Pulls finishing nails from the back of removed trim. Use with a block of wood to provide leverage and protect trim.

Staple gun
Staples wire mesh backing for patches in deep holes.

Combination square
For marking 45- and 90-degree angles.

Tin snips
For cutting wire mesh backing to patch deep holes.

Caulking gun
For applying panel adhesive.

Safety goggles
Protect eyes from fumes and sawdust; always wear them when using power tools.

Wood chisel
For making fine cuts in wood; should be kept very sharp. Strike only with a mallet.

Cold chisel
Chips old adhesive and scraps of panel off wall, furring or studs.

Paintbrush
Small, general-purpose brush spreads stain or chemical stripper.

Coping saw
Makes finely contoured cuts in molding for coped joints.

Keyhole saw
For cutting nails to remove trim or for cutting holes in panels; can be fitted with various blades.

Putty knives
Narrow and wide blades for filling holes with patching compound, stripping paint and loosening trim for removal.

Paint scraper
Removes old paint from flat wood surfaces; scrapes dried panel adhesive from furring or wall.

WOOD TRIM AND PANEL ANATOMY

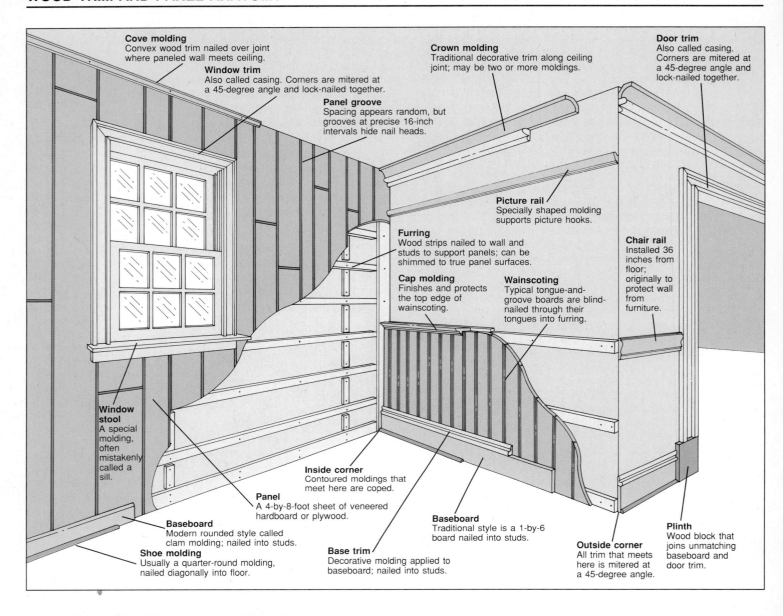

Cove molding
Convex wood trim nailed over joint where paneled wall meets ceiling.

Window trim
Also called casing. Corners are mitered at a 45-degree angle and lock-nailed together.

Panel groove
Spacing appears random, but grooves at precise 16-inch intervals hide nail heads.

Crown molding
Traditional decorative trim along ceiling joint; may be two or more moldings.

Door trim
Also called casing. Corners are mitered at a 45-degree angle and lock-nailed together.

Picture rail
Specially shaped molding supports picture hooks.

Furring
Wood strips nailed to wall and studs to support panels; can be shimmed to true panel surfaces.

Cap molding
Finishes and protects the top edge of wainscoting.

Wainscoting
Typical tongue-and-groove boards are blind-nailed through their tongues into furring.

Chair rail
Installed 36 inches from floor; originally to protect wall from furniture.

Window stool
A special molding, often mistakenly called a sill.

Panel
A 4-by-8-foot sheet of veneered hardboard or plywood.

Baseboard
Modern rounded style called clam molding; nailed into studs.

Shoe molding
Usually a quarter-round molding, nailed diagonally into floor.

Inside corner
Contoured moldings that meet here are coped.

Baseboard
Traditional style is a 1-by-6 board nailed into studs.

Base trim
Decorative molding applied to baseboard; nailed into studs.

Outside corner
All trim that meets here is mitered at a 45-degree angle.

Plinth
Wood block that joins unmatching baseboard and door trim.

WOOD FILLERS AND PATCHING COMPOUNDS

TYPE	CHARACTERISTICS	APPLICATIONS
Putty stick	Wax-based, very easy to use; incompatible with lacquer.	Filling countersunk nail holes and small scratches on varnished wood; coloring other fillers.
Shellac stick	Difficult to use, especially on vertical surfaces.	Fine furniture and woodwork repair; perfecting final finish.
Wood putty	Accepts stain, easy to use; some are pre-colored, or color may be added before use.	Most repairs to finished woodwork where there will not be heavy wear.
Wood dough (or plastic wood filler)	May be pre-colored; difficult to apply and to sand. Very strong; sets quickly.	Areas of wear such as corners.
Plaster of paris	Accepts paint; easy to use. Very strong; sets very quickly.	Good base for building up large or heavily contoured areas.
Spackling compound	Accepts paint; easy to use. Premixed or dry powder; can be thinned with water.	Repairs on wood surfaces to be painted.
Caulk	Flexible, moisture-resistant. Some types accept stain or paint.	For areas of heavy moisture.
Sawdust and glue	Mixture of sawdust from the wood to be repaired and wood glue. Accepts stain.	For final surface repairs.
Epoxy preservative	Strengthens wood fibers eaten away by rot.	A primary treatment before filling wherever there is evidence of wood rot.

TROUBLESHOOTING GUIDE

SYMPTOM	POSSIBLE CAUSE	PROCEDURE
Finish dirty	Buildup of grime or kitchen grease; air pollution	On paint or varnish finish, wash with mild detergent-and-water solution or commercial cleaner □○; on oil, shellac or lacquer finish, wash with detergent suds *(p. 50)* □○
Finish dull	Humidity has softened shellac or lacquer finish	Restore the finish *(p. 50)* ▭○
Wax buildup on finish	Old wax not stripped periodically	Remove wax with turpentine or mineral spirits on a soft cloth □○; if necessary, restore the finish *(p. 50)* ▭○
Clear finish discolored or stained	White water marks, spills	On shellac or lacquer finish, wipe spot gently with proper solvent on cloth or cotton swab □○; on varnish finish, rub gently with very fine steel wool and mineral oil in direction of grain □○
Scratch on painted finish	Normal wear and tear	On a shallow scratch, feather in a paint touch-up *(p. 50)* □○; on a deep scratch, apply a filler *(p. 51)* □○, then touch up
Scratch on clear finish	Normal wear and tear	On shellac or lacquer, stroke lightly with proper solvent *(p. 50)* on a cotton swab □○; on any clear finish, apply liquid color or felt pen *(p. 50)* □○; on a deep scratch, apply putty stick *(p. 51)* □○
Alligatored clear finish (a network of cracks in surface)	Aging of finish; fluctuations in temperature or humidity	Restore finish with the proper solvent *(p. 50)* ▭○
Paint blistered or cracked	Fluctuations in temperature or humidity; water seeps under paint; paint applied over unprepared surface	Scrape flaking paint, fill and sand *(p. 51)* ▭◐
Small hole in clear-finished trim or panel	Countersunk nail head; wire or cable removed	Fill with a putty stick *(p. 51)* □○; for larger hole, apply filler *(p. 51)* □○ and touch up *(p. 56)* □○
Small hole in painted trim or panel	Countersunk nail head; wire or cable removed	Fill with crayon in same color; for larger hole, apply filler *(p. 51)* □○
Gap between trim and wall	Trim warped; nails loose; wall not straight	Reseat trim; if unsuccessful, fill the gap *(p. 52)* □○
Large hole, deep dent, broken or worn corner in trim	Electrical outlet removed from baseboard; lock removed from door trim	On a painted finish, fill the damaged area *(p. 52)* ▭◐; on a clear finish, install a wood patch *(p. 54)* ■◐ if possible; or fill the damaged area *(p. 52)* ▭◐ and grain the surface *(p. 56)* ▭○
Missing piece of baseboard or other trim	Radiator or baseboard heater removed; doorway walled in; trim never installed	Cut and install new moldings *(p. 55)* ▭◐
Conspicuous patch in clear-finished trim	Repair not finished to match surrounding wood	Sand off old finish; stain and grain patch *(p. 56)* ▭◐
Excessive paint buildup on trim	Careless or unnecessary repainting	Strip and sand wood *(p. 57)* ▭◐
Extensive damage to trim	Paint buildup that can't be stripped in place; water or fire damage	Remove trim *(p. 58)* ▭◐; cut replacement pieces if necessary *(p. 59)* ▭◐; install trim *(p. 60)* ▭◐
Door or window trim extensively damaged or missing	Same as above; also new door or window installed; trim removed to install panels	Remove trim *(p. 58)* ▭○; cut replacement pieces, if necessary *(p. 59)* ▭○; and install trim *(p. 61)* ▭◐
Plywood or hardboard panel loose or bowed	Panel not allowed to reach room temperature and humidity for 48 hours before installation; fluctuations in temperature or humidity; wall moist	Resecure panel *(p. 63)* ▭○
Large hole in plywood or hardboard panel	Access hole cut for work on wall; electrical outlet or built-in cabinet removed	Patch the hole with a scrap piece of panel *(p. 62)* ▭◐; or remove damaged panel *(p. 63)* and cut and install replacement panel *(pp. 65, 67)* ▭◐
Panel surface marred beyond repair; panel permanently warped	Water or fire damage; damage to wall under panel	Remove panel *(p. 63)* ▭◐; check and correct damage to wall; cut *(p. 65)* and install *(p. 67)* a new panel ▭◐

DEGREE OF DIFFICULTY: □ **Easy** ▭ **Moderate** ■ **Complex**
ESTIMATED TIME: ○ **Less than 1 hour** ◐ **1 to 3 hours** ● **Over 3 hours** *(Does not include drying time)*

RESTORING AN ALLIGATORED CLEAR FINISH

1 **Washing the surface.** Shellac and lacquer are softened and clouded by water; if this occurs as you clean, stop, rinse and dry the finish and go to step 2. A varnish finish may be scrubbed more vigorously. Mix a mild solution of detergent and water, whipping up a good froth. Using a soft-bristled brush, scrub the alligatored area thoroughly with the suds *(above)*, lifting off any loose flakes of varnish. Take care not to scrub water into the wood grain. Rinse the area well with a moist sponge and wipe it dry.

2 **Restoring the finish.** For a varnish finish, mix a rubbing compound of two parts turpentine, three parts alkyd varnish, and four parts boiled linseed oil. Wearing rubber gloves, dip a folded cloth pad into the mixture and work it into the alligatored surface in smooth strokes *(above)*. Let the finish dry. If the cracks are still apparent, repeat the process. If the cracks do not diminish, strip the wood *(page 57)* and refinish it. For a shellac or lacquer finish, amalgamate the cracks by applying the appropriate solvent—denatured alcohol for shellac, lacquer thinner (acetone) for lacquer—stroking lightly in one direction with a varnish brush.

DISGUISING SCRATCHES

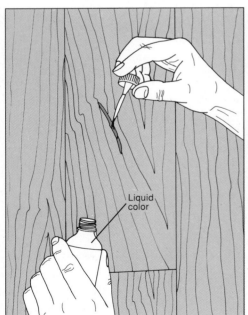

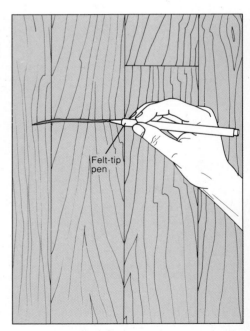

Applying liquid color. Also called furniture dye, liquid colors are available in many wood shades and come in a bottle with an applicator top. Test the shade on a scrap of matching wood or in an out-of-the-way corner before applying it. Two colors may be mixed to obtain the right shade. Brush the liquid into the scratch *(above, left)*, then wipe it with a soft cloth *(above, right)*. If desired, feather the color into the undamaged area to help blend the repair.

Using a felt-tip pen. Special wood-tone retouching pens are available, but an ordinary felt-tip pen works as well. Test the color in an inconspicuous location, then color in the scratch *(above)*. A felt-tip pen can also be used to recreate grain lines on a patch *(page 56)*.

REPAIRING CRACKED OR BLISTERED PAINT

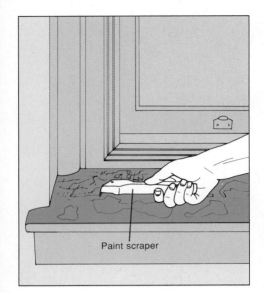

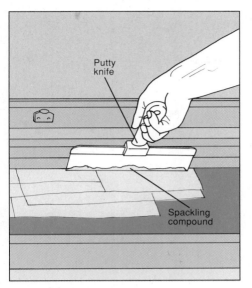

Putty
knife

Spackling
compound

Paint scraper

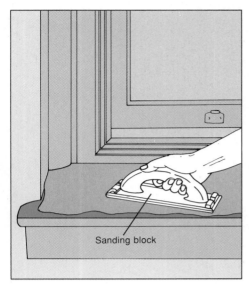

Sanding block

1 **Scraping off loose paint.** When paint loses its grip on the wood beneath it, the result may be either a network of cracks called alligatoring, or a bubbled surface called blistering. To smooth the damaged surface for a new coat of paint, first use a paint scraper to dislodge all loose chips and flakes *(above)*, taking care not to scratch the wood underneath. Paint that adheres well may be left on the wood, but if the surface is very thick or bumpy, you may need to strip the wood with heat or chemicals before repainting *(page 57)*.

2 **Filling the surface.** Spread a thin layer of spackling compound over the damaged area with a wide, flexible putty knife *(above)*. Flex the blade of the knife firmly, filling in cracks and depressions without building up the surface. Two or three thin coats fill better than one thick coat; allow each coat to dry 2 hours between applications. Fill contoured moldings as on page 53, step 5. Sand the compound between coats *(step 3)*.

3 **Sanding the surface.** Using fine sandpaper on a sanding block, smooth the filled surface *(above)*. Cut the filler down just to the original paint surface, without exposing any high spots. Sand contoured molding as described on page 53, step 6. Seal the repair with primer or shellac before painting.

FILLING SMALL HOLES

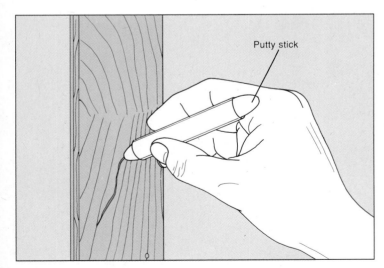

Putty stick

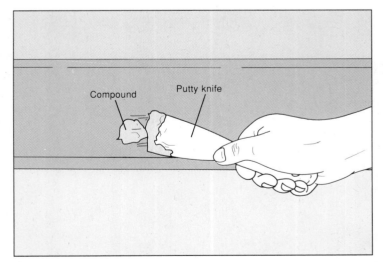

Compound   Putty knife

Using a putty stick. Sold in various wood tones, putty sticks can be used to cover countersunk nails and deep scratches. Rub the tip of the stick into the depression to bring it level with the finished surface *(above)*. Warm the tip between your fingers to help the filler spread, or use a knife blade to cut off and press in a small amount. A child's wax crayon or a wax-based shoe polish may also be used.

Filling with a patching compound. To fill holes and depressions up to an inch wide, select the appropriate compound from the chart on page 48. Use a putty knife to push the compound into the hole *(above)*. If the hole is deep, apply several layers, allowing the compound to dry after each application. Smooth the repair with fine sandpaper and apply shellac or primer before painting.

CLOSING A BASEBOARD GAP

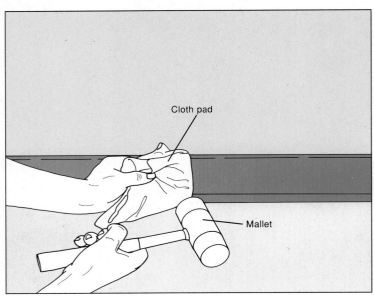

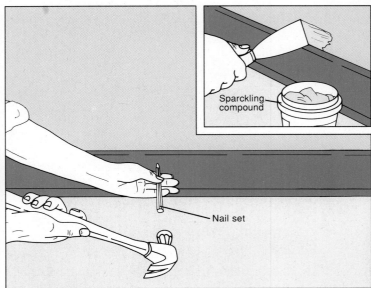

Reseating the molding. If trim molding has "sprung," leaving a gap along the wall, try tapping it back in place using a rubber mallet padded with a piece of cloth *(above, left)*. Use a hammer and nail set to countersink any nail heads that rise to the surface *(above, right)*. To secure the sprung trim, hammer several large finishing nails through the trim into the studs behind it (to locate studs, see page 136). Countersink the nail heads. If this method fails to reseat warped molding, a last resort is to fill the gap with spackling compound, using a flexible putty knife *(inset)*. Smooth the compound with fine sandpaper after it dries. Due to expansion and contraction of the wood, such a patch is usually temporary.

PATCHING A LARGE, DEEP HOLE

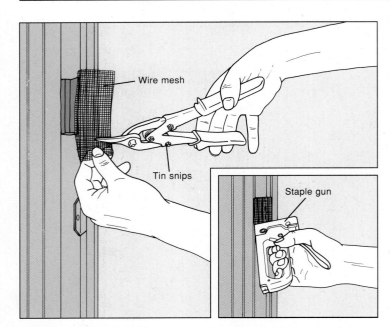

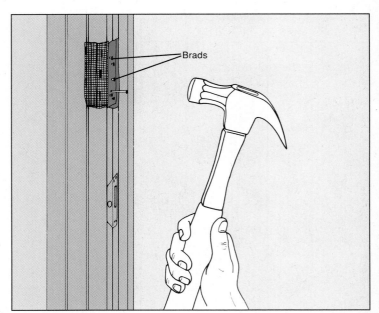

1 Installing a backing. To help anchor patching compound in a deep hole, use tin snips to cut a backing of fine wire mesh—window screening, in this example—1/2 inch larger than the hole *(above)*. Bend up the edges of the screening and secure it in the hole using a staple gun *(inset)*, ensuring that all the wire edges are beneath the surface of the molding.

2 Adding brads for support. To provide a gripping surface for patching compound in a shallow depression at a corner or in an area of wear, hammer in several small tacks or brads *(above)*. Allow their heads to protrude slightly, but not beyond the surface of the molding. Alternatively, provide a rough surface for the patching compound by punching a number of small holes in the wood with an awl.

PATCHING A LARGE, DEEP HOLE (continued)

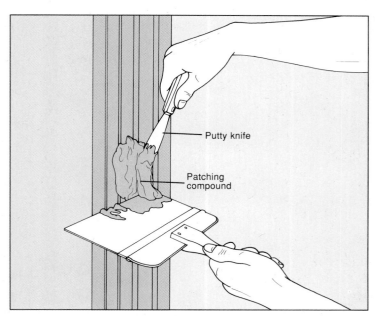

3 **Filling with plaster of paris.** Strong and quick-setting, plaster of paris makes a good first coat for an area that is difficult to fill or will be subject to wear and tear—a door jamb, in this example. Mix a small quantity of plaster powder and water to a smooth paste. Using a flexible 2-inch knife, squeeze plaster through the wire mesh backing or around the brads. Build up this first layer to approximately 1/8 inch below the surface of the wood, leaving a rough-textured base for the next coat. Allow the plaster to dry about an hour.

4 **Applying patching compound.** Select the best patching compound for the molding from the chart on page 48. Using a flexible 2-inch knife, spread a thin layer of the compound over the plaster of paris *(above)*. Depending on the size, depth and contours of the area, several applications may be necessary; allow each layer to dry before applying the next. After applying the final layer, go directly to step 5 before it dries.

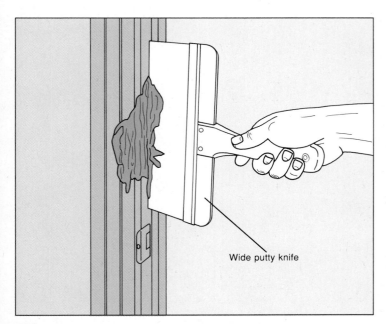

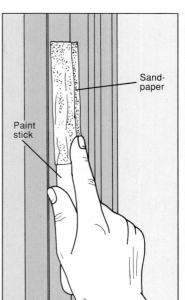

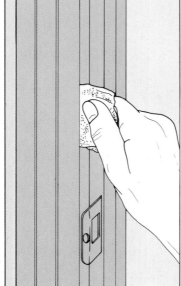

5 **Shaping the contours of the molding.** Position the blade of a wide putty knife so that it spans the entire patch and the molding on each side of it. Closely following the contours of the molding, pull the blade across the patch, shaping it to the same contours *(above)*. Let the patching compound dry. If the contours are not filled completely in one pass, repeat this technique.

6 **Sanding the patch.** Smooth all flat areas of the patch with fine sandpaper on a sanding block. To smooth contours, wrap the sandpaper around a piece of wood—a paint-stirring stick in this example—that fits the contour *(above, left)*. To define sharp angles, fold the sandpaper and use the folded edge to sand *(above, right)*. After sanding, use your finger to fill slight imperfections with compound. Finally, smooth the entire patch with very fine steel wool and apply shellac or primer.

INSTALLING A WOODEN PATCH

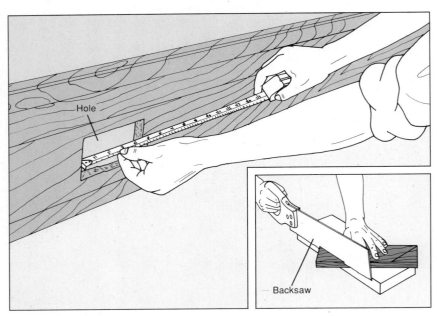

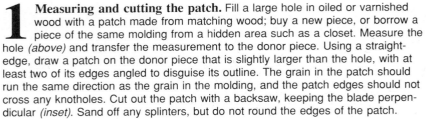

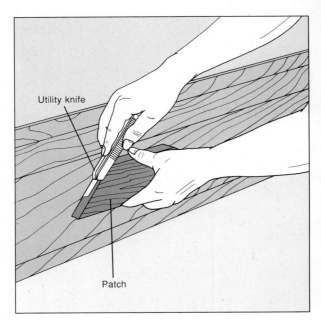

1 **Measuring and cutting the patch.** Fill a large hole in oiled or varnished wood with a patch made from matching wood; buy a new piece, or borrow a piece of the same molding from a hidden area such as a closet. Measure the hole *(above)* and transfer the measurement to the donor piece. Using a straight-edge, draw a patch on the donor piece that is slightly larger than the hole, with at least two of its edges angled to disguise its outline. The grain in the patch should run the same direction as the grain in the molding, and the patch edges should not cross any knotholes. Cut out the patch with a backsaw, keeping the blade perpendicular *(inset)*. Sand off any splinters, but do not round the edges of the patch.

2 **Scribing the patch outline.** Hold the patch securely over the hole and trace its exact outline on the molding with a sharp utility knife *(above)*. Take care not to scratch the surrounding wood finish. Set the patch aside and use the utility knife to deepen the cut.

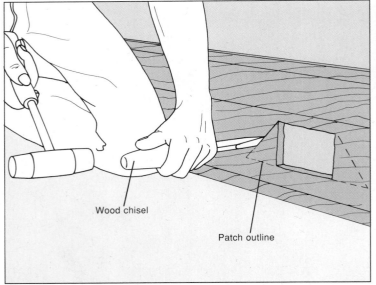

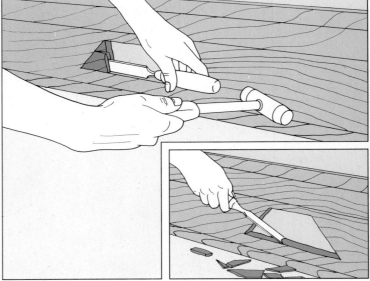

3 **Chiseling the outline.** Set the blade of a very sharp wood chisel in the outline cut, its bevel facing in toward the hole. Tap the chisel lightly with a mallet *(above, left)*, driving the blade in about 1/8 inch. Reposition the chisel along the outline and continue deepening the cut all the way around. Then set the chisel blade in the hole with its bevel facing out, and tap the chisel to dislodge thin chips of wood from within the outline *(above, right)*. Repeat this procedure, cutting the outline deeper and chiseling out the chips, until the opening is as deep as the thickness of the patch. If you dislodge any chips of wood beyond the outline, save them— they can be glued back in place. Smooth the opening without enlarging it or rounding its edges, using the chisel bevel side down *(inset)*.

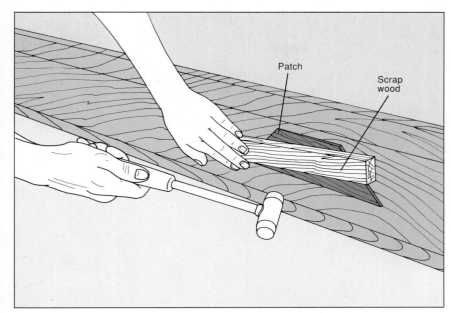

Patch

Scrap wood

4 **Inserting the patch.** Test the patch for size by pushing it slightly into the opening; it should fit very snugly. If the edges don't fit at all, try sanding a bit of wood off the rear corners of the patch. Spread a thin coat of white glue on the inside perimeter of the opening and the edges of the patch, and let it set for a minute. Push the patch into the hole again. Hold a long piece of scrap wood across the patch and tap it lightly with a mallet *(left)*, working the patch into the opening until its surface is flush with the surrounding wood surface. Do not drive the patch too deep—it cannot be pulled out. Wash off oozing glue with a moist sponge. Fill the joint *(page 51)* if necessary, and finish the patch to match the surrounding wood *(page 56)*.

REPLACING A MISSING SECTION OF TRIM

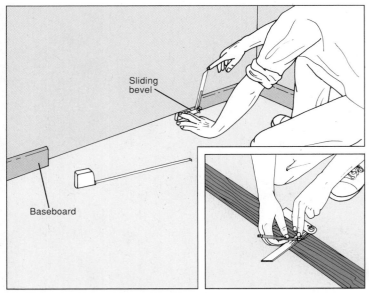

Sliding bevel

Baseboard

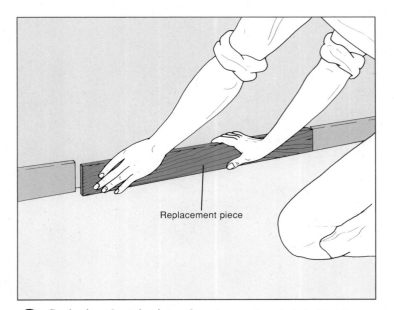

Replacement piece

1 **Measuring and cutting a new section.** Replace a missing section of trim—a baseboard in this example—with a matching piece; if the molding style is no longer made, try to borrow a piece from a hidden area such as a closet. Measure the space between the ends of the existing trim and mark this measurement, plus 1/8 inch, on the replacement piece. Because the ends of the existing trim may not have been cut at a 90-degree angle, use a sliding bevel to measure the angle of each end of the trim *(above)*. Transfer the angles to the marks on the replacement piece by tracing the bevel blade *(inset)*. Cut the replacement piece with a backsaw just outside the marks, keeping the saw blade perpendicular. If the replacement piece will meet an inside corner, make a coped cut if necessary *(page 60)*. If it will meet an outside corner, make a miter cut *(page 59)*.

2 **Springing the trim into place.** Locate the studs behind the space to be filled *(page 136)* and lightly pencil their positions on the wall. Fit one end of the replacement piece against the corresponding end of the trim, bend the piece slightly, and spring its free end into place against the other end of the trim *(above)*. The new piece should fit snugly without bowing; if it is too long, remove it and trim one end slightly with a wood chisel. Drive a finishing nail at each end and at each stud location, and countersink their heads with a nail set. Measure, cut and install other trim elements, such as shoe molding, in the same way.

STAINING AND GRAINING A PATCH

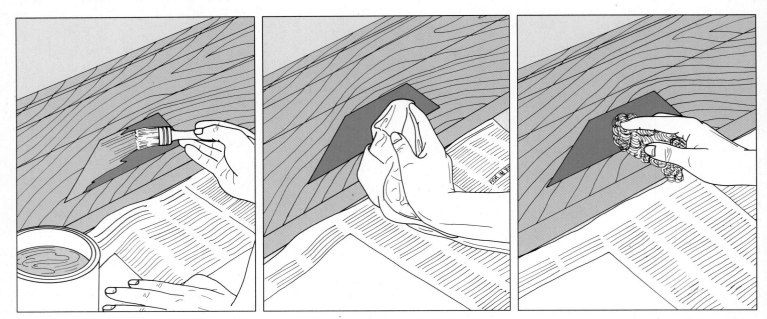

Staining a patch. Arriving at a close color match is an experimental process; before staining the patch, mix several shades of stain and test them on samples of the wood or filler. Apply the varnish or oil that will be used over the stain before judging the final color. Apply a clear pre-stain sealer to the wood patch or filler to keep the stain from penetrating too quickly and deeply. Apply the stain with a varnish brush or a rag in the direction of the wood grain *(above, left)*. If the stain appears too dark, wipe it with a dry rag *(above, center)*; if it is too light, apply a second coat. After each coat dries, remove raised "hairs" of wood by rubbing with fine steel wool *(above, right)*, then dust the surface with a tack cloth. To duplicate the patina of old wood, brush orange shellac over the stain. Duplicate grain lines as described below. Protect the patch with penetrating oil or clear varnish *(page 85)*, but do not apply polyurethane varnish over shellac. Blend the finish coat beyond the edges of the patch.

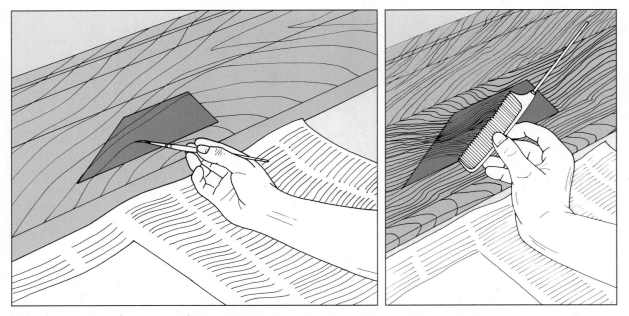

Imitating wood grain on a patch. To reproduce the grain pattern of surrounding wood, the stain can be manipulated in several ways. After staining the patch to its base color, but before varnishing it, use an artist's brush dipped in stain to draw grain lines across the patch *(above, left)*, continuing the lines beyond the patch. A felt-tip pen *(page 50)* may also be used to draw grain lines. Alternatively, apply a coat of stain and, before it dries, drag the teeth of a comb through it *(above, right)*, matching the swirls of the surrounding wood grain. If you are dissatisfied with the effect, wipe off the stain with a dry cloth and try a different technique or tool. Let the stain dry and finish the patch as described above.

STRIPPING PAINT AND VARNISH

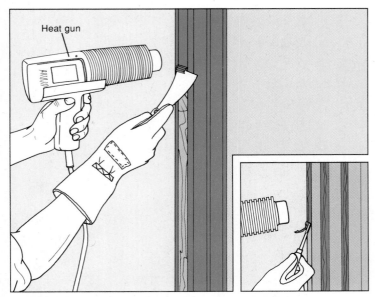

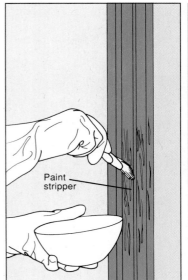

Stripping with a heat gun. A heat gun can blow air heated up to 750° F. Aim the gun carefully and wear heavy gloves. Holding the heat gun 3 to 6 inches from the wood surface, move the nozzle back and forth in short strokes just until the paint begins to blister. As the paint separates from the wood, immediately scrape it off flat areas of the trim with a putty knife *(above)*. Work in the direction of the grain, taking care not to burn or gouge the wood, and use heavy cardboard to shield nearby surfaces not being stripped. To strip paint from crevices, select the scraping tool that best fits the contours of the trim—a dulled wood chisel, in this example *(inset)*.

Stripping with chemicals. Consult the Emergency Guide *(page 8)* for information on the safe use of strippers. Ventilate the area well, and protect surrounding surfaces from drips *(page 141)*. Follow the label instructions for using the stripper. Wearing heavy rubber gloves, brush the stripper in one direction onto a small area of the wood *(above, left)*. When the paint has wrinkled and bubbled, use a putty knife to scrape it off flat surfaces *(above, right)*, wiping the blade frequently with old newspapers. Scrape paint from crevices with the tool that best fits the trim contours. Clean off bits of paint using medium steel wool moistened with the stripper and rinse the wood as recommended on the stripper label.

SANDING STRIPPED WOOD

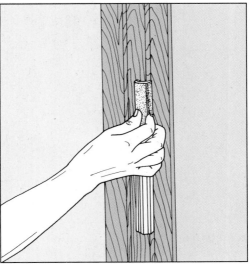

Sanding trim to a uniform finish. First sand all flat areas of the trim, using fine sandpaper on a sanding block *(above, left)* and working in the direction of the wood grain. Then sand contours, wrapping fine sandpaper around a suitably-shaped dowel or scrap of molding *(above, center)*. Use the folded edge of the sandpaper to define narrow recesses. Finally, smooth the entire wood surface with medium, and then fine steel wool *(above, right)*. Wipe the surface free of dust with a dry rag, then with a tack cloth. Before staining and finishing the wood, fill any scratches, dents or holes as described in this chapter.

REMOVING WOOD TRIM

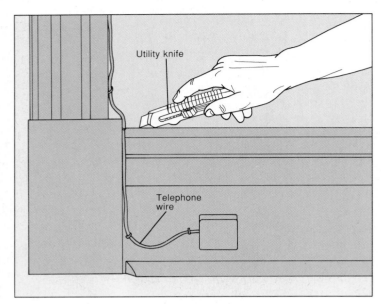

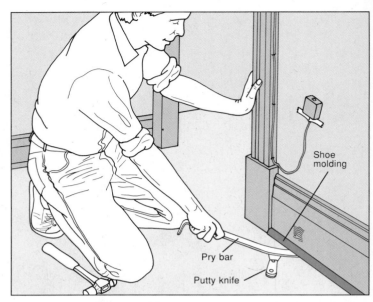

1 **Cutting paint and removing wires.** Layers of paint may obscure the joint between trim and wall; use a utility knife to slice through the paint without marring the wood *(above)*. If a telephone wire is attached to the trim, as shown above, pull out the staples with pliers and remove the connection box. Tape wires out of the way on the wall. In older homes, electrical outlets may have been installed through the baseboard; turn off power to the circuit *(page 137)* and disconnect the outlets *(page 138)*. When removing trim from more than one wall, first draw a sketch of the room. Number the back of each piece as you remove it and note its position on the sketch.

2 **Removing shoe molding.** When removing baseboard trim, take off the shoe molding first. Check the inside corners of the room and start with strips of molding that have coped ends *(page 60)*. At one end, separate the molding from the floor by pushing the blade of a putty knife between them; tap in the blade with a hammer if necessary. Gently insert the end of a pry bar between the knife and the molding, and ease the molding up *(above)*. Continue along the length of the molding. Shoe molding is sometimes nailed to the baseboard instead of the floor; follow step 3 to remove it. If the molding breaks, save the pieces and glue them back together before reinstallation.

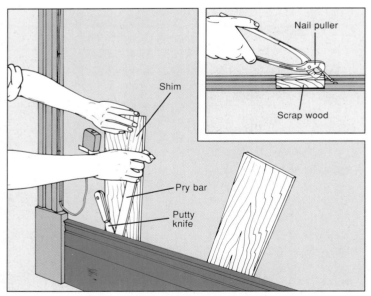

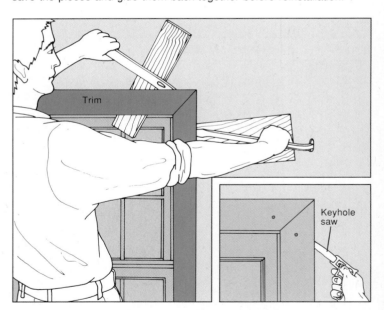

3 **Removing baseboard molding.** A fancy baseboard may be topped with an extra piece of molding that is removed separately, as in this example. Near one end of the molding, insert a putty knife blade between molding and wall. Push in a wood shim behind the knife, and work the end of a pry bar between them *(above)*. Pry the molding out 1/2 inch and wedge a second shim behind it about 2 feet away. Insert the putty knife in front of the second shim, work the pry bar between them, and continue prying off the molding. After removing the molding, use a nail puller to pry nails out from the back *(inset)*. Use the same technique to remove the baseboard.

4 **Removing door and window trim.** Follow step 3 to remove the trim around a door or window, working up from the bottom of the side trim. Use care as you approach the corner joints; two pieces of trim are often nailed to each other there. Try to hammer the corner nails through the joint using a nail set. If the trim pieces remain joined, pry off both pieces at the same time *(above)*. If the wood starts to split, insert a a keyhole saw with a metal-cutting blade, or a hacksaw, behind the trim and cut through the nails *(inset)*.

INSTALLING NEW BASEBOARD TRIM

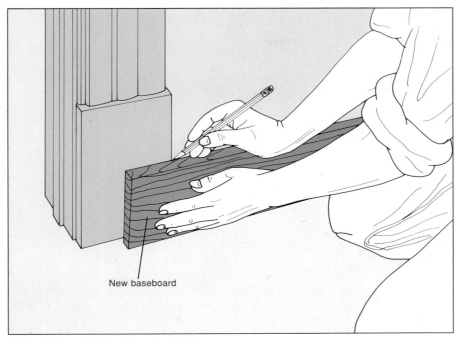

New baseboard

1 **Measuring and marking the new baseboard.** The first trim piece installed is the baseboard. If the baseboard will span the wall from corner to corner, measure the wall and mark the replacement piece. If it will run into door trim, butt one end in the corner and mark the other end where it meets the door trim *(left)*. Check the exact angle of the corner or trim with a sliding bevel *(page 55)*. Use a butt cut *(step 2)* to trim these pieces 1/8 inch longer than their measured length. If two short replacement pieces will meet in mid-wall, join them with a scarf joint, overlapping their ends at a 45-degree angle. Make the scarf cut first *(step 2)*, then butt cut the ends to fit the wall. Shoe molding, and any fancy molding added to the baseboard *(page 58)*, are cut as described above, but their inside-corner joints are coped *(page 60)*. Outside-corner joints for any molding are mitered at a 45-degree angle *(page 60, step 4)*.

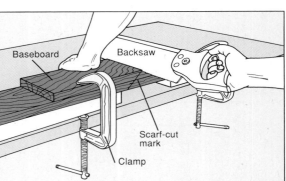

Baseboard

Backsaw

Scarf-cut mark

Clamp

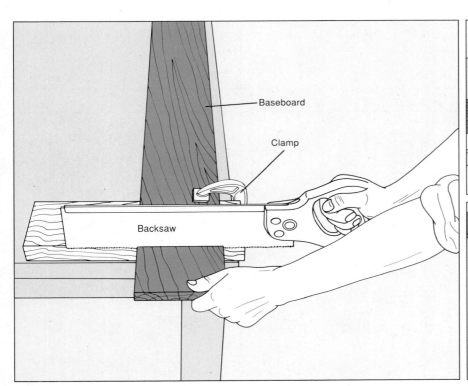

Baseboard

Clamp

Backsaw

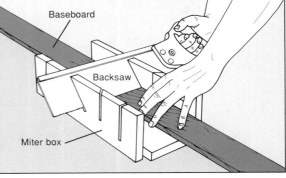

Baseboard

Backsaw

Miter box

2 **Making butt cuts and scarf cuts.** To make a simple butt cut in a baseboard, support the piece on scrap wood and clamp it securely. Place the teeth of the backsaw just outside the marked line, and saw straight down *(above, left)* without wobbling the blade. Hold the free end of the piece as shown so that it doesn't break off. To make a scarf cut in a baseboard, overlap the ends of two pieces, both face up, and clamp them together. Using a straightedge, draw a guideline across the face of the top piece, and continue it at about a 45-degree angle across the edges of the pieces. Place the teeth of the backsaw along the guideline and cut down at an angle *(above right, top)*, closely following the angled line on the edges of the pieces. Make sure the cut doesn't wander.

To make a scarf cut in a contoured molding, or to make a 45-degree miter cut in any trim that will meet at an outside corner, use a miter box with a slot angled for 45-degree face cuts *(above right, bottom)*. Cut the trim one piece at a time, making sure to situate each piece in the miter box so that the cut ends will join properly when installed.

INSTALLING NEW BASEBOARD TRIM (continued)

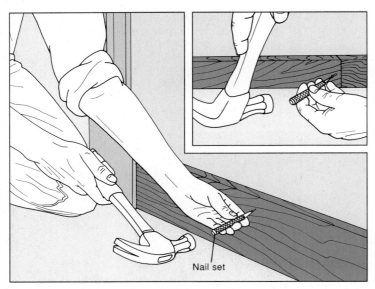

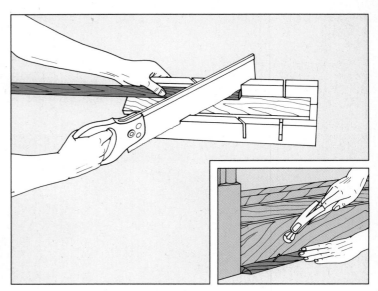

3 **Nailing the baseboard to the wall.** Locate the studs *(page 136)* and mark their positions on the wall. Hold the baseboard firmly in place and hammer a finishing nail straight through it into each stud. (If the baseboard is more than 4 inches wide, drive a pair of nails, 2 inches apart, into each stud.) Drive each nail the last 1/4 inch using a nail set, and countersink its head *(above)*. To secure a scarf joint, drive a pair of finishing nails through the joint at an angle and countersink their heads *(inset)*. Fill the nail holes with a putty stick *(page 51)*.

4 **Installing shoe molding.** Cut shoe molding as described on page 59. Where it will meet door trim, use a backsaw and miter box to cut the end of the molding at a 45-degree angle *(above)*. Install the shoe molding that butts an inside corner first; the piece that joins it will be coped to fit *(below)*. Hold the shoe molding in place against the baseboard and the floor. Drive finishing nails diagonally through the molding into the floor at 16-inch intervals *(inset)*, and countersink their heads.

MAKING A COPED JOINT

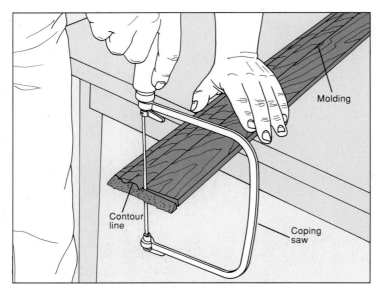

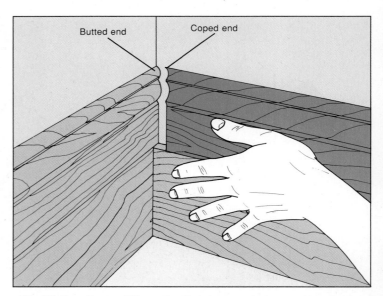

1 **Coping a contoured molding.** Practice coping a scrap piece of the same molding before cutting the final piece. Cut the end of the molding at a 45-degree angle *(page 59, step 2)*; this reveals a contour line on the face of the molding to be followed with the coping saw. With the end hanging over a table edge, slowly and carefully cut along the contours of the molding with the coping saw blade perfectly upright *(above)*. If the molding is heavily contoured, cut across the waste wood periodically to remove small pieces.

2 **Fitting the molding.** Position the coped piece against the butted corner piece *(above)*; the fit should be perfect. Reshape any slight irregularities using a round file or fine sandpaper wrapped around a dowel. If you cannot correct the fit, recope the molding. Once the coped joint fits perfectly, measure and cut the other end *(page 59)*, using a butt cut at an inside corner or a doorway, or a 45-degree miter cut at an outside corner. Install the molding as for a baseboard *(step 3, above)*, using finishing nails.

INSTALLING DOOR OR WINDOW TRIM

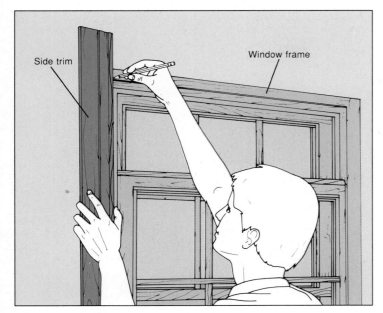

1 **Measuring the side trim.** Butt cut the bottom end of the side trim molding piece *(page 59)*. Hold the piece alongside the window, flush with the inside edge of the window jamb. Mark the inside edge of the molding where it meets the top corner of the window jamb *(above)*. Take down the molding and use a combination square to draw a 45-degree guideline across its face at the mark. Cut and mark the second piece of side trim molding the same way.

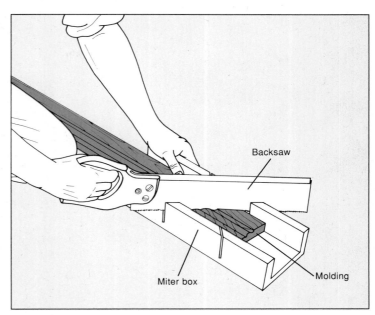

2 **Cutting the trim in a miter box.** Place the side trim molding in the miter box face up, and align the guideline with the box's 45-degree angle slot. Support the free end of the molding on scrap wood. Insert the backsaw blade in the slot, rest its teeth on the molding just outside the guideline, and saw gently on the pull stroke only *(above)*. Cut the second piece of side trim molding the same way.

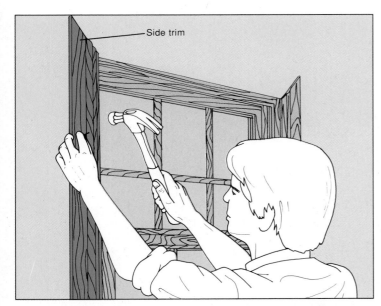

3 **Installing the side trim.** Hold a side trim piece in place against the window jamb. Drive several finishing nails through the trim partway into the window jamb; the rest of the nails will be added after all trim pieces are checked for fit. Tack the second side trim piece in place the same way *(above)*. To make the top trim piece, measure between the inside corners of the side trim pieces and mark this distance on a piece of molding. Mark and cut the ends at a 45-degree angle as described in step 2.

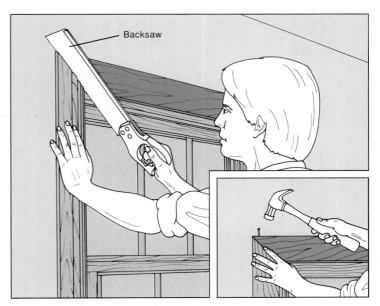

4 **Installing the top trim piece.** Fit the top trim piece between the side trim pieces, and tack it in place. The corner ends should align exactly. If there is an uneven gap at the joint, try sawing along the joint with a backsaw to straighten it *(above)*; lock-nailing the corner later will close the gap. When the trim fits properly, drive finishing nails through it at 8-inch intervals, into both the window jambs and the studs. Then lock-nail the corners by driving finishing nails down through the top trim *(inset)* into the side trim, and through the side trim into the top trim. Use a nail set to countersink all nail heads.

PATCHING A PANEL

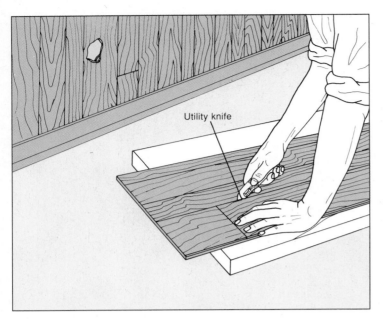
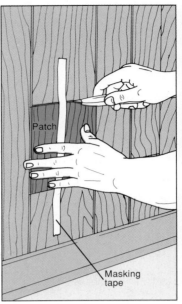
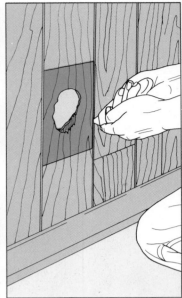

1 **Cutting the patch.** Compare the wood-grain pattern on a scrap panel to the grain in the damaged area to find the best match for the patch. With the panel face up, use a sharp utility knife to cut a rectangular patch a bit larger than the damaged area *(above)*. Make several clean, shallow passes with the knife to cut through each side of the patch. Cut the sides of the patch within the panel grooves to disguise the joints.

2 **Cutting out the damaged area.** Tape the patch over the damaged area, positioning it carefully so that the grooves and grain pattern match. With a utility knife, trace the exact outline of the patch onto the panel *(above, left)*. Remove the patch and, using the utility knife, cut through the panel along the outline *(above, right)*, taking care not to mar the surrounding surface. Several passes with the knife may be necessary. Pull out the damaged piece without tearing the surface of the panel; if the panel is glued to the wall, pry it out carefully with a putty knife.

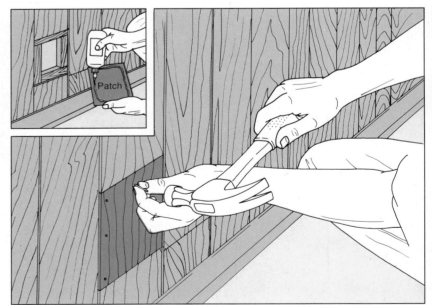

3 **Installing backing for the patch.** If the panel is mounted on furring, nail or glue a 1-by-3 block behind each edge of the hole to support the edges of the patch *(above)*. Position each support so that it will be half under the panel and half under the patch.

4 **Installing the patch.** Spread white glue or panel adhesive on the supports and run a bead of glue around the back edges of the patch *(inset)* and on the furring strips. Wait two minutes, then fit the patch into the hole. Allow the glue to become slightly tacky, then push the patch into position. Hold a block of scrap wood over the patch and tap it with a hammer to seat the patch edges. Wash off any oozing glue. Drive finishing nails at 3-inch intervals around the perimeter of the patch, 1/4 inch from the edges *(above)*. Countersink the nail heads and fill the holes with a putty stick *(page 51)*; the putty stick can also be used to disguise the patch joint.

SECURING A LOOSE PANEL

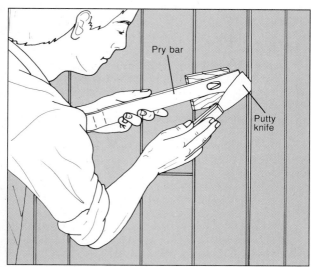

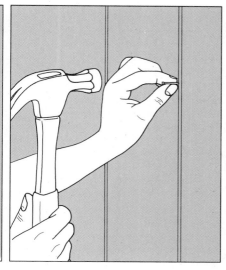

Assessing damage to the panel. If an edge of the panel is bowed or loose, carefully pry it out slightly with a putty knife and a cloth-padded pry bar *(above, left)*. If the nails have pulled through or the adhesive has let go, inject white glue or panel adhesive behind the edge *(above, center)*, wait for it to become tacky (follow label directions) and then push the panel back in place. Drive several panel nails along the loose edge to secure it *(above, right)* and cover their heads with a putty stick *(page 51)*. If the panel bulges in the middle, try to locate the furring strips behind the bulge by rapping on the panel. Drive panel nails through the panel grooves at that location to secure it. If the panel itself is warped, you may need to remove the panel *(below)* and reinstall or replace it.

REMOVING A PANEL

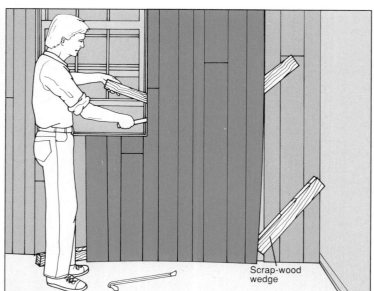

1 Working the panel loose. Remove all trim from the panel *(page 58)*. Cut electrical power to the wall's circuit *(page 137)* and disconnect switches and outlets from the panel *(page 138)*. A panel may be mounted on furring strips, on studs or directly on the wall, and may be glued, nailed or both. Rap against the panel. A hollow sound indicates furring strips or studs; otherwise, the panel is probably glued directly to the wall and will have to be ripped off in pieces *(page 64)*. Check the panel grooves for nail heads at regular intervals. If the heads are small, drive them through with a nail set *(inset)*. Near bottom of the panel, carefully work a putty knife into the joint and insert a wedge of scrap wood to hold it open. Slip a pry bar into the crack *(above, left)* and work the panel off its supports. Watch for nails that may still be securing the panel. Drive the nails through or pull the panel very carefully to dislodge them. Work up the panel in this way, inserting wedges behind both edges *(above, right)*. If the panel doesn't separate readily from the furring or studs, it may be glued; go to page 64 to remove it.

REMOVING A PANEL (continued)

Furring   Panel

2 **Taking down the panel.** Standing on a stepladder, pull the panel free from the wall *(left)*. If nails near the center of the panel resist, reach behind the panel with a piece of scrap wood to pry them up. Check the panel for permanent warpage, cracks or water damage before reusing it. If you are cutting a new panel, use the old one as a template.

REMOVING A GLUED PANEL

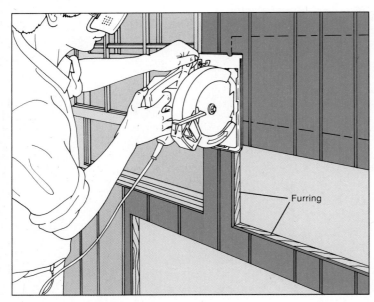

Furring

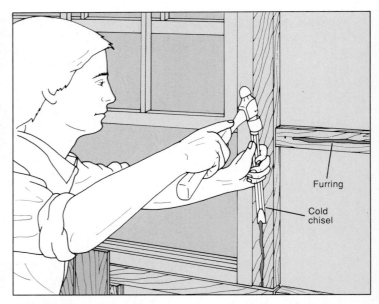

Furring

Cold chisel

1 **Cutting the panel into pieces.** Prepare to remove the panel as on page 63, step 1. If you must cut a glued panel apart to remove it, fit a circular saw with an old blade—the cuts don't have to be clean. Set the cutting depth of the saw to 1/4 inch. Wearing safety goggles, cut through the panel 3 or 4 inches from each edge *(above)*, then cut across the panel at 1-foot intervals. If the saw ejects plaster or drywall dust, set a shallower cutting depth. Rows of nails indicate that the panel is mounted on furring strips or studs; cut along each side of the nails. Pry off the panel sections with a pry bar. Use a putty knife to scrape off pieces that are glued.

2 **Cleaning the wall.** Save a few large panel sections for future patching jobs; discard the rest. Pull out any nails remaining in the furring or the wall with a pry bar or claw hammer. Use a paint scraper or a ball-peen hammer and cold chisel to clean adhesive and bits of panel from the furring *(above)* or the wall, leaving a flat, smooth surface. Replace or resecure any damaged furring strips before installing a new panel.

CUTTING A REPLACEMENT PANEL

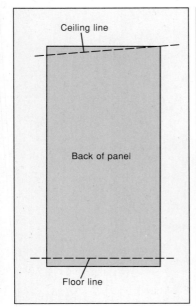

Ceiling line

Back of panel

Floor line

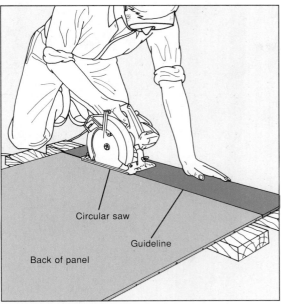

Circular saw

Guideline

Back of panel

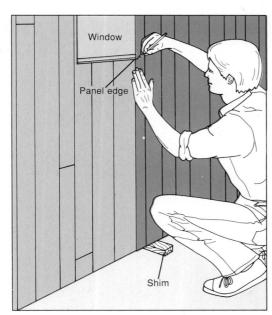

Window

Panel edge

Shim

1 **Measuring and cutting the panel.** If the old panel came off in one piece, use it as a template for marking the new one. If not, first determine whether the ceiling above the opening slants by holding a level along it. Measure the amount of slant and mark a corresponding guideline across the top edge on the back of the panel. (Remember that the positions of the marks will be reversed on the front.) Then measure the height from floor to ceiling along each edge of the opening, subtract 1/2 inch, and mark the height on each panel edge, measuring down from the ceiling guideline. Finally, draw a guideline across the bottom of the panel connecting the two height marks *(above, left)*. Set a circular saw to a cutting depth of 1/2 inch and, supporting the panel face down on scrap lumber, cut along the guidelines *(above, right)*. If the panel is being installed around a window, go to step 2; if it is being installed around an electrical outlet, go to page 66.

2 **Marking the panel at a window.** Position the panel in the opening, inserting shims at the bottom to raise the top edge to the ceiling and fitting its edges flush with the neighboring panels. If necessary, drive a pair of panel nails near the top of the panel to hold it. Mark the panel edges where they overlap the edges of the window framing *(above)*, then take the panel down. Use the same technique to mark the panel for a door. If the panel covers an electrical outlet, mark its position at the same time *(page 66)*.

Window frame

Existing panel

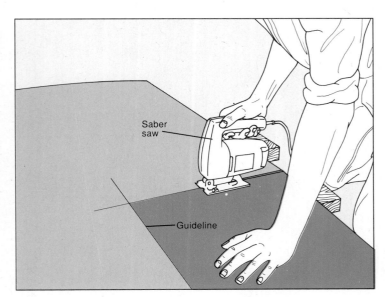

Saber saw

Guideline

3 **Measuring and marking the opening.** Using a measuring tape or straightedge, measure the window from the edge of the existing panel to the inside edge of the window frame *(above)*. Take measurements at the top and bottom of the opening. Transfer these measurements to the back of the panel, using a carpenter's square to draw a guideline of the correct length from each mark you made on the panel edge. Connect the ends of these guidelines to form the outline of the window.

4 **Cutting the opening with a saber saw.** Place the panel face down on scrap-wood supports at least 2 inches thick. Fit a saber saw with a plywood-cutting blade and, wearing safety goggles, cut along the guidelines. When you get to a corner, round the corner with the blade and trim it square later. Install the panel as described on page 67.

CUTTING AN ELECTRICAL BOX OPENING

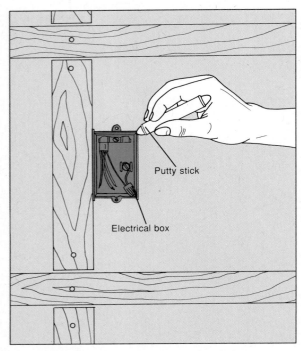

1 **Marking the electrical box.** Turn off power to the circuit (page 137) and disconnect the electrical outlet from the wire. Mark the corners of the electrical box with a putty stick *(above)*, chalk powder, paint or other substance that will rub off when the back of the panel is pressed against it.

2 **Transferring the marks to the panel.** Position the panel in the opening *(page 65, step 2)*. Hold a piece of cloth or scrap wood against the panel surface in the area of the electrical box and tap it lightly with a mallet or hammer *(above)*, imprinting the marks on the back of the panel. Take down the panel.

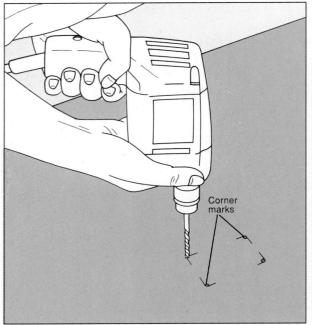

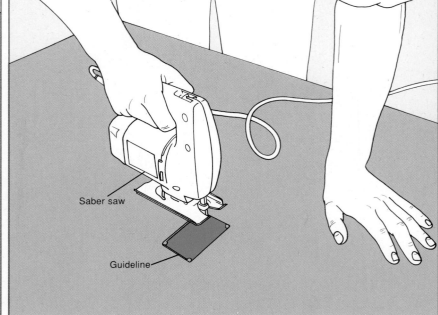

3 **Cutting the opening.** Place the panel face down on scrap-wood supports at least 2 inches thick. Use a straightedge to connect the electrical-box corner marks. At each corner, drill a 1/4-inch pilot hole for the saber saw blade *(above, left)*. Fit the saw with a plywood-cutting blade and, wearing safety goggles, cut the opening 1/8 inch outside the guidelines *(above, right)*.

INSTALLING A PANEL

1 **Applying adhesive.** To install a panel on furring strips, use a caulking gun to apply a narrow bead of panel adhesive to each strip *(above)*. Apply the adhesive sparingly to strips that support the edges of existing panels. If the panel will be mounted on studs, apply adhesive to the studs in the same way. To install a panel directly on the wall, apply the adhesive in vertical lines, ceiling to floor, at 16-inch intervals.

2 **Installing the panel.** Position the panel in the opening *(page 65, step 2)*, pushing it firmly against the adhesive *(above)*. Fasten the top edge of the panel by driving panel nails through the grooves 1 inch from the ceiling *(inset)*.

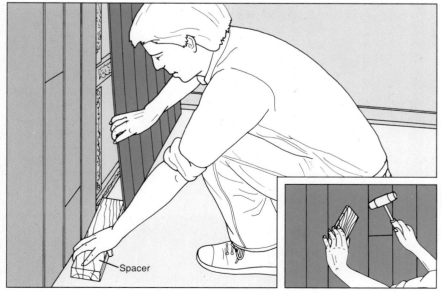

3 **Setting the adhesive.** To help the adhesive cure, pull out the bottom edge of the panel and slip a scrap-wood spacer between the panel and wall at each side *(left)*. Wait the length of time recommended by the adhesive manufacturer (usually a few minutes), then pull out the spacers and press the panel back in place. Working down from the top of the panel, place a block of wood against the surface and tap the block with a hammer or mallet, setting the panel firmly in the adhesive *(inset)*. Add panel nails for extra support, spacing them 1 foot apart, 1/2 inch from the panel edges and at 2-foot intervals along the other furring strips or studs.

PAINT

A fresh coat of paint makes a room look like new, but paint alone cannot cure most wall, ceiling or woodwork problems. Locate and correct the underlying cause of paint failure before repainting; consult other chapters in this book, or call in a professional if necessary.

The Troubleshooting Guide on page 70 walks you through a range of problems with painted surfaces—and with painting itself. Unlike most other household repairs, the usual repair for damaged paint is to do the job over again from scratch. This is simpler than it sounds; modern paints and equipment make painting a wall almost as easy as washing it.

No one paint covers all surfaces equally well. Latex and alkyd paints are used for most indoor surfaces, with latex usually the first choice for walls and ceilings because it dries quickly and cleans up easily with water. Alkyd paint, the odorless successor to oil-based paint, is faster drying than oil-based, but slower than latex. Alkyd paint makes a more dura-

ble coating for woodwork; its main drawback is that it must be thinned and cleaned with mineral spirits. Alkyd and polyurethane varnishes are suitable clear finishes for wood trim; polyurethane is more durable but some people find its hard, plastic-like finish unattractive.

Paints and solvents are dangerous to skin, eyes and lungs. Familiarize yourself with the safety information in the Emergency Guide *(page 8)* before using these materials. The interior of an older home may contain toxic lead paint. If your old paint is chipping or peeling, ask your local health department to test it for lead content. Take special precautions when sanding or stripping lead paint *(page 79)*.

When choosing a paint, first consider its covering ability. High-quality paint will cover most surfaces with a single coat; cheaper brands often require two coats (and therefore twice the work). Consult the paint chart on page 71 to help you find the best paint for the job.

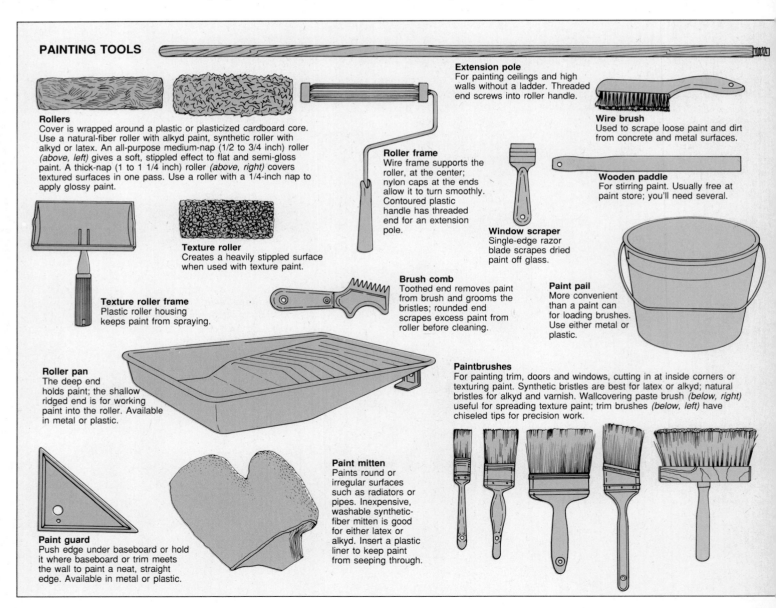

PAINTING TOOLS

Rollers
Cover is wrapped around a plastic or plasticized cardboard core. Use a natural-fiber roller with alkyd paint, synthetic roller with alkyd or latex. An all-purpose medium-nap (1/2 to 3/4 inch) roller *(above, left)* gives a soft, stippled effect to flat and semi-gloss paint. A thick-nap (1 to 1 1/4 inch) roller *(above, right)* covers textured surfaces in one pass. Use a roller with a 1/4-inch nap to apply glossy paint.

Texture roller
Creates a heavily stippled surface when used with texture paint.

Texture roller frame
Plastic roller housing keeps paint from spraying.

Roller pan
The deep end holds paint; the shallow ridged end is for working paint into the roller. Available in metal or plastic.

Paint guard
Push edge under baseboard or hold it where baseboard or trim meets the wall to paint a neat, straight edge. Available in metal or plastic.

Extension pole
For painting ceilings and high walls without a ladder. Threaded end screws into roller handle.

Roller frame
Wire frame supports the roller, at the center; nylon caps at the ends allow it to turn smoothly. Contoured plastic handle has threaded end for an extension pole.

Window scraper
Single-edge razor blade scrapes dried paint off glass.

Brush comb
Toothed end removes paint from brush and grooms the bristles; rounded end scrapes excess paint from roller before cleaning.

Wire brush
Used to scrape loose paint and dirt from concrete and metal surfaces.

Wooden paddle
For stirring paint. Usually free at paint store; you'll need several.

Paint pail
More convenient than a paint can for loading brushes. Use either metal or plastic.

Paint mitten
Paints round or irregular surfaces such as radiators or pipes. Inexpensive, washable synthetic-fiber mitten is good for either latex or alkyd. Insert a plastic liner to keep paint from seeping through.

Paintbrushes
For painting trim, doors and windows, cutting in at inside corners or texturing paint. Synthetic bristles are best for latex or alkyd; natural bristles for alkyd and varnish. Wallcovering paste brush *(below, right)* useful for spreading texture paint; trim brushes *(below, left)* have chiseled tips for precision work.

A variety of simple, inexpensive tools *(below)* simplifies the chore of painting. Synthetic-bristle brushes are used to apply both latex and alkyd paint. Use natural bristle brushes with alkyd paint or varnish only—the water in latex swells natural bristles. For big jobs, rollers cover large, flat areas faster and with less effort than a brush. Rollers come in short nap for applying glossy paint, medium nap for flat paint and thick nap for rough or heavily textured surfaces. A paint mitten comes in handy for odd shapes such as radiators and banisters *(page 76)*, and disposable tools like the sponge brush are handy for touch-ups.

To make certain that new paint will stick, prepare the surface thoroughly. Scrape off loose paint with a paint scraper or putty knife. Wash heavily soiled or greasy surfaces with a solution of trisodium phosphate (TSP) and water *(page 74)*. Make all necessary repairs to the wall, ceiling or trim, then sand the painted surface lightly by hand or with an orbital sander *(page 81)* to provide a "tooth" (a slightly roughened surface) for the new paint, especially if applying latex over non-latex or glossy paint. Seal repaired areas and bare drywall or concrete with a latex primer before painting. If you must paint over wallpaper, use alkyd rather than latex—latex will swell and loosen paper.

The label on the paint can lists its average coverage; divide this into the surface area of the walls and ceiling to determine the number of cans you will need. Add 25 percent more paint if covering a textured surface.

Read the Tools & Techniques section *(page 132)* for information on using ladders and scaffolding safely, and for tips on protecting floors and furniture. Paint the ceiling first, the walls next, and finish off with the baseboards and trim.

When the job is done, clean rollers and brushes immediately *(pages 86-87)*. Store leftover paints and solvents in well-sealed containers, in a cool place.

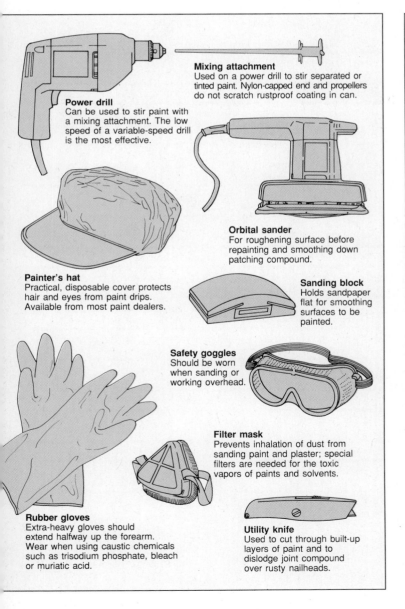
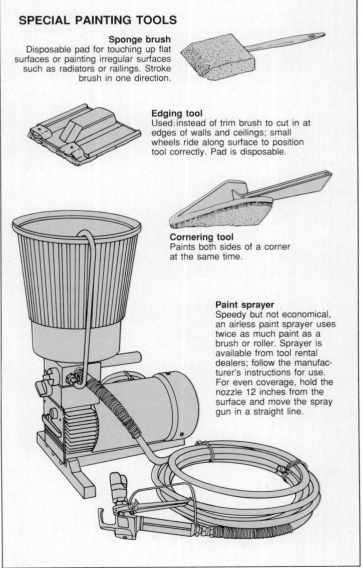

TROUBLESHOOTING GUIDE

SYMPTOM	POSSIBLE CAUSE	PROCEDURE
Paint or varnish on wall, ceiling or woodwork blistering, peeling, flaking or alligatoring (network of small cracks)	Underlying problem in wall, ceiling or woodwork; surface not prepared properly before painting; paint improperly mixed or prepared	Repair wall, ceiling or woodwork before correcting paint problem. Wash wall or ceiling (p. 74) or woodwork (p. 50), prepare room for painting (pp. 81, 141), and paint ceiling (p. 82) or wall (p. 83) or woodwork (p. 84), or varnish woodwork (p. 85) ▣●
Paint flaking over patched area of wall or ceiling	Patch not primed	Scrape loose paint, fill, prime (p. 78), then paint patch (p. 74) ▣◑; if desired, repaint entire ceiling (p. 82) or wall (p. 83) ▣◑
Painted wallpaper lifting from wall	Water in latex paint absorbed by paper	Strip wallpaper (p. 100) ▣●; repaint wall (p. 83) ▣◑
Raised fibers on drywall surface	Alkyd paint applied to unprimed drywall	Sand surface (p. 81); apply latex primer to ceiling (p. 82) or wall (p. 83) ▣◑
Powdery white deposits on painted masonry	Efflorescence (mineral deposits leaching through masonry)	Scrape, remove deposits with muriatic acid and repaint (p. 77) ▣◑
Paint sags or wrinkles	Paint brushed or rolled on too thickly	If paint is wet, brush out surface with an almost dry brush; if dry, sand (p. 81) and feather in matching paint (p. 75) □○
Paint faded or blotchy	Low-quality paint; paint applied too thinly	Prepare surface and room (pp. 81, 141), repaint ceiling (p. 82) or wall (p. 83) ▣◑
Dark area behind object hung on wall	Paint faded around object; water condensation behind object	Wash wall (p. 74), match leftover paint (p. 73) and touch up area (p. 75) or repaint wall (p. 83) ▣◑
Rust stain on wall or ceiling	Rusty heat register, duct vent, metal curtain-rod support, picture frame	Clean (p. 76) or replace rusty object; sand stained area; tint leftover paint to match (p. 73); touch up area (p. 75) or paint entire ceiling (p. 82) or wall (p. 83) ▣◑
Rusty spots on drywall	Heads of drywall nails rusted	Uncover and clean nailheads and daub on metal primer (p. 75) □○; touch up paint
Rust on painted radiator	New paint applied over rust; latex paint used	Clean, prime and repaint radiator (p. 76) ▣◑
Black or gray spots on painted surface	Mildew growth caused by high humidity	Wash with bleach-and-water solution (p. 74); if mildew returns, repaint ceiling (p. 82) or wall (p. 83) with mildew inhibiting paint ▣◑; improve ventilation in room
Dark streaks above vents	Dirt circulated by air	Wash wall or ceiling (p. 74), tint leftover paint to match (p. 73) and touch up area (p. 75); if desired, repaint ceiling (p. 82) or wall (p. 83) ▣◑
Grease on walls and ceiling	Cooking fumes	Wash walls and ceiling (p. 74); repaint ceiling (p. 82) and walls (p. 83) ▣◑ if necessary
Stains bleeding through new paint	Ink or crayon marks; soluble dye in painted-over wallcovering	Seal stain with shellac (p. 75) □○; touch up area or repaint wall (p. 83) ▣◑
New coat of paint doesn't dry	Damp surface or excessive humidity	Ventilate room; do not paint in humid weather
Paint being applied dries too fast	Surface or room too hot or dry; not enough drying inhibitor in paint	Wait for surface or room to cool; mix a small amount of boiled linseed oil into alkyd paint, or water into latex paint (p. 72) □○
Roller fibers or brush hairs come loose while painting	Poor-quality tool; surface too porous; paint applied on hot surface	Choose a quality brush or roller (p. 71); seal surface with primer (p. 79) or shellac (p. 75) □○; wait until surface cools
Cosmetic flaws in otherwise sound wall or ceiling	Poorly-made repairs	Apply texture paint to area (p. 80) or to entire ceiling (p. 82) or wall (p. 83) ▣◑
Stored paint does not match painted surface	Paint surface discolored with age	Tint paint (p. 73) □○
Paint drips down side of can	Paint overflows lip of can after pouring	Punch holes in lip of can (p. 72) □○
Paint in can separated	Paint left standing too long or not mixed properly	Stir paint by hand or with power drill, or "box" paint (p. 72) □○
Skin on surface of paint in can	Air dries paint	Remove paint skin, strain paint (p. 72) □○
Brushes and rollers dirty	Fresh or dried paint on applicator	Wash off paint with water (p. 86) or solvent (p. 87), wrap (p. 87) and store □○

DEGREE OF DIFFICULTY: □ Easy ▣ Moderate ■ Complex
ESTIMATED TIME: ○ Less than 1 hour ◑ 1 to 3 hours ● Over 3 hours *(Does not include drying time)*

PAINTS AND THEIR PROPERTIES

PAINT	CHARACTERISTICS	REMARKS
Latex	Made of acrylic or polyvinyl resins; flat or semi-gloss; dries in 2-4 hours; odor free; thinned and cleaned with water; flows easily; durable; washable, but stains easily.	Use latex primer on new drywall, plaster and masonry or under gloss finishes; do not apply latex too thinly; do not apply to unsealed wood or over wall sizing.
Alkyd	Made of alkyd and other synthetic resins; flat, semi-gloss or gloss finish; dries in 6-8 hours; little odor; thinned and cleaned with mineral spirits; flows on stickier than latex; washable and durable when dry.	Alkyd primer needed before applying gloss or semi-gloss to plaster or wood; gives glossier finish than latex; not to be used on unprimed plaster, masonry or drywall.
Metal	Contains zinc or other rust inhibitors. Available as a flat primer or an enamel topcoat. Latex metal primer dries in 2-4 hours; odorless; thinned and cleaned with water. Alkyd primer and enamel topcoat dry in 6-8 hours; almost odorless; thinned and cleaned with mineral spirits.	Use either latex or alkyd metal paint on iron or steel. Galvanized steel needs a zinc-rich primer. Latex available in flat only; alkyd comes in flat, semi-gloss, gloss and metallic.
Varnish	Made from alkyd, phenolic or polyurethane resins. Gloss or semi-gloss. Dries in 24 hours but can be recoated in 6-8 hours. High resistance to wear, moisture or stains.	High-gloss varnishes are the most durable. Touch-ups will not blend into old varnish. If painting over varnish, sand and clean surface, then apply an alkyd paint.
Shellac	Made of a natural resin in solution with denatured alcohol. May be clear or orange. Dries in 1-3 hours to a transparent finish; thinned and cleaned with alcohol. Use on bare or stained wood; do not apply over paint. Easily damaged by water or alcohol.	Finish is not as hard as varnish. Premixed shellac has a 1- to 2-month shelf life; concentrated shellac resin in 4- or 5-pound "cuts" can be mixed as needed by adding 1 gallon of denatured alcohol to the 5-pound cut, or 3/4 gallon to the 4-pound cut.
Texture	Stiff latex paint covers plaster, drywall or wood. Dries in 15 to 30 minutes; cleaned with water. Can be tinted. Apply with a wallcovering paste brush or texture roller. Difficult to wash.	Hides irregularities and flaws. A textured surface can be painted over with a thick-nap roller; requires approximately 25 percent more paint than a smooth surface.

CHOOSING A BRUSH OR ROLLER

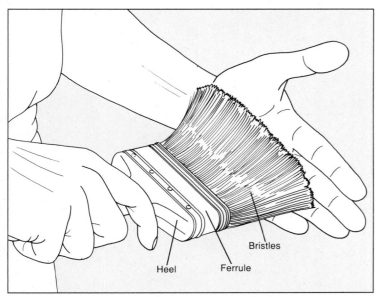

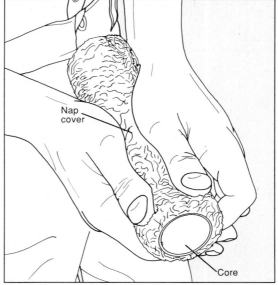

Selecting quality tools. The handle of a good paintbrush is made of varnished wood or sturdy plastic. Check that it is firmly fastened to the ferrule by grasping the bristles in one hand and twisting the handle with the other; there should be no movement. Now splay the bristles out *(above, left)*; they should fan out evenly and not form clumps. Choose a brush with synthetic bristles for latex paint, natural bristles for varnish. Alkyd paint can be applied with either type.

A good roller has a densely napped cover which has been cut into a spiral form and glued to either a plastic or plasticized cardboard core. Separate the nap between your thumbs *(above, right)*; if you can see the core, the nap is too thin and won't hold enough paint. A spring-cage roller frame is stronger than the spindle type and less likely to become clogged with paint.

PREPARING THE PAINT

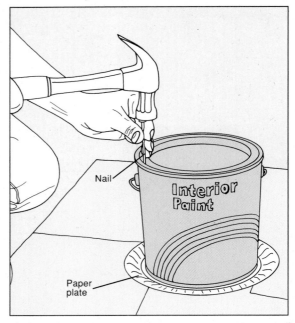

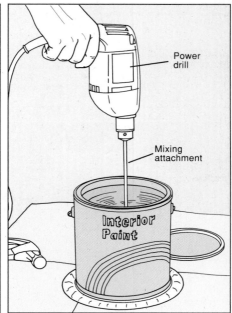

Preventing drips. Glue a paper plate to the bottom of a paint can with a little rubber cement to stop drips from reaching the floor. Then pry off the lid of the can with a wide screwdriver or the rounded end of a can opener and place the lid on newspaper. For a gallon can, make seven or eight evenly spaced holes in the lip with a hammer and 3-inch nail *(above)* to allow paint to drip back into the can. Don't try this on a small can; it might bend so that it can't be resealed.

Stirring paint. Stir paint before using, even if it has just been mixed mechanically at the store. Use a wooden paddle *(above, left)* or foot-long piece of clean wood, and repeatedly draw a figure eight through the paint without striking the can bottom. Don't use a metal stirrer; scratching the can's rustproof coating could ruin leftover paint.

You can also stir paint with a mixing attachment on a standard power drill *(above, right)*. With the drill off, lower the mixer until the propellers are beneath the paint surface but not touching the bottom of the can. Turn on the drill and use the figure-eight motion described above. Turn off the drill before removing it from the paint.

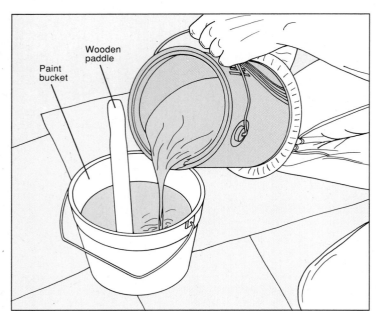

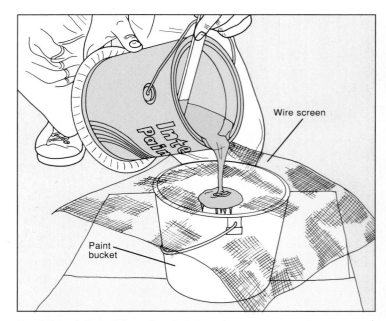

"Boxing" paint. Mix paint that has settled by pouring part of the thin liquid at the top into a pail *(above)*. Stir the remaining paint with a wooden paddle or drill attachment until uniform. Pour some of the thin paint back into the can and stir again. Continue until all the paint has been thoroughly mixed together. For uniform color, box paint before starting any job requiring more than one can of tinted paint. Use a third container to mix the paint together thoroughly.

Straining dried oil-based paint. Remove any skin from the paint surface with a wooden paddle, wrap it in newspaper and discard. (The forming of a thin paint skin does not affect the quality of the paint.) If the paint has separated, mix it with a paddle. Then cut a square of window screening and lay it on top of an empty bucket. Slowly pour the paint onto the screen *(above)* to strain out any lumps or debris; discard the screen.

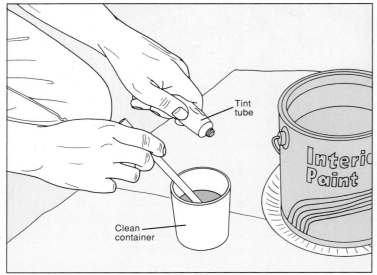

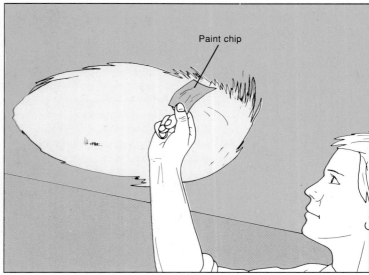

Tinting leftover paint. Since painted surfaces darken with age, use tints called raw umber or lampblack, available from most paint stores, to adjust the color of leftover paint for touch-ups or patching. Pour some of the leftover paint into a clean container. Add a few drops of tint while stirring *(above, left)*, then mix by hand or with a drill attachment *(page 72)* until the tinted paint is uniform in color. Smear some of the paint onto white blotter paper, which will absorb and dry the paint quickly to give you an instant paint chip. Compare the chip to the area to be painted *(above, right)*. If the color is too light, add more tint to darken it. If too dark, mix in some of the original paint until the color matches.

LOADING A BRUSH OR ROLLER

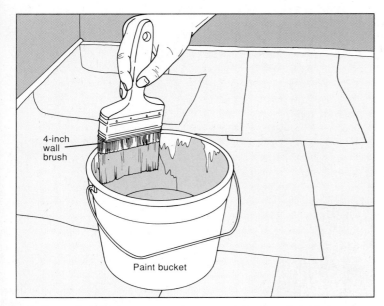

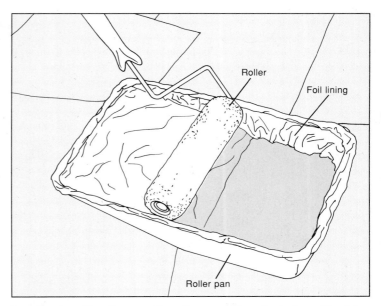

Loading a brush. Before using latex paint, dampen the paintbrush bristles lightly with water. For alkyd or oil-based paint, dampen the bristles with mineral spirits. Wipe away the excess with a clean cloth. Dip the brush into the paint one-third to one-half the bristle length, and swish it around to load the bristles with paint. Lift the brush and gently slap the bristles against the inside of the pail or can *(above)* to knock off excess paint. Do not wipe a loaded brush along the edge of the pail; this removes too much paint and can damage a natural-bristle brush.

Loading a roller. Dampen the roller nap with water before using latex paint, or with mineral spirits before applying alkyd or oil-based paint. Run the dampened roller over an absorbent surface such as paper towels. Line the pan with aluminum foil for easy cleanup, then pour in paint about 1 inch deep and dip half the roller into the deep end of the pan. Work paint into the nap by pushing the roller back and forth across the ridges of the pan. Repeat several times, until the roller is heavily loaded but not dripping with paint.

CLEANING PAINTED SURFACES

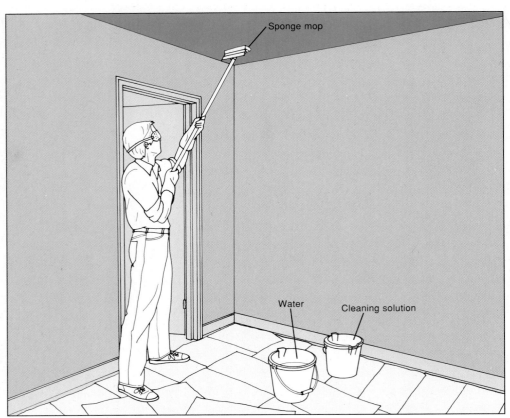

Washing a ceiling. Though dirt and grease collect most often on kitchen ceilings, these rooms are often easiest to clean because they have been previously painted with semigloss or high-gloss paint. For a good general cleaner, add two or three tablespoons of trisodium phosphate (TSP) to a gallon of warm water and stir. If you do not plan to repaint the ceiling, avoid using too much TSP; it can degloss the surface.

Put on rubber gloves and safety goggles or glasses, cover the floor with newspaper or drop cloths, and load a sponge mop with the cleaning solution. Squeeze out excess water until the mop is damp. Starting in a corner, wash a portion of the ceiling *(left)*. Rinse the mop out in clean water and reload with cleaning solution. Start where you left off and clean another portion. Go over the area once more if it is not completely clean.

Other ceilings can be washed the same way, but bear in mind that flat paint is harder to clean. Dusting or light mopping with water, then a fresh paint job will give the best results.

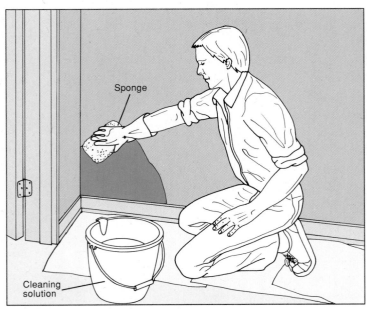

Washing walls. Protect the floor with newspaper, and prepare a TSP cleaning solution *(step above)*. Starting in a corner at the bottom of the wall, wash a three-foot-wide strip up to the ceiling, rinsing out the sponge as it gets dirty. If you do not plan to repaint, avoid streaks by mopping up drips with the sponge or a dry cloth. Remove mildew by washing with a solution of 1 cup bleach to a gallon of warm water. If mildew returns, prime the wall with an undercoat *(page 79, step 5)* containing a fungicide, and either touch up with matching paint *(page 73)* or repaint the entire surface *(page 83)*.

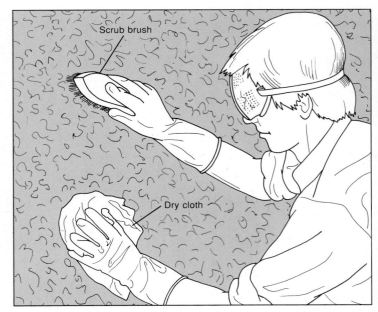

Cleaning a textured surface. Wear rubber gloves and safety goggles, since the cleaning solution will spray off the bristles of the brush. Protect the floor with newspaper, and prepare a TSP solution *(step above)*. Start near the floor and scrub with a medium- or stiff-bristled brush, mopping up drips with a dry cloth to prevent streaking *(above)*. Rinse the brush frequently and replenish it with cleaning solution. Wash a textured ceiling the same way, starting at one corner and cleaning small sections at a time. If texture paint comes off with washing, use a lighter touch and a softer brush.

REMOVING STAINS

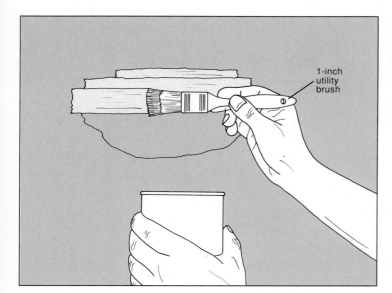

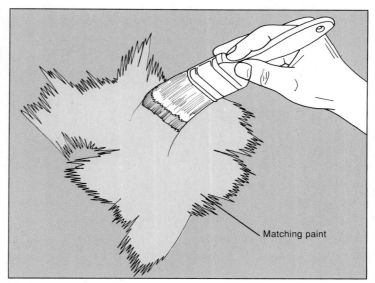

Matching paint

1 **Sealing a stain.** Seal any water, rust or ink stains that might bleed through a fresh paint job by applying white or orange shellac. If the stain is rough or glossy, sand with fine or medium-grit sandpaper. Pour shellac into a container, brush a thin coat over the stain *(above)*, and let it dry for an hour. Two coats may be necessary if the shellac soaks in. To seal bleeding knots in wood, scrape off the resin with a knife, sand with fine or medium-grit sandpaper and brush on a coat of shellac.

2 **Touching up a stain.** To touch up a sealed stain without repainting the entire wall, match leftover paint by tinting *(page 73)*. Then start at the center of the stain to brush paint over the area, feathering the edges to blend into the rest of the wall. Applying paint with a dry roller may more closely match the original painted surface. A 3-inch roller can be used for this purpose.

SEALING A RUSTY NAILHEAD

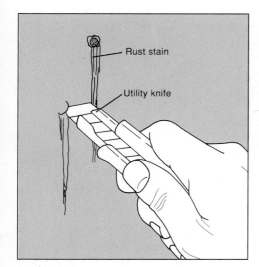

Rust stain

Utility knife

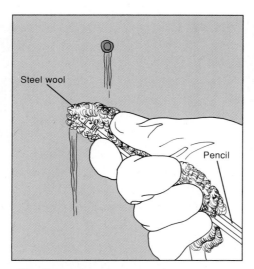

Steel wool

Pencil

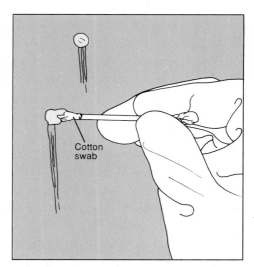

Cotton swab

1 **Exposing the nailhead.** If a rust stain reappears even after sealing with shellac, it may be caused by a rusty drywall nail. Dig out the compound covering the rusty nailhead with a sharp blade *(above)*.

2 **Removing the rust.** Wrap fine steel wool around the eraser end of a pencil and push it into the depression formed by the countersunk nailhead *(above)*. Twist the pencil to scrape off all traces of rust on the nail. Repeat for other exposed nailheads.

3 **Sealing the nailhead.** Dip a cotton swab in metal primer paint, a rust inhibitor, and coat each nailhead *(above)*. Let the paint dry before filling the holes *(drywall, page 12; plaster, page 30)*. Let the patching compound dry for 24 hours, then sand, apply shellac and paint.

PAINTING A RADIATOR

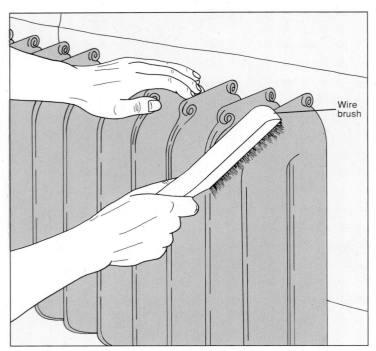

1 **Cleaning the surface.** Spread newspapers beneath the radiator to catch debris, then use a paint scraper to dislodge flaking, peeling and blistered paint. Scrape away as much rust as possible with a stiff wire brush *(above)*. Apply rust remover to any deposits that cannot be scraped or brushed away *(step 2)*. If no rust remains after brushing, go to step 3.

2 **Applying rust remover.** Wearing rubber gloves, apply rust remover with a small paintbrush *(above)* following label directions. Leave the remover on for 10 minutes, then wipe it off with a wet cloth. If any rust remains, scrape it again with a wire brush, then reapply the rust remover.

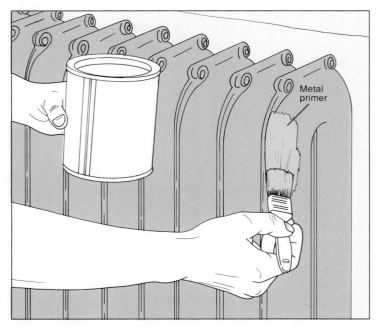

3 **Priming exposed metal.** Sand rough areas and the edges of old paint with medium-grit sandpaper. To get at hard-to-reach spots, wrap sandpaper around a sponge to make a flexible sanding block. Touch up bare spots with a liberal coat of metal primer, using a 1-inch trim brush *(above)*. Let the primer dry before painting the rest of the radiator *(step 4)*.

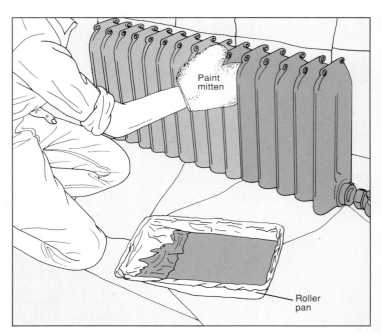

4 **Applying paint.** Dip a paint mitten into a pan of metal finishing paint *(page 71)* and carefully shake off any excess. Starting at the top of the radiator at one side, rub the mitten up and down, using the tip to paint between the coils. A small trim brush or curved "radiator brush" may help in some areas. Avoid applying too much paint—overpainting makes a radiator less heat-efficient.

PAINTING MASONRY

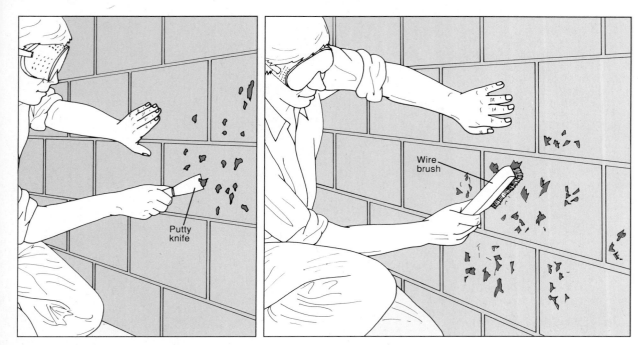

1 Cleaning the surface. Lift off any peeling paint on the surface of the masonry with a paint scraper or putty knife *(above, left)*. Then scrub the peeling areas with a wire brush *(above, right)*, scraping off any white powder (mineral deposits known as efflorescence). If this fails to remove efflorescence, or the deposits return, go to step 2. Finally, run the scraper over the entire area again to remove any less apparent peeling or blistering.

2 Removing persistent efflorescence. Protect the floor with a thick layer of newspapers, put on heavy rubber gloves and safety goggles, and open the windows or doors for ventilation. In a plastic pail, mix muriatic acid (available at hardware stores) with water in the proportions indicated on the container. **Caution:** pour acid into water—not water into acid—to avoid bubbling. Dip a scrub brush into the solution and work it over the mineral deposits *(above)*. Wait for the fizzing reaction to stop, then rinse the acid off the masonry thoroughly, using a hose if there is a floor drain, or a mop and pail.

3 Applying paint. If necessary, wash the masonry with a TSP solution *(page 74)*. If the old paint is glossy, sand with medium-grit sandpaper to provide a tooth for the new paint. Brush latex primer on any bare or patched areas, and let it dry. Load a wide wall brush with the recommended paint *(page 71)* and force the bristles into depressions and gaps in the masonry surface *(above)*. Spread paint over the rest of the area, using the wall brush for seams and depressions and a 9-inch long-nap roller to finish up.

PATCHING PEELING PAINT

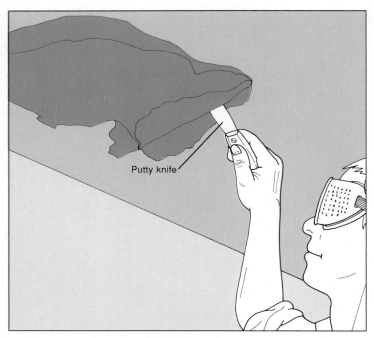

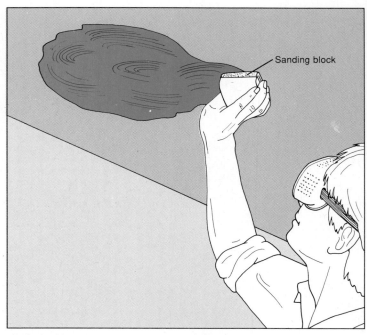

1 **Removing peeling paint.** Use a rigid putty knife to scrape peeling paint off walls and ceilings before repainting. Wear safety goggles when working overhead. Slip the knife edge underneath peeling paint *(above)*, and push loose flakes off the surface. Twist the blade under a loose edge to remove stubborn chips.

2 **Smoothing the edges.** Smooth down rough edges left by missing paint with medium-grit sandpaper on a sanding block *(above)*. If the block cannot reach all areas, fold the sandpaper over your hand. If it is difficult to sand the edges of thick paint flush with the surface, go to step 3. If not, go to step 4.

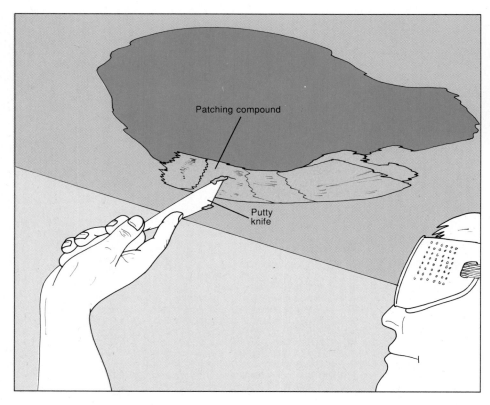

3 **Patching a crater.** Apply spackling compound or premixed joint compound to conceal the edges of a crater formed when large chips of thick paint are removed. Prepare the compound as directed, and spread it on the wall or ceiling with a flexible putty knife *(left)*, covering the edges to be concealed. Smooth and feather out the compound with a large putty knife until it is even with the surface *(page 140)*, and let it dry.

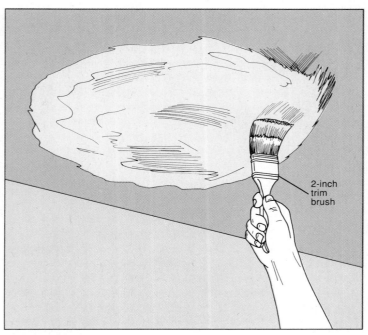

2-inch
trim
brush

4 **Sanding the patch.** If the repaired area is on a ceiling, wear a filter mask and safety goggles. With fine sandpaper on a sanding block, smooth down the compound so that the edges taper into the wall. Dust the patched area with a damp cloth.

5 **Applying an undercoat.** Load a 2-inch trim brush *(page 73)* with primer *(page 71)* or with regular paint. Start at the center of the repair and brush outward *(above)*, feathering the edges onto the painted surface *(page 75)*. If you plan only to touch up the patched area, you may need to tint leftover paint *(page 73)* to match the old surface. In many cases it is easier simply to repaint the entire surface.

THE DANGERS OF LEAD PAINT

The walls and woodwork in some pre-1960 homes have paint with a high lead content that can be hazardous. Children can be poisoned by eating sweet-tasting lead paint chips or dust; you are at risk if you inhale dust while sanding a lead-painted surface. To check the paint's lead content, take a paint chip for analysis. (Contact your local health department.)

Protect your family by covering or removing lead paint, but take special care when doing so. Wear an adjustable respirator, safety goggles, gloves, and work clothes that cover your arms and legs. Keep all this gear in the work place, and do not eat, drink or smoke there. Seal off doorways with plastic sheets and work with windows open. When finished, clean up thoroughly and promptly.

To cover old lead paint that is well adhered to the wall or ceiling, hand sand with medium-grit paper. Do not use a power sander; the fine dust is too easily inhaled. Apply a quality alkyd undercoat to seal the surface, then an alkyd top coat.

If a painted surface is peeling or chipping, scrape off all the loose paint *(page 78)*, fill craters with joint compound, and sand and repaint as described above.

Cover a lead-painted wall or ceiling that is beyond repair with new drywall *(page 12)* or paneling *(page 46)*, after removing as much of the loose paint as possible.

If you decide to strip lead-based paint from woodwork, protect the surrounding area *(page 141)*. Ventilate the room by opening all windows and aiming a fan out a window to draw away fumes. If possible, remove doors and woodwork and work outside. Don't let stripped paint get tracked around; transfer it directly from the scraper to a metal can that can be covered with a lid. Never use a blowtorch or heat gun to strip lead-based paint: high heat vaporizes the lead and produces toxic fumes.

Discard drop cloths, rags and paint residue. Clean the floor with a workshop vacuum cleaner, then mop it with a solution of 4 tablespoons of trisodium phosphate (TSP) in a gallon of water.

PATCHING WITH TEXTURE PAINT

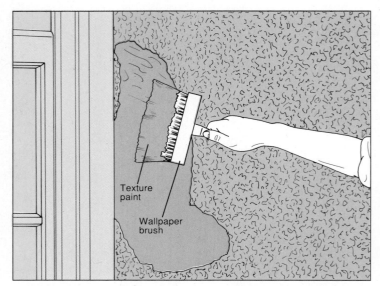

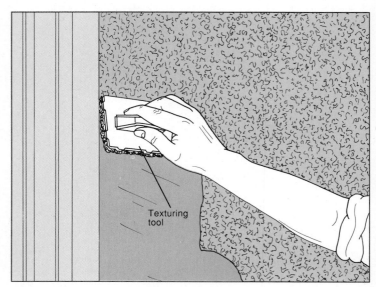

1 Applying texture paint to a patch. To repair the finish on a textured surface, use special texture paint, which has a yogurt-like consistency. (For a small repair, you may substitute joint compound.) Protect the floor with newspapers. Dip a wallcovering-paste brush into the paint, or scoop paint onto the brush with a putty knife. Apply the paint to the wall in an upward direction; for a ceiling, use smaller amounts on the brush and wear safety goggles. Spread out the paint *(above)* until the patched area is evenly coated. If any paint gets on the old textured surface, scrub it off with a brush before it hardens. Go to step 2 to match the texture.

2 Matching the textured surface. Finding a tool to reproduce the surface already on your wall or ceiling may take some experimentation. For a stippled effect, try using a nylon or plastic-fiber paint edger *(above)* or roller, available in texture-paint kits. Dabbing a sponge or a crumpled ball of heavy paper on the surface will produce a stippled effect. Make a swirl pattern by pushing the bristles of a paint-brush into the texture paint, then twisting. Let dry, then repaint *(below)*.

REPAINTING TEXTURED SURFACES

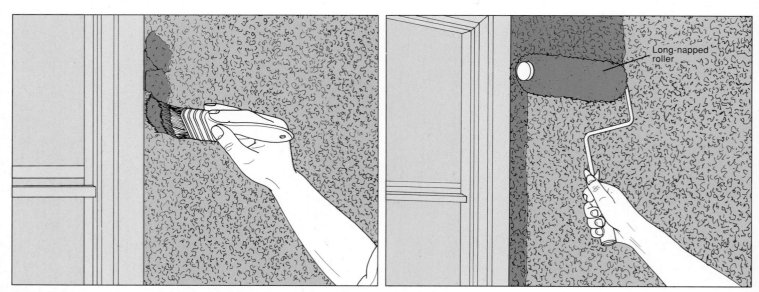

Painting over textured walls and ceilings. Use a regular brush to touch up patches or to paint in corners and around doors, windows and baseboards. Dab the paint into the textured surface *(above, left)*, then fill in with a smooth brushstroke.

To cover large textured areas, use a 9-inch, long-nap roller *(above, right)*. Protect your eyes with goggles when painting a ceiling. Start near a corner of a wall or ceiling, and roll the tool away from your body. For the fastest coverage of a very large area, roll on the paint in a W or M pattern *(page 83)*. Fill in one area before going on to the next.

PREPARING A ROOM FOR PAINTING

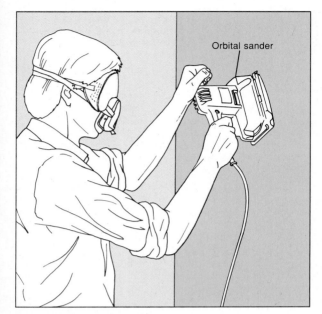

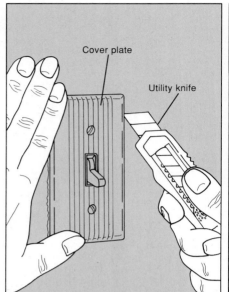

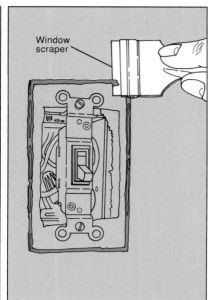

1 **Preparing the surface.** Wash soiled walls and ceilings before painting *(page 74)*. A strong TSP solution removes grease and deglosses smooth surfaces, providing a tooth for the new paint. Sand glossy surfaces with an orbital sander and fine to medium-grit sandpaper. If you are sanding lead-based paint, wear a respirator and take the proper safety precautions *(pages 8, 79)*. For other paint, a dust-filter mask is recommended. Begin sanding in a corner and use light, sideways strokes *(above)*. When finished, damp-mop all surfaces to be painted.

2 **Removing a painted-over cover plate.** Turn off power to the circuit before working on switches or outlets *(page 137)*. Run a sharp utility knife along the edge of the cover plate *(above, left)* to break the paint seal, and remove the plate. Use a window scraper *(above, right)* or paint scraper to remove any ridges of old paint caused by repeated overpainting, being careful not to nick the wall. Finish by sanding with medium-grit sandpaper until the surface is flat. If the power must be left on, paint carefully around uncovered outlets and switches: the paint could conduct electricity, giving you a shock or blowing a fuse. For the neatest results after a fresh paint job, replace used cover plates with new ones.

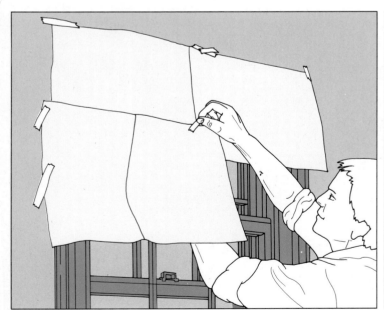

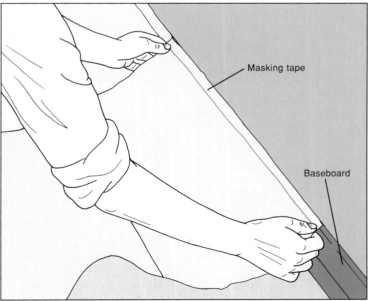

3 **Masking trim and baseboards.** Accomplished painters use a brush technique called "beading" *(page 83, step 1)* instead of masking baseboards and door and window trim. Non-professionals may want to take the time to cover these surfaces if they are being painted a different color or with a different type of paint, or not being painted at all. Protect a window when painting the ceiling by taping a few layers of newspaper across the top *(above, left)*. For baseboards and other wood trim, measure a length of masking tape a few inches longer than a full sheet of newspaper. Attach half the tape to the paper and half to the edge of the wood trim *(above, right)*. Press the masking tape down firmly to keep paint from seeping underneath, but remove it as soon as you complete the paint job to avoid damaging the finish of the woodwork.

PAINTING A CEILING

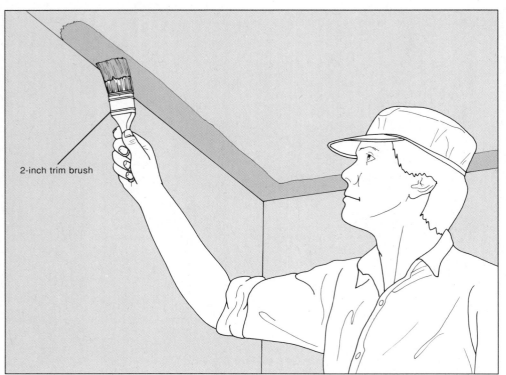

2-inch trim brush

1 **"Cutting in" at the ceiling.** Use a 2-inch trim brush to paint the edges of the ceiling. Stand on a stepladder *(page 132)*, load the brush and start applying the paint in a 2-inch-wide strip *(left)*. Work the brush slowly and evenly to avoid splatters and drips; pressing too hard or going over your work can leave visible brushstrokes. When the brush feels empty, "tip off," or feather, the final stroke by lifting the brush gradually. Reload the brush and start at an unpainted part of the ceiling one brush length from where you stopped. Work back toward the previously painted strip. To avoid lapmarks from the cutting in, feather the edges lightly toward the center of the ceiling.

Hang a clean, absorbent rag on the ladder or tuck it in a pocket of your work pants to wipe up the inevitable drips and spills. For the neatest results, wrap the cloth tightly around the first two fingers. Rub any partially dried splatters with a cloth dampened in solvent or paint thinner (alkyd paint) or water (latex paint). You'll save yourself a lot of work later by cleaning up mistakes promptly.

2 **Using a roller.** Choose a short-nap roller for high-gloss surfaces, a medium nap for most others. The easiest way to cover the rest of the ceiling is by attaching the roller to an extension pole. Paint across the width of the ceiling to help prevent lapmarks. Starting near a corner, push the roller away from you and paint in a W or M pattern *(above, left)* about three feet across. Roll the paint on slowly to avoid spraying and splattering. Fill in the area completely *(above, right)*, then move to an unpainted section about one-and-a-half roller widths away. Blend the areas together. You may have trouble checking the coverage if you are repainting in the same color, or if the ceiling needs a second coat. Light from a window or ceiling fixture should help you catch any missed areas; also look for slight differences in sheen.

PAINTING A WALL

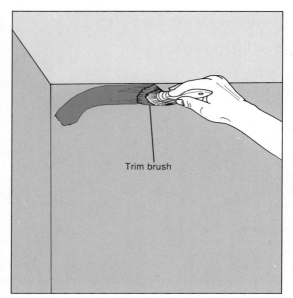

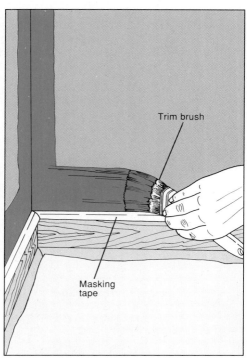

1 **Beading in the wall.** If the walls and ceiling are being painted different colors, use the technique called "beading." Dip a 2-inch trim brush in paint, without overloading it. Grasp the ferrule and let the handle rest between your thumb and index finger. Start the first brushstroke near a corner, about an inch below the ceiling *(above)*. Press the brush up, allowing the paint to form a thin line along the wall at the ceiling. Pull the brush along firmly, flexing your arm only at the shoulder. After beading, relax and widen the paint strip to 2 inches.

2 **Cutting in the wall.** If the walls and ceiling in a room are being painted the same color, cut in the tops of the walls, as well as the corners, with a 2-inch trim brush as you did the ceiling *(page 82, step 1)*. You will also need to cut in around doors, windows and fixtures and above the baseboards *(above, left)*. Either use masking tape to protect the baseboards and wood trim, or paint the areas where the wall meets the trim by beading the paint *(above, right)* as described in step 1.

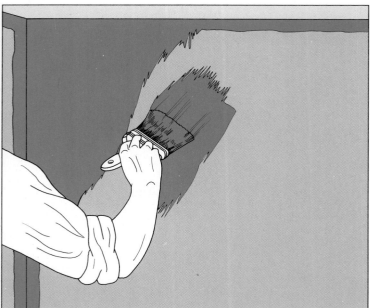

3 **Painting with a roller.** Start with a loaded roller several inches away from the corner of the wall. Push the roller away from you on the upstroke, and paint a rough M or W pattern on the wall *(above, left)*. Spread the paint evenly, filling in the area completely. Repeat the same strokes about a roller width away, and blend in the two patches of paint. Avoid rolling too quickly, especially close to

ceilings or trim, as this causes paint to splatter on the surrounding area.

When painting an entire wall with a brush, load a 3- to 4-inch wall brush and start applying paint near a top corner of the wall. Paint diagonally across the wall. Reload the brush and go to a section about two brush lengths away. Smooth out the paint, brushing back toward the recently painted area *(above, right)*.

PAINTING WOODWORK

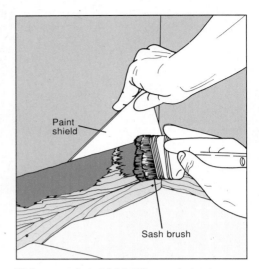

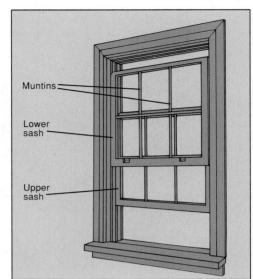

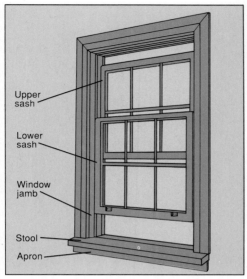

Using a paint shield. When painting baseboards, keep paint off the wall and floor by using a triangular paint shield. Place its long edge along the top of the baseboard *(above)* and paint the upper half of the baseboard with smooth, even strokes, using a long-handled sash brush for greater accuracy. Then push the edge of the paint shield into the crack between the molding and the floor and paint the lower half of the baseboard. Wipe the edge of the shield frequently with a clean cloth to avoid paint smears.

Painting a window frame. Remove handles and locks to provide a smooth painting surface. Handles can be painted by dipping them into paint. Do not paint locks—paint can clog the mechanism and prevent it from working properly. Place masking tape on the glass less than 1/16 inch from sashes and muntins, or simply use the beading technique *(page 83, step 1)* if you have a steady hand. Apply paint with a 1 1/2-inch sash brush. Pull down the upper sash and raise the lower one to paint the inside and top of the sash strip and an inch or two of the muntins. Leave the bottom edge of the upper sash for exterior paint. Then slide the window sections past one another, leaving them open a few inches at each end. Finish painting any previously inaccessible parts of the sash. Paint the horizontal muntins, then the vertical muntins, and finally the stool and apron. Paint the window jambs after all the other sections have dried.

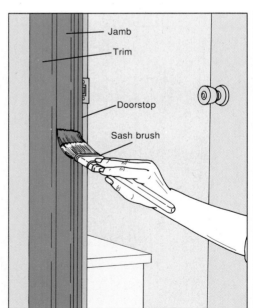

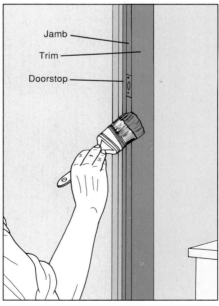

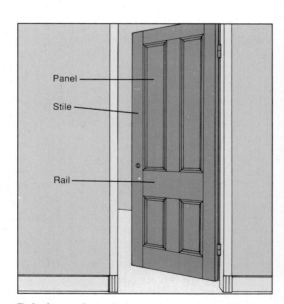

Painting a door frame. Remove hardware attached to the frame and wash the frame with TSP solution *(page 74)*, or sand a glossy surface with medium-grit sandpaper. Use a sash brush for best results. Begin painting at the top of the door frame, then move on to the sides, painting the jamb and then the trim. If the door opens out of the room being painted *(above, left)*, paint that part of the doorstop and door frame facing you the same color as the trim in the room. If the door opens into the room being painted *(above, right)*, paint the door frame inside the room and just the edge of the doorstop that the door touches.

Painting a door. Remove the doorknob. Wash the door *(page 74)*, including the top edge. Sand a painted door lightly with medium-grit sandpaper. Use a roller to paint a flat door quickly, after first painting the edges with a brush. To paint a panel door *(above)*, begin with the panels, then paint the horizontal rails, and finally the vertical stiles. Paint the edge of a door the color of the room into which it opens.

VARNISHING WOOD TRIM

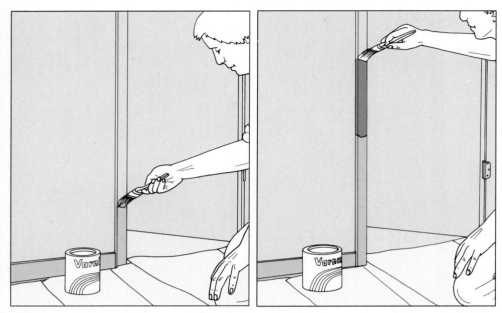

1 **Applying varnish.** For unfinished trim, brush on a clear wood sealer or a synthetic clear finish such as polyurethane before applying varnish. On a previously finished surface, remove any unsightly old varnish with paint stripper and wipe with a clean cloth soaked in mineral spirits. Dip a trim brush in varnish and apply with long, smooth strokes in one direction to avoid air bubbles. Apply varnish to vertical surfaces *(above, left)* from the bottom to the top to avoid runs. Start a second stroke at the point where the first ended *(above, right)*, trying not to overlap strokes.

2 **Adding a second coat.** When the first coat of varnish is dry, sand it lightly by hand *(above)* with very fine sandpaper. Clean the surface with a tack cloth *(page 46)*, let it dry and brush on a second coat.

TAKING A BREAK

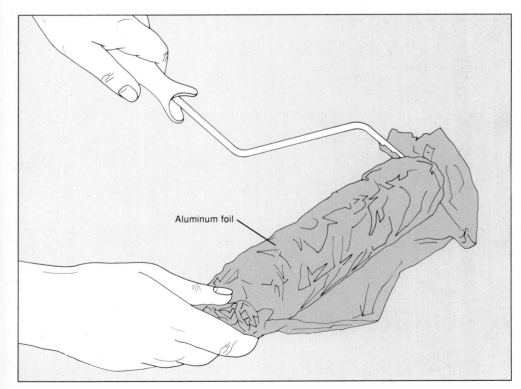

Aluminum foil

Wrapping up rollers and brushes.
Whether you're stopping work for 15 minutes or overnight, the easiest way to store rollers and paintbrushes is to wrap them in aluminum foil. For overnight storage, press brushes and rollers onto paper towels to work out excess paint, then cover them with cloths soaked in water (for latex paint) or mineral spirits (for alkyd paint). Take a sheet of heavy aluminum foil at least one and a half times the width of the roller or length of the brush and wrap the tool securely *(left)* so that it will not dry out. Lay the roller on its end to avoid flattening the nap. Rollers and brushes can also be stored in plastic bags. During a short break, cover the roller pan with aluminum foil to keep paint fresh. For overnight storage, however, pour the paint back into its tin and fasten the lid down securely.

CLEANING UP

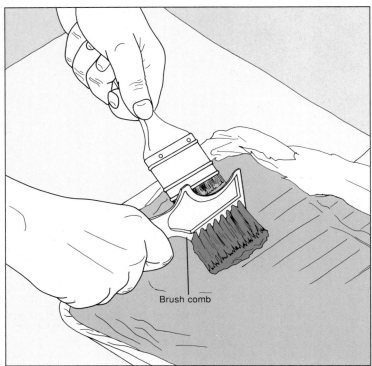

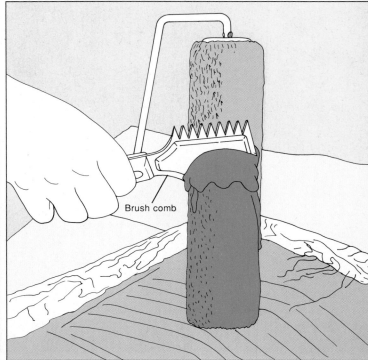

Removing excess paint from a brush. Before cleaning, press excess paint out of brushes with a brush comb *(above)* or by painting onto newspaper. To restore a gummed-up or dried-out brush, suspend it overnight or longer in a container of paint-and-brush softener *(page 87)* or strong TSP solution. Then comb out the brush over newspaper, scraping off the paint and separating the bristles.

Removing excess paint from a roller. The least messy way to remove excess paint from a roller before cleaning is with the rounded end of a brush comb. Place the roller in the pan and start at one end, pulling the rounded end of the tool along its length *(above)*. Keep turning and scraping the roller until you have removed as much paint as possible without damaging the nap.

WASHING LATEX PAINT FROM TOOLS

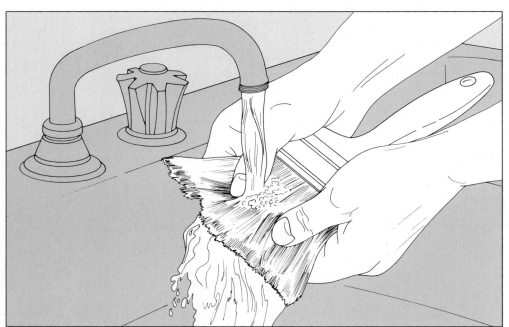

Rinsing out brushes and rollers. Remove latex paint from brushes and rollers by rinsing them with plenty of warm water. Hold the brush under running water and separate the bristles between your thumbs *(left)* to let the water penetrate. Rub the bristles closest to the ferrule first to get at any paint that may have backed up, then move down to the ends of the bristles. Finish by applying a drop of dishwashing detergent to the top of the bristles. Work it through with your fingers and rinse a final time.

Clean a roller the same way; apply plenty of running water, and rub the nap with your fingers until the water runs clear. Shake out the excess water over newspaper before storing brushes and rollers *(page 87)*.

CLEANING ALKYD PAINT FROM TOOLS

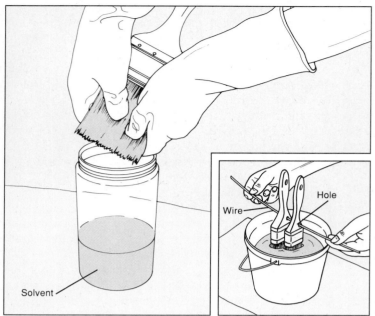

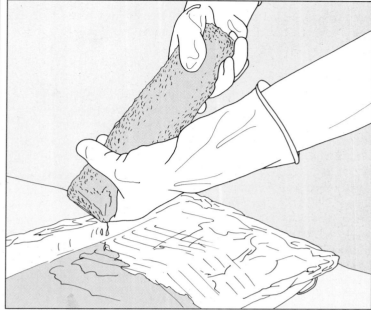

Cleaning with solvent. Use solvent (either paint thinner, mineral spirits or turpentine) to clean alkyd and oil-based paint off brushes and rollers. First, remove excess paint *(page 86)*. For brushes, pour solvent into a wide-mouthed container. Wear rubber gloves and work in a well-ventilated area. Agitate the brush in the solvent, pushing the bristles up and down against the jar bottom. When the solvent becomes cloudy, pour it into another container and use a fresh batch. Pour clean solvent onto the bristles and work it into them by hand *(above, left)*. If the brushes do not come clean, suspend them overnight in solvent.

Drill holes in the heels of the brush handles, insert a stiff wire, and hang the brushes in solvent up to their ferrules *(inset)*.

Since rollers are inexpensive, you may wish to discard used ones and start each new paint job with a fresh roller; if not, clean rollers in the pan. Change the foil, pour in solvent and soak the roller. Wearing rubber gloves, work the solvent through the nap by hand *(above, right)*, changing the solvent as it gets cloudy. To dry, stand the roller on one end on a dry cloth laid over newspaper. Do not discard used solvent in a sink or septic system; pour it down an outside drain or throw it away.

STORING PAINTING TOOLS

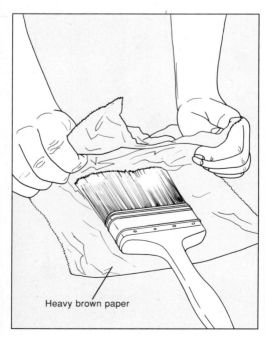

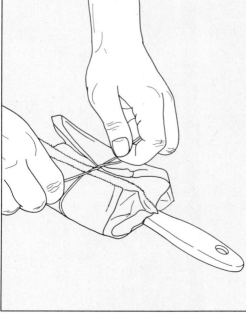

Wrapping brushes and rollers. To wrap a cleaned paintbrush, cut a sheet of heavy brown paper the length of the brush and twice its width. Fold the sheet in half, place the brush in the center of one half and fold the other half over it *(far left)*. Then fold both sides over onto the brush, and fasten the envelope with string *(left)* or a rubber band.

Store rollers on their ends in their original packages, or wrap in a clear plastic bag punctured with a few holes to prevent mildew from forming.

WALLCOVERINGS

Wallpaper was once considered the essential finishing touch for a properly-clad home. Even ceilings were always papered years ago. In the busy and practical 1950s and '60s, styles were streamlined, but times have changed again. Wallcoverings are back in vogue, with modern improvements that have made the word "wallpaper" archaic.

The most durable—and most popular—wallcoverings today are made of vinyl, laminated to a paper or cloth backing. Less washable wallcoverings are made of vinyl-coated paper. The most delicate are such specialties as foil, flocked, grasscloth, burlap and synthetic suede, which may be hung over lining paper to minimize wall defects.

However well a wallcovering is installed and cared for, it is inevitable that daily wear will result in soiling at high-traffic areas such as light switches and corners. Most vinyl wallcoverings are not only washable but "scrubbable," and thus suitable for kitchens, bathrooms and playrooms. Test all wallcoverings for water resistance before washing *(page 91)*.

Many homes are decorated with older or more fragile wallcoverings that cannot survive rough treatment. Refer to the Troubleshooting Guide on page 90 for the most effective ways to clean all types of wallcoverings. To lift a persistent stain you may need to try several cleaners. Permanent stains and tears can be concealed by a variety of patches. If you have no leftover scraps for patching a discontinued pattern, you can sometimes borrow a piece of strippable wallcovering from a hidden area of the wall.

Some wallcovering problems result from poor installation, defects in the wall, or the environment in the house. Walls not treated with the proper primer can cause loose seams and air bubbles. The wrong paste, incomplete coverage and incorrect seam rolling can lead to trouble, too.

Bulges in the wallcovering surface often signal problems in the wall itself. You may need to strip away the damaged paper to inspect the wall surface. Consult the chapters on drywall *(page 12)* or plaster *(page 30)* to make any necessary repairs.

High humidity causes wallcovering to peel off the wall. Improved ventilation usually solves this problem. If not, you may need to replace the wallcovering with a highly water-resistant vinyl, after first treating the wall with a mildew-

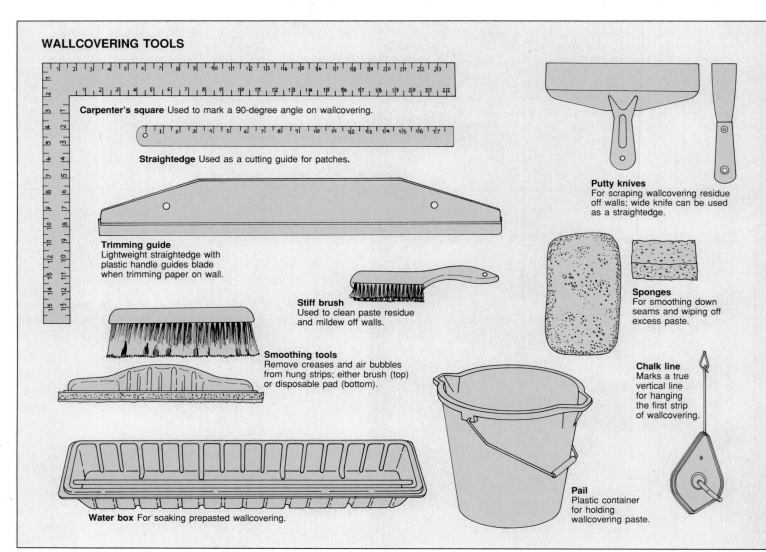

WALLCOVERING TOOLS

Carpenter's square Used to mark a 90-degree angle on wallcovering.

Straightedge Used as a cutting guide for patches.

Trimming guide
Lightweight straightedge with plastic handle guides blade when trimming paper on wall.

Stiff brush
Used to clean paste residue and mildew off walls.

Smoothing tools
Remove creases and air bubbles from hung strips; either brush (top) or disposable pad (bottom).

Water box For soaking prepasted wallcovering.

Putty knives
For scraping wallcovering residue off walls; wide knife can be used as a straightedge.

Sponges
For smoothing down seams and wiping off excess paste.

Chalk line
Marks a true vertical line for hanging the first strip of wallcovering.

Pail
Plastic container for holding wallcovering paste.

inhibiting primer. Use a vinyl adhesive rather than an organic product such as cellulose or wheat paste, since humid conditions encourage these pastes to host mold and mildew. If spots appear on the surface of your wallcovering, clean them off immediately with a bleach solution *(page 91)* before they develop into a permanent stain. If the growth is underneath the paper, you have no choice but to strip off the wallcovering, scrub the wall with a bleach solution and start again.

Wallcoverings are sold in single or double rolls. Whatever the width, each single roll has 36 square feet. To estimate your needs, measure the walls and count on one single roll for every 30 square feet. Deduct from the wall area only for large picture windows, double doors and built-in cabinets. Round up the final number of rolls and add one roll in case of mistakes—and for later patching. Check that every roll is marked with the same lot number, or there may be noticeable color variations.

Wallcovering installation requires careful preparation, including the application of primer or sizing to seal the wall and promote adhesion. It is seldom advisable to hang new wallcovering over old. The better the surface you start with,

the more durable your finished wall will be. But new primers make it possible to paper directly over old wallpaper, provided it is smooth and solidly anchored.

Read all the instructions that come with the wallcovering, and select your primer and paste according to the manufacturer's recommendation. Some wallcoverings are prepasted and must be soaked in water to activate the adhesive. But many people prefer to apply paste themselves. Pasting allows more time to work with each strip and often results in better adhesion. You may apply paste to a prepasted wallcovering; dilute the paste a bit to improve its bond.

Wallpapering requires few special tools. Most of those shown below will already be in your tool box; others can be improvised. A large sponge will substitute for a smoothing brush. In place of a chalk line, make a plumb bob by tying a small tool to a string.

Assemble everything you need before you begin, and sweep and dust the room. Wipe up any smeared paste immediately; dried paste can be hard to remove. Methodically following directions will bring you a professional-looking job.

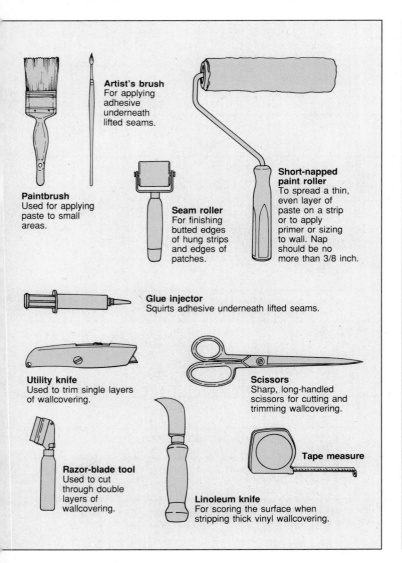

Paintbrush
Used for applying paste to small areas.

Artist's brush
For applying adhesive underneath lifted seams.

Seam roller
For finishing butted edges of hung strips and edges of patches.

Short-napped paint roller
To spread a thin, even layer of paste on a strip or to apply primer or sizing to wall. Nap should be no more than 3/8 inch.

Glue injector
Squirts adhesive underneath lifted seams.

Utility knife
Used to trim single layers of wallcovering.

Scissors
Sharp, long-handled scissors for cutting and trimming wallcovering.

Razor-blade tool
Used to cut through double layers of wallcovering.

Tape measure

Linoleum knife
For scoring the surface when stripping thick vinyl wallcovering.

ELECTRIC WALLCOVERING STEAMER

Some older, nonstrippable wallcoverings can be especially hard to remove with chemicals. An electric wallcovering steamer can do a more efficient job on large expanses of paper. Steamers can be rented from a wallcovering dealer or a tool rental company. Most resemble the one shown below. Follow the manufacturer's instructions for operating your particular model. Prepare the room *(page 141)* and fill the steamer tank as directed. With the water-level gauge at full, plug in the steamer and wait for vapor to emerge from the perforations in the steamer plate. Hold the plate firmly against the wall for 2 to 3 minutes, or until paper around the plate appears damp. Move to an adjacent spot on the same strip and repeat. Once you have steamed half a strip, use a large flexible putty knife to scrape the steamed paper off the wall and clean off paste residue *(page 100)*.

Water-level gauge

Water tank

Steamer plate

TROUBLESHOOTING GUIDE

SYMPTOM	POSSIBLE CAUSE	PROCEDURE
Wallcovering dirty (washable)	Normal wear; air pollution	Test for water resistance (p. 91), then wash with mild detergent-and-water solution (p. 91) □●
Wallcovering dirty (nonwashable)	Normal wear; air pollution	Clean with kerosene or cleaning dough (p. 92) □●; to make wallcovering more washable, spray with vinyl sealant (p. 95) □●
Paint spots on vinyl wallcovering	Wall not protected while painting	Wipe off immediately with a cloth dampened in the proper solvent; wash with detergent-and-water solution (p. 91) □○
Ballpoint ink on vinyl wallcovering	Child's artwork	Wipe off immediately with a cloth dampened in rubbing alcohol □○
Tar or asphalt on vinyl wallcovering	Bicycles, outdoor toys or auto tires stored against wall	Wipe off immediately with a cloth dampened in kerosene or cleaning naphtha, rubbing toward the center to avoid spreading stain; rinse with water □○
Grease stain on nonwashable wallcovering	Kitchen spill; cooking splatters	Cover stain with brown paper and apply warm iron (p. 92) □○, or clean with fuller's earth paste (p. 93) □○
Deep stain in nonwashable wallcovering	Nonwashable wallcoverings are porous and absorbent	Apply dry-cleaning fluid (p. 93) □○; on delicate grasscloth, silks or flocks, gently rub on detergent suds □○
Black, gray or green spots on wallcovering	Mold or mildew feeding on paste residue; contamination caused by high humidity	Clean away paste residue with paste remover □○; or clean washable wallcovering with mild bleach solution (p. 91) □○; improve ventilation in room
	Mold or mildew growing on wall behind wallcovering	If mold reappears after cleaning surface of wallcovering, remove wallcovering (p. 100) ◲●; treat wall with fungicide □○; replace wallcovering (p. 101) with fabric-backed vinyl, applied with mildew-inhibiting paste ◲●; spray with vinyl sealant (p. 95) □○
Bulges under wallcovering	Small air blister	On newly hung wallcovering, if paste is still damp, prick blister with needle and press out air □○; on older wallcovering, cut a slit and squirt in adhesive with glue injector (p. 94) □○
	Large air bubble	Cut open bubble and repaste (p. 94) □○
	Defect in plaster or drywall	Remove wallcovering (p. 100) ◲●; repair plaster (p. 30) or drywall (p. 12); replace wallcovering (p. 101) ◲●
Seams lifting	Adhesive wrong type or dried out; prepasted paper soaked too long in water; seams rolled too hard when hanging	Apply acrylic seam paste (p. 95) □○
Wallcovering peeling	Adhesive wrong type or dried out; prepasted paper soaked too long in water	Repaste peeling section (p. 95) □○
	High humidity	Improve ventilation by installing exhaust fan or dehumidifier; repaste peeling section (p. 95) □○; treat wallcovering with vinyl sealant (p. 95) □○
	"Hot spots" from uncured patching compound on wall	Paint hot spot with alkyd primer; let dry 24 hours □●; replace wallcovering (p. 101) ◲●
	Moisture in wall caused by seepage, condensation or plumbing leak	Remove wallcovering (p. 100) ◲●; correct problem and repair wall; replace wallcovering (p. 101) ◲●
Wallcovering damaged along top of wall	Flooding from floor above; plumbing problem inside wall or ceiling	Correct problem causing water damage; repair wall if necessary; install decorative border (p. 96) ◲●
Holes, tears and permanent stains	Normal wear and tear, accident	Make an overlay patch with leftover paper or material stripped from a hidden spot (p. 97) □○; or for paper and thin paper-backed vinyls, make a torn patch (p. 99) □○ For thick vinyl and strippable wallcoverings, make a double-cut patch (p. 98) □○ For wallcovering with large pattern, make appliqué patch (p. 99) □○
Wallcovering being removed doesn't strip off easily	Wallcovering nonstrippable	Score wallcovering; apply wallpaper remover (p. 100) ◲●
Wallpaper remover not effective	Old adhesive reacted with wall surface	Remove wallcovering with electric steamer (p. 89) ◲●
Mold or mildew on wall to be covered	Excessive humidity; wall surface or paste residue contaminated	Wash with trisodium phosphate-and-bleach solution (p. 100) □●; treat wall with fungicide and mildew-inhibiting primer (p. 101) □●; use a mildew-inhibiting paste

DEGREE OF DIFFICULTY: □ Easy ◲ Moderate ◼ Complex
ESTIMATED TIME: ○ Less than 1 hour ◔ 1 to 3 hours ● Over 3 hours *(Does not include drying time)*

TESTING WALLCOVERINGS FOR WASHABILITY

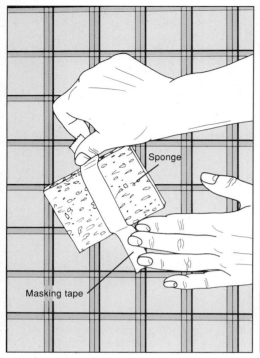

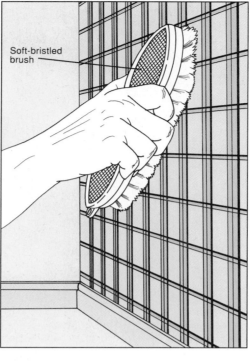

Soft-bristled brush

Sponge

Masking tape

Determining wallcovering durability.
Before cleaning any wallcovering, test it for water and abrasion resistance. In an inconspicuous corner, attach a damp sponge to the wall with masking tape *(far left)*. Leave it in place for several minutes. If water does not penetrate the wallcovering, it is washable and well adhered to the surface. To check whether your wallcovering is scrubbable, rub a soft-bristled brush over the damp area *(left)*. If the covering does not tear or wear away, it can be scrubbed clean with a brush. Before washing even a water-resistant wallcovering, test the cleaner you intend to use in an inconspicuous corner. Wear rubber gloves when using any cleaner other than a mild detergent, and protect your eyes when cleaning the ceiling.

CLEANING WASHABLE WALLCOVERINGS

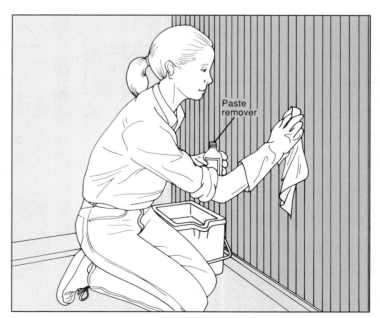

Paste remover

Washing with a detergent solution. Clean vinyl-coated wall-coverings with mild detergent diluted in a pail of water. (Be sure to test any cleaning solution in an inconspicuous corner before proceeding.) Protect the floor from spills. Using a large sponge, start washing at the bottom of the wall and work up *(above)*. Do not let water seep into the seams. Rinse the wallcovering, then dry it immediately with a soft towel. To remove heavy dirt, try a weak solution of an ammonia-based cleaner and water.

Removing mold and mildew. Paste residue on the surface of a vinyl wallcovering may remain invisible until it breeds mold or mildew. To clean away the paste, wear rubber gloves and apply a commercial paste remover with a cloth *(above)* or sponge, following label directions. Do not let the paste remover seep into the seams. Clean away mold and mildew with a solution of 1 cup bleach in a gallon of water. Persistent mildew indicates the need for better ventilation. If the growth returns repeatedly, the wall behind the covering is affected; remove the wallcovering and clean the wall *(page 100)*.

DRY-CLEANING NONWASHABLE WALLCOVERINGS

Brown paper

Cleaning with kerosene. Small quantities of kerosene will pick up accumulated dirt from many wallcoverings. Wearing rubber gloves and working outdoors, fold a towel in quarters and dampen it in grade K-1 kerosene. Wring out the towel as much as possible, then air it outdoors until nearly dry. Tie the towel around a mop or broom head and pass it over the wallcovering vertically from floor to ceiling *(above)*, cleaning the wallcovering one strip at a time.

Removing grease stains. Grease stains can be drawn out of most nonwashable wallcoverings by applying heat. Place a double thickness of brown paper over the stained area. Hold a warm iron (without steam) on the paper for several minutes *(above)*. Fold the paper over to a fresh side and reapply heat until the stain lifts. If this method is unsuccessful, try using a paste cleaner *(page 93)*.

CLEANING WALLCOVERINGS WITH DOUGH

Using a dough cleaner. A general-purpose cleaning dough for wallcoverings can be made by mixing salt, aluminum potassium sulfate (alum—available in drugstores), flour and kerosene. In a saucepan over low heat, dissolve 1 cup of salt and 2 tablespoons of alum in 2 cups of water. Remove from heat and add 5 cups of flour and 1 tablespoon of kerosene. Mix, then knead to a bread-dough consistency. To apply the dough, roll it over soiled areas with the palm of your hand *(far left)*. As the surface of the dough collects dirt, fold it to a clean section. Continue until the dirt is removed. For especially grimy areas, such as child-high corners, press dough onto the stain *(left)* and leave in place for about 30 minutes. Lift the dough off the wall or brush it into a dustpan. Leftover dough can be stored in a sealed jar.

CLEANING WALLCOVERINGS WITH PASTE

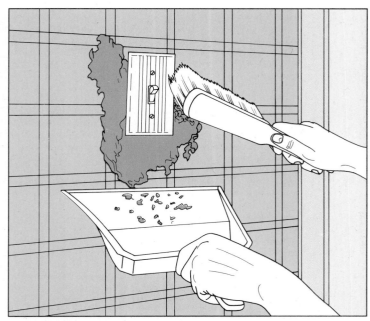

1 Preparing and applying a paste cleaner. An absorbent cleaner for grease stains can be made with fuller's earth and kerosene. In a plastic container mix several ounces of fuller's earth (available at drugstores) with 1 tablespoon of kerosene. The mixture should be the consistency of wet cake frosting. Wearing rubber gloves, daub small handfuls of paste onto the soiled area *(above)*.

2 Removing the paste. Leave the paste on the wallcovering for 30 minutes, or until dry. With a soft-bristled brush, sweep the mixture off the wall into a dustpan. Then wipe the area clean with a cloth slightly dampened in kerosene.

CLEANING SPECIAL WALLCOVERINGS

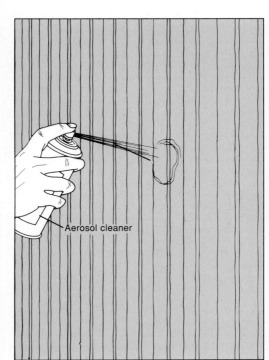

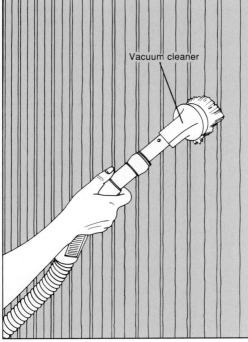

Using an aerosol spray cleaner. Stains on delicate wallcoverings such as silks, grasscloths and flocks can often be cleaned with commercial dry-cleaning fluid, available in aerosol sprays. Test the cleaner in an inconspicuous corner, spraying a small amount on the wall. Wait 30 minutes and wipe it off. If no discoloration occurs, apply the spray to the stained area *(far left)*. Let it dry several minutes, then remove with the soft-bristled brush attachment of your vacuum cleaner *(left)*.

REMOVING SMALL BLISTERS

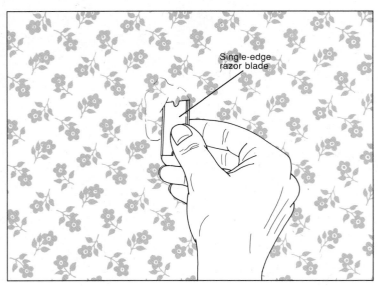
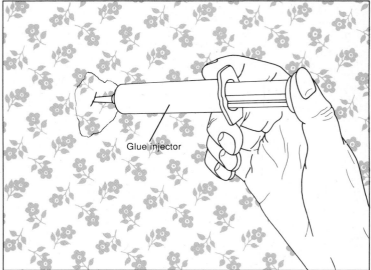

Opening and gluing the blister. Purchase a syringe-style glue injector specially designed for wallcovering repair. Using a single-edge razor blade, cut a slit in the blister *(above, left)* no larger than the tip of the injector. Insert the tip and squirt out a small amount of glue *(above, right)*. Pull out the tip, press down the repaired area with a damp sponge and wipe away any excess glue. For fine work, try using a hypodermic needle and syringe filled with diluted wallpaper paste.

REMOVING LARGE BUBBLES

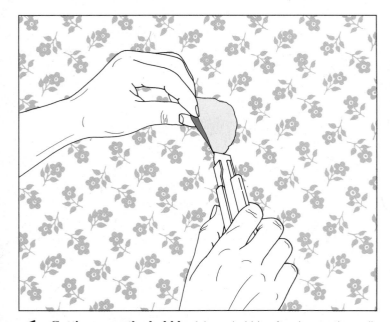
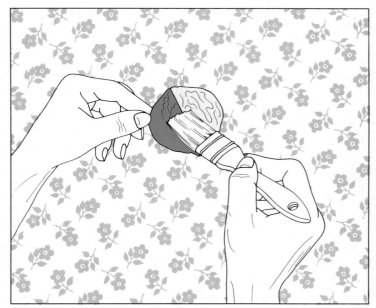

1 **Cutting open the bubble.** A large bubble often leaves the wall-covering over it especially brittle. Avoid damaging the surface during repair by first dampening the affected area with a sponge to soften the wallcovering. Then cut a semicircle around the edge of the blister with a sharp utility knife *(above)*.

2 **Pasting down the flap.** Carefully lift the cut flap and hold it away from the wall. With a small brush, apply paste to the underside of the flap and to the wall *(above)*. Let the paste stand for 5 minutes, then gently smooth the flap back into place with your fingers. For a vinyl wallcovering, press the edge with a seam roller; for more delicate non-vinyls, smooth the bubble down with a damp sponge. Wipe away excess paste with the sponge.

REPAIRING LOOSE SEAMS

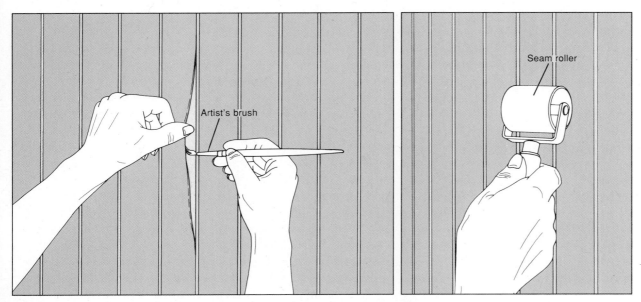

Securing the seam. With a fine artist's brush, apply acrylic seam paste to both the loose edges of the wallcovering and the wall *(above, left)*. Let the paste stand for 3 to 5 minutes, then press the edges together with your hands. Let stand for about 5 more minutes, or until you can apply pressure without glue seeping out. For a vinyl wallcovering, flatten the seam with a seam roller *(above, right)*; for more delicate non-vinyls, press the seam edges together with a slightly damp sponge. Wipe away excess glue with a damp sponge. To prevent persistent loose seams due to high humidity, see below.

REPAIRING PEELING WALLCOVERING

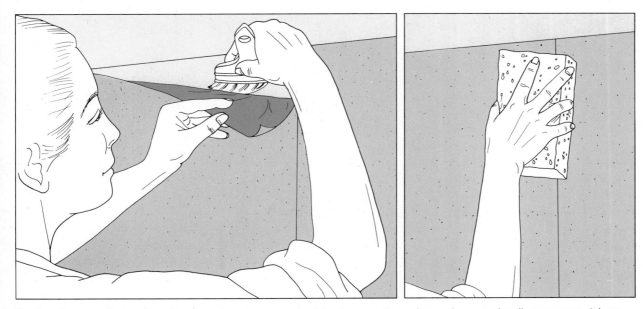

Pasting loose wallcovering. Brush paste onto as much of the loose wallcovering and exposed wall as you can *(above, left)*. Let it stand for several minutes until tacky, then press the pasted flap back into place with your hands. Use a large sponge to smooth out any wrinkles or air pockets *(above, right)*. Peeling wallcovering is a frequent problem in such high-humidity areas as bathrooms, finished basements and laundry rooms. Better ventilation, perhaps installing an exhaust fan or dehumidifier, often prevents peeling. Another solution is to treat the wallcovering with vinyl sealant, a clear acrylic coating. Start with dry, clean wallcovering, and keep the room well ventilated as you work. Spray on an aerosol sealant, or use a brush or roller for liquid sealant. (Such a sealant can also make a nonwashable wallcovering washable.) For persistent peeling, remove the existing wallcovering *(page 100)* and replace it with a fabric-backed vinyl *(pages 101-105)*.

INSTALLING A WALLCOVERING BORDER

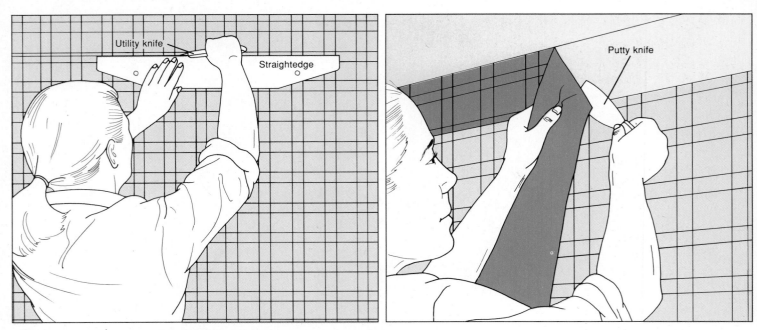

1 **Removing the damaged wallcovering.** Peeling or discolored wallcovering caused by water damage at the ceiling level can be replaced by a decorative border. Measure the damaged area at its widest spot, and use a straightedge and sharp utility knife to score a horizontal line of that distance from the ceiling around the room *(above, left)*. Remove all wallcovering above the cut line *(page 100)*; peel off strippable wallcovering or, if necessary, apply wallpaper remover. Scrape off any remaining paste or paper with a sharp tool such as a putty knife *(above, right)*, taking care not to nick the wall. Sand the wall smooth.

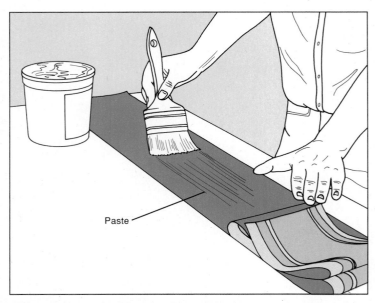

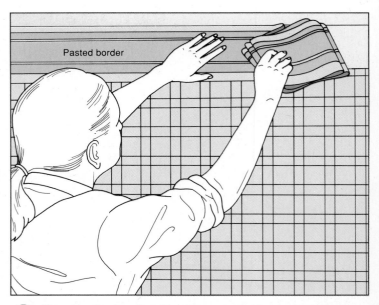

2 **Preparing the border.** Buy special border wallcovering or make your own from leftover paper or a coordinating roll. If cutting your own border, measure the width you need. Spread the paper on a clean worktable and cut it into strips using a straightedge and sharp blade. Cut slowly and firmly; pulling quickly or too hard may tear the paper. Cut a border strip to the length of the wall. Spread out an arm's length of border and brush on paste *(above)*, or water on prepasted paper. Then gather up the length into 9-inch folds, pasted side in. Repeat this process for an entire strip, ending with an accordion-pleated bundle which you can hold in one hand.

3 **Hanging the border.** Stand on a stepladder *(page 132)* at one end of the wall, and pick up the pasted bundle in one hand. Lay an arm's length of border against the wall abutting the ceiling. Straighten it and smooth it lightly in place with your hand, a sponge or a smoothing brush. Continue with another arm's length. If the border begins to run crooked, lift it at one end and straighten it. Once an entire strip is hung, return to the start and smooth out any air bubbles with a moist sponge.

MAKING AN OVERLAY PATCH

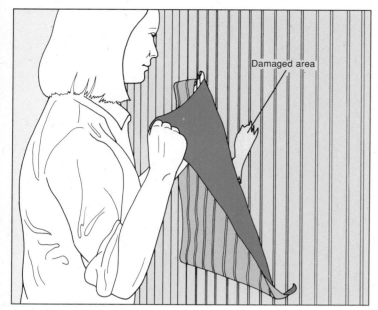

1 **Preparing the patch material.** If you have leftover wall-covering or can purchase a new roll of the same material, find a section of the pattern that matches the damaged area. Using a sharp blade or sharp scissors, cut a patch several inches wider and longer than the damaged area to be covered. Center the patch material over the damaged area and align it with the pattern on the wall. If you have a strippable wallcovering but no extra pieces, you might be able to remove a reusable section from a place hidden by furniture or in a closet. The least conspicuous patch on strippable wallcovering, however, is the double-cut method shown on page 98.

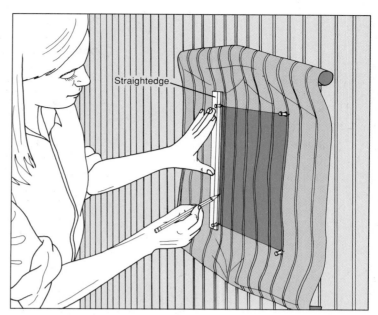

2 **Outlining the patch.** Holding the patch material in place with one hand, lift an upper corner to see where the upper edge of the patch should fall to cover the damage. Push a pin through the patch material an inch or two beyond that spot. Repeat the procedure for the other three corners, making sure the pins are placed outside the damaged area. With a pencil and straightedge, draw a rectangle on the patch material, using the pins as guides *(above)*.

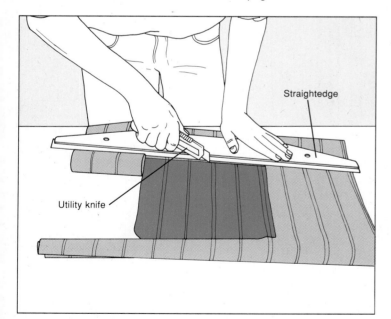

3 **Cutting the patch.** Remove the patch material from the wall and place it pattern side up on a clean worktable. With a straightedge and sharp utility knife, cut along the guidelines *(above)*. Apply a thin, even layer of paste to the back of the patch with a small brush. If you are pasting a vinyl patch on top of vinyl wallcovering, use special vinyl-to-vinyl adhesive. Fold the patch in half, glued sides together, and place it in a plastic bag. Let the paste cure for 10 minutes and remove the patch.

4 **Applying the patch.** Hold the pasted patch by the top corners and place it over the damaged area. Align the patch with the pattern on the wall and smooth it down with your fingers. Use a damp sponge to remove wrinkles and air bubbles and to press down the edges. Gently roll the edges of a vinyl wallcovering patch with a seam roller *(above)*. Wipe off any excess paste with the damp sponge.

MAKING A DOUBLE-CUT PATCH

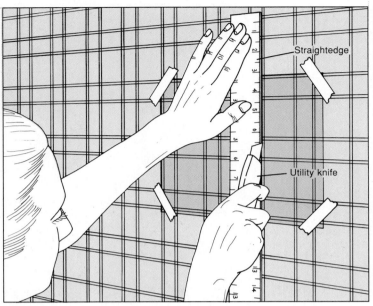

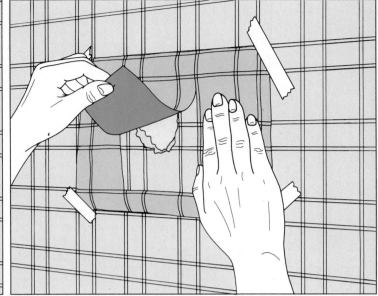

1 **Cutting the patch.** Match the pattern on a piece of leftover wallcovering and, if necessary, use the push-pin method *(page 97)* to cut a piece of patching material larger than the damaged area to be covered. (Make the patch no smaller than 3 inches square, or it will be difficult to handle.) If the wallcovering has an enclosed pattern such as the geometric design shown here, cut a patch along the outline of the pattern. Place the patch material over the damaged area,

aligning thepatterns, and secure it temporarily with masking tape. Position a straightedge over the patch material. If the wallcovering has vertical lines, use them to align the straightedge. Holding the straightedge firmly, cut along its edge with a sharp blade *(above, left)*, slicing through both the patch material and the wallcovering underneath. Turn the square and repeat to cut the other three sides. Remove the freshly cut patch *(above, right)* and untape the leftover scraps.

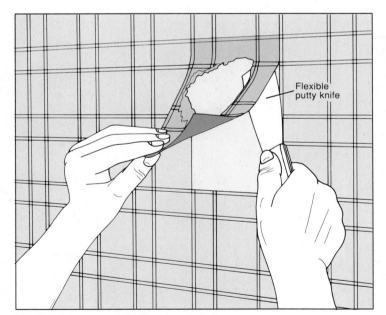

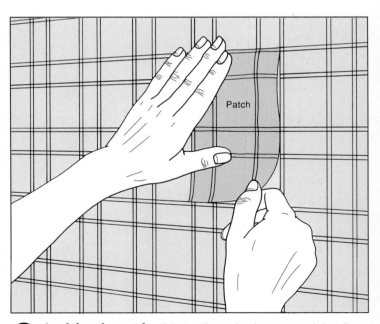

2 **Removing the damaged area.** You may need to rescore the cuts on the wall to free the section of damaged wallcovering. Then, with strippable wallcovering, insert a flexible putty knife beneath a corner of the damaged section and peel it off, being careful not to nick the wall *(above)*. It may be necessary to apply wallpaper remover *(page 100)* to other types of wallcovering before you can remove it. Once the damaged material is gone, clean off all traces of paste with a damp sponge and dry the wall.

3 **Applying the patch.** If the wallcovering is prepasted, brush the patch with water. Otherwise, use the adhesive recommended by the manufacturer, applying it to the bare wall with a small paintbrush. Let the paste set for a few minutes. Insert the patch in the space, pressing it into place with your fingers *(above)*. Smooth out any air bubbles with a damp sponge and wipe away excess paste. If the wallcovering is a heavy vinyl, gently use a putty knife to push in the edges of the patch, and press the seams flat with a seam roller.

MAKING A TORN PATCH

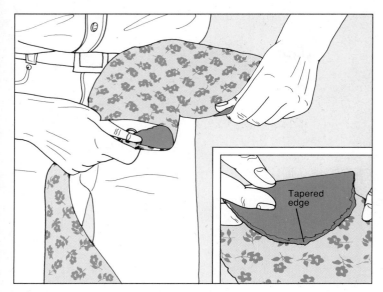

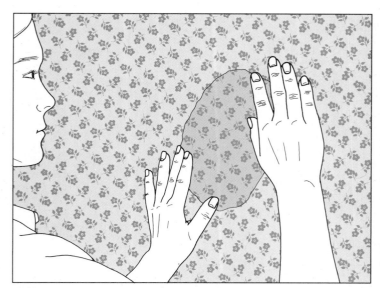

1 Preparing the patch. On small, busy patterns, a round patch is less visible than a square one. (Note: This method is not suitable for fabric-backed vinyl wallcoverings.) Obtain a matching piece of patch material. Hold it in both hands, pattern side up, with one thumb on the underside and the other on top *(above)*. Tear out a patch by pulling the excess down and away from the patch. The tapered edge this produces *(inset)* will be less conspicuous when the patch is glued down over the damaged area. Practice on a scrap piece first.

2 Applying the patch. If the wallcovering is prepasted, brush the patch with water. For unpasted paper, apply the manufacturer's recommended adhesive to the wall with a small paintbrush and let it set for several minutes. If you are gluing a vinyl patch on top of vinyl wallcovering, use special vinyl-to-vinyl adhesive. Position the patch over the damaged area, matching the pattern with the wallcovering underneath *(above)*. Smooth with a damp sponge, and press vinyl edges with a seam roller. Wipe off any excess paste with the sponge.

MAKING AN APPLIQUÉ PATCH

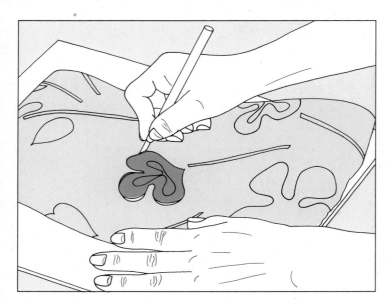

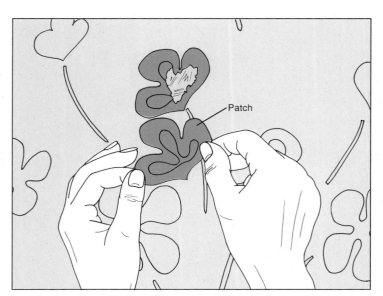

1 Preparing the patch. Damaged wallcovering with large, distinctive shapes in the pattern can be repaired almost invisibly by using the pattern to disguise the patch. If the damaged area is within a shape in the pattern, cut the same shape out of a scrap of matching wallcovering with a sharp blade *(above)*.

2 Applying the patch. If you have a strippable wallcovering, use a sharp blade to outline the shape around the damaged area, then lift out that section and discard it. For other wallcoverings, simply paste the appliqué over the damaged area. If the wallcovering is prepasted, brush water onto the patch; for unpasted paper, apply a thin, even layer of the recommended paste to the area to be patched. Place the patch in position and pat it smooth with a sponge; roll vinyl edges with a seam roller. Sponge away any excess paste.

REMOVING WALLCOVERING

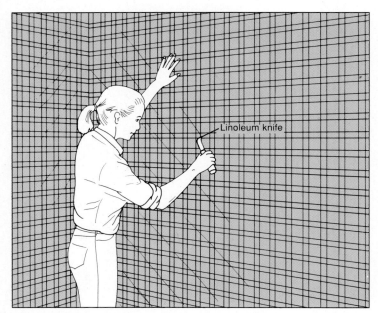

1 **Stripping or scoring.** Many vinyl wallcoverings, as well as some fabrics and foils, are strippable. To test, push a flexible putty knife under the top corner of a strip. Take the corner and pull down. If the strip comes away easily, continue around the room, then proceed to step 4. For nonstrippable wallcoverings, first score the surface with a sharp knife (here, a linoleum knife is used on thick vinyl) or a special scoring tool resembling a pizza cutter. Draw the blade across the wallcovering, cutting through it without damaging the wall.

2 **Applying wallpaper remover.** Mask baseboards with tape and cover the floor with a drop cloth *(page 141)*. Mix wallpaper remover, following the manufacturer's directions, in a bucket (as shown) or a spray bottle. Wearing rubber gloves, and eye protection if working on the ceiling, liberally apply remover to the cuts in the wallcovering with a large sponge *(above)* or by spraying. Soak the paper so the remover penetrates to the paste. Complete one wall before moving on to the next. If using a spray bottle, 2 to 3 applications will be necessary. Let the remover stand for at least 30 minutes.

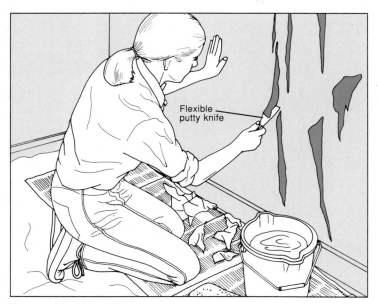

3 **Pulling off the wallcovering.** Have a large plastic garbage bag ready to catch sodden paper. Insert the blade of a flexible putty knife at the bottom of a strip or at one of the cuts and push upwards, being careful not to nick the wall. As the paper lifts, pull it up in strips. Non-coated papers will peel off less evenly than vinyl-coated ones. Do not force paper off the wall; if it doesn't lift easily, apply more wallpaper remover as in step 2.

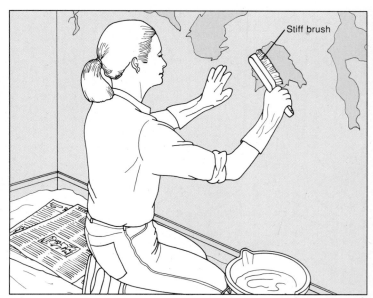

4 **Cleaning the wall.** Strippable wallcovering leaves behind a fuzzy residue which may need to be removed before recovering—follow the paper manufacturer's recommendation. If you used wallpaper remover to strip the paper, clean the walls of any paste residue with a stiff brush and the remaining wallpaper remover *(above)*. Rinse the walls, and let them dry. To remove mold or mildew from the wall, prepare a solution of 1 cup bleach in a gallon of water. Open a window for ventilation, put on rubber gloves, and scrub the solution onto the walls with a stiff brush. Let dry.

PREPARING TO HANG NEW WALLCOVERING

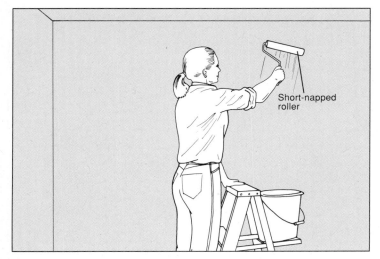

1 Priming the wall. Repair any defects in the wall following instructions in this book. Clean previously papered walls (page 100, step 4). Use a short-napped paint roller to apply a coat of acrylic primer or cellulose sizing (above), according to the wallcovering manufacturer's directions. Previously unpapered glossy paint should be roughened with medium-grit sandpaper, dusted, washed, then primed. Test flat latex paint by taping on a damp sponge and leaving it for 15 minutes. If the paint washes off, sand, dust and prime the wall. Seal wall patches with shellac, or neutralize with vinegar (acetic acid).

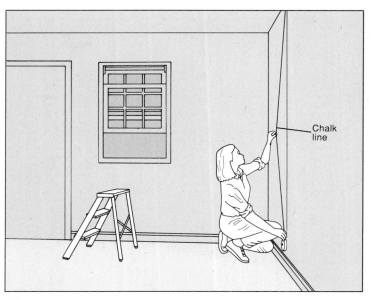

2 Drawing a vertical line. Since few rooms are exactly symmetrical, you cannot use a corner to align the first sheet of wallcovering. Instead, mark a true vertical by using a chalk line as a plumb bob. At the middle of the wall, tack the ring near the ceiling. Draw the string out from the spool to within 6 inches of the baseboard, and close the handle to lock the spool. Let the case hang free so that the string is taut and vertical. Hold the case, pull the string out (above) and let it snap back against the wall, leaving a line of chalk. You can also use a level and a pencil to draw a vertical line on the wall.

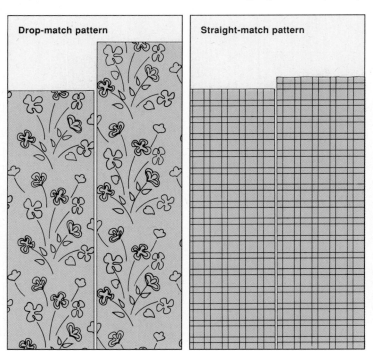

3 Matching patterns. Most patterned wallcoverings fall into one of two categories: straight-match and drop-match, sometimes stamped on the back of the paper. Determine what type of pattern you have before cutting the wallcovering. If the elements of the same design are directly opposite each other on the left and right edges of the strip, the paper is a straight-match (above, right); the pattern repeats horizontally from strip to strip. All others are drop-match patterns, with elements that begin near the edge of one sheet completed on the next (above, left), and a design that repeats diagonally on the wall.

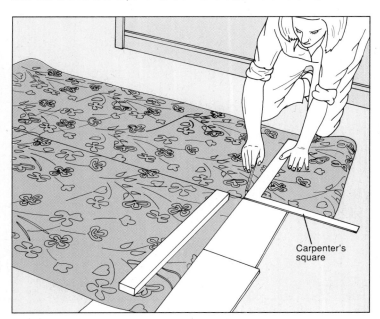

4 Measuring and cutting. For a straight-match pattern, cut several sheets at a time from a single roll. The most efficient way to cut strips for a drop-match pattern is to start with two rolls. On a clean surface, unroll both rolls several feet. Pull one end ahead until the designs match. With a utility knife and carpenter's square, cut the longer end even with the other (above). Pencil an A on the top back of one roll and a B on the other. Now measure the height of the walls in several places. Add 4 inches to the longest measurement, allowing 2 inches for trimming at the top and bottom of the strip. Cut sheets alternately from roll A and roll B. Mark the top of each strip in pencil.

HANGING THE FIRST STRIPS

1 **Pasting and folding a strip.** If you are using prepasted wallcovering, go to step 2. Otherwise, choose a paste according to the wallcovering manufacturer's recommendation. Prepare powdered paste as directed on the label. Cover a worktable with plastic and spread out a strip of wallcovering (strip A if a drop match), pattern side down, with half the strip hanging over the edge. Weight the strip to keep it from curling. Drop a dollop of paste onto the surface and use a short-napped roller or paste brush to work it out to the edges *(above,*

left), covering the entire area with a thin coat. Fold the pasted section over on itself, pattern side out. Do not crease the fold. Turn the strip around so the pasted half drapes over the edge of the table. Paste and fold the other half *(above, center)*. Allow the pasted strip to set following the manufacturer's instructions, usually 3 to 10 minutes. Then pick up the strip at the center, lifting it by the sides so that it folds in the middle *(above, right)*.

2 **Positioning the strip.** Carry the pasted strip, folded in quarters, to the starting point marked by the chalk line. Mount the stepladder, grasp the top of the strip and allow the rest to drop to a three-quarter length. Align a side edge with the chalk line near the top *(above)*, allowing a 2-inch overlap to curl at the ceiling. Use both hands to press the sheet lightly against the top of the wall. Smooth the rest as far down as you can reach. For a prepasted wallcovering *(inset)*, place a water box on newspapers or plastic directly beneath the chalk-line area. Fill the box two-thirds full. Roll a cut strip loosely from bottom to top, pattern side in, place it in the water and soak it for the length of time recommended by the manufacturer. If the rolled strip floats above the water, insert a straightedge through its middle to weigh it down. Pull the paper up out of the box and apply it to the top of the wall, aligning a side edge with the chalk line and allowing a 2-inch overlap at the ceiling.

3 **Straightening the strip.** Step down the ladder and unfold the remaining section of the strip. Align the edge with the chalk line and pat the strip into place. If the edge does not follow the chalk line to the baseboard, do not pull it; instead, gently lift the strip up and out from the bottom, and shift it until it hangs straight.

4 **Smoothing the strip.** Sweep in short, firm strokes from the center of the strip to the edges with a clean, damp sponge or a smoothing brush *(above)*. This will flatten the wallcovering, brush out air bubbles and spread the paste underneath. Smooth the top half of the sheet, then repeat on the lower half. If a wrinkle develops, pull the sheet up from the bottom until it flattens. Go over each strip carefully as it is hung: you must remove wrinkles or large air bubbles before the paste sets. Very small bubbles generally disappear as the paper dries.

5 **Hanging the second strip.** Apply this strip to the wall as you did the first, matching the pattern carefully. (If using a drop match, this should be strip B.) Since wallcoverings generally shrink as they dry, butt the two edges together until they buckle slightly; this will result in a tight seam. Use both hands to slide the new strip into position *(above)*, being careful not to stretch the edges. Adjust delicate wallcoverings using a sponge, since your hands could tear the material.

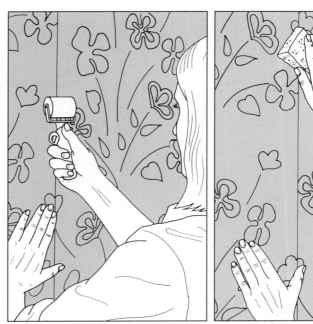

6 **Trimming the excess.** When two sheets have been hung, trim both at top and bottom. Hold a trimming guide at a 45-degree angle and push it firmly into the corner where the wall and ceiling meet. Draw a sharp blade along the trimming guide halfway across the first strip *(above)*, shift the trimming guide and continue the cut. Repeat along the baseboard. Wipe paste off the ceiling and baseboard with a damp sponge.

7 **Finishing the seams.** Twenty minutes after hanging the third sheet, go back and press all the seams flat with a seam roller *(above, left)*. Keep a light touch—too much pressure squeezes out needed paste. Substitute a sponge for the roller when pressing the seams of fragile or textured wallcoverings. Use a damp sponge to wipe off excess paste *(above, right)*, and dry with a towel. If large amounts of paste ooze from seams, let the paste set for five more minutes. If paste still oozes out, you are applying too much. Spread paste more thinly on remaining sheets.

WORKING AROUND A CORNER

1 **Measuring the corner.** When you are within one strip's width of a corner, measure the distance between the last strip hung and the corner at the top, middle and bottom of the wall *(above)*. Add 1/4 inch to the widest measurement, and use a straight-edge and sharp blade to trim a strip that will barely overlap the corner. (Unless the remaining piece is only 1 or 2 inches wide, put it aside to be used in step 3.)

2 **Hanging the corner strip.** Paste and hang the corner strip *(page 102)*, butting the untrimmed edge against the last full sheet. Use a smoothing brush to press the strip firmly into the corner *(above)*, creasing it so that the overlap curls around to the adjacent wall.

3 **Hanging the remaining strip.** Measure the width of the remainder of the strip cut in step 1. (If only a thin piece is left over, start with a fresh strip.) Mark a new vertical line *(page 101, step 2)* at a distance from the corner equal to the width of the strip. Align the pasted strip with the chalk line *(above)* and press the edge into the corner. If the cut edges overlap too far, double-cut them *(page 105, step 3)*.

WORKING AROUND A WINDOW

Hanging wallcovering around a window. Position the pasted strip at the ceiling, allowing it to hang over the window. Use long-handled scissors to clip diagonally at the corners, then cut away an outline of the window *(above, left)*, leaving about 2 inches overlapping the trim. Press the wallcovering on the wall above and below the trim. With a trimming guide and utility knife, fit the wallcovering tight against the sides of the window trim *(above, center)*. Repeat for the other side of the window *(above, right)*. Sponge paste off the window trim.

HANGING THE FINAL STRIP

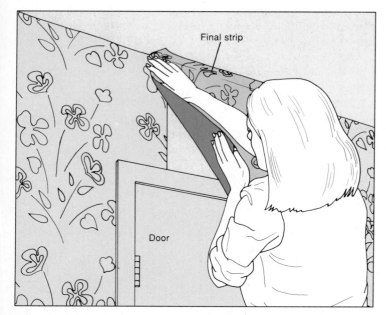

1 **Positioning the strip.** The last two sheets hung should meet in an inconspicuous place, such as above a door, since the patterns are not likely to match. (To end where you want, you'll probably need to work in both directions from your original starting point.) Paste the final strip and position it over the door *(above).* If possible, overlap an adjacent strip that has just been hung so that the paste is still damp.

2 **Trimming the strip.** Smooth the final strip onto the wall, creasing it into the angle made by the wall and door trim. Cut off the excess at top and bottom with a trimming guide and utility knife. Wipe paste off the door trim with a damp sponge.

3 **Double-cutting the overlap.** Smooth down the overlapping section of the final strip—a putty knife will do—on top of the adjacent strip. With a small straightedge and a sharp blade, make a vertical cut approximately in the middle of the overlap *(above),* slicing through both layers of wallcovering.

4 **Finishing the final seam.** Pull off the cut piece of wallcovering on the outside; lift the last installed strip and pull off the cut section underneath it *(above).* Press the edge of the strip back into place by hand; roll a vinyl seam with a seam roller. Wipe off any excess paste with a damp sponge. If this mismatched seam is unsightly, you might be able to cut out missing parts of the pattern from a leftover scrap and paste these appliqués on top *(page 99),* using a vinyl-to-vinyl adhesive, if necessary. Save all leftover paper for future patching.

TILE

Back in the days of Henry Ford's Model T, bathroom and kitchen tiles were available in any color you wanted—as long as it was white. Nowadays, colorful ceramic tile walls have come into their own as home decorating accents, without sacrificing any of their old-fashioned practicality.

In its most demanding application—a bathtub enclosure like the one pictured below—a modern tile wall starts with a backing of water-resistant drywall, or a concrete and glass-fiber backer board, or even plywood. A layer of Type I water-proof mastic, a special adhesive, holds the tiles in place and helps seal the backing. Joints between tiles are filled with a cement-based or silicone grout, and the tub rim is sealed with

silicone or latex caulk. During the 1950s and '60s, plastic tiles were installed in some bathrooms. In old bathrooms, ceramic tiles may have been set in mortar rather than mastic—repairs to such a wall may require professional service. And kitchen wall tiles may be applied with a less water-resistant, Type II mastic directly over drywall or plaster.

Caulk and grout joints are chinks in the armor of a tile wall. Unless sealed with silicone *(page 110)* and properly maintained, they allow moisture to pass through to the backing, the main cause of tile wall deterioration. By the time loose tiles or a warped wall have become noticeable, the backing itself often needs to be replaced.

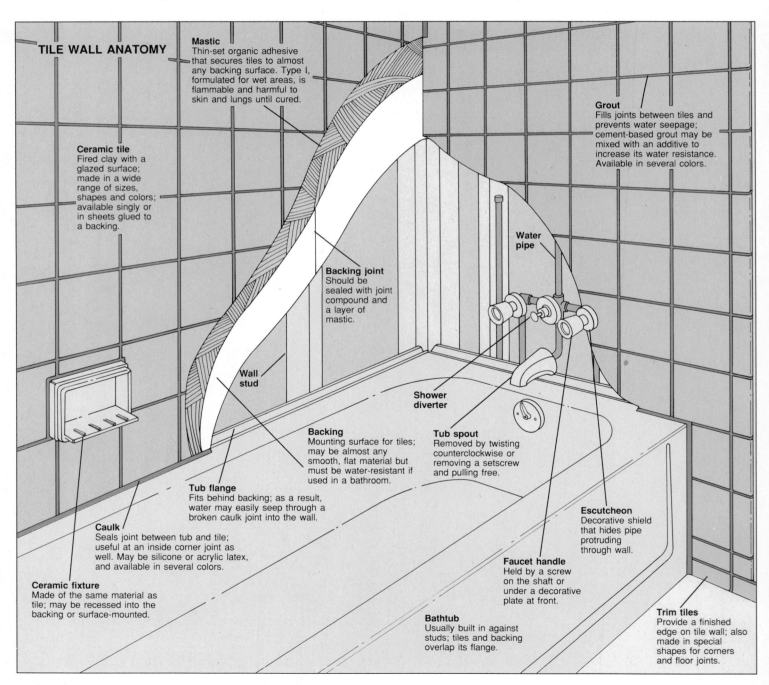

TILE WALL ANATOMY

Mastic
Thin-set organic adhesive that secures tiles to almost any backing surface. Type I, formulated for wet areas, is flammable and harmful to skin and lungs until cured.

Ceramic tile
Fired clay with a glazed surface; made in a wide range of sizes, shapes and colors; available singly or in sheets glued to a backing.

Grout
Fills joints between tiles and prevents water seepage; cement-based grout may be mixed with an additive to increase its water resistance. Available in several colors.

Backing joint
Should be sealed with joint compound and a layer of mastic.

Water pipe

Wall stud

Shower diverter

Backing
Mounting surface for tiles; may be almost any smooth, flat material but must be water-resistant if used in a bathroom.

Tub spout
Removed by twisting counterclockwise or removing a setscrew and pulling free.

Tub flange
Fits behind backing; as a result, water may easily seep through a broken caulk joint into the wall.

Caulk
Seals joint between tub and tile; useful at an inside corner joint as well. May be silicone or acrylic latex, and available in several colors.

Escutcheon
Decorative shield that hides pipe protruding through wall.

Faucet handle
Held by a screw on the shaft or under a decorative plate at front.

Ceramic fixture
Made of the same material as tile; may be recessed into the backing or surface-mounted.

Bathtub
Usually built in against studs; tiles and backing overlap its flange.

Trim tiles
Provide a finished edge on tile wall; also made in special shapes for corners and floor joints.

Many of the procedures listed in the Troubleshooting Guide *(page 108)* should be considered regular maintenance. Inspect caulk, grout and the glazed surface of tiles weekly, and make spot repairs immediately. Do not attempt to patch faulty caulk, however; replace the entire caulk seal *(page 109)*.

Most tile wall repairs can be accomplished with the tools pictured below and a few standard materials: tubes of acrylic-latex or silicone caulk, powdered grout mix (buy a liquid additive to make it more water-resistant), ready-mixed Type I

mastic and, if replacing the backing, panels of water-resistant drywall or backer board. If you must remove tiles to make a repair, save as many as possible; colors and styles can be hard to match. If you cannot find matching replacement tiles, buy contrasting tiles of the same size and use them as accents.

Caulk, grout and mastic can all harm skin; in addition, mastic and some caulks produce toxic fumes as they cure, and may be flammable. Wear rubber gloves when using these materials, and ventilate the room until they are dry.

TILE TOOLS

Mallet
Plastic face for striking tools with wooden handles.

Ball-peen hammer
For striking a cold chisel.

Cold chisel
Used to break and remove damaged tiles and break holes through backing.

Razor-blade tool
Safety handle for single-edge razor blades; used for stripping damaged caulk.

Putty knife
An all-purpose tool for scraping old grout, prying up tiles and cleaning backing surface.

Grout saw
Rough tungsten-carbide blade scrapes away old grout.

Notched knife and notched spreader
For spreading mastic on large areas of backing; notches should be spaced according to recommendations of mastic manufacturer.

Pry bar
Also called utility bar; for removing loose tiles from wall.

Safety goggles
Worn when chipping tiles or cutting dusty backing.

Tile nippers
Bite out tiny chunks of tile for creating irregular shapes.

Grout float (disposable)
Rubber-padded face of float pushes grout into joints between tiles.

File
Smooths rough edges of cut tiles.

Caulking gun
Fitted with a tube of caulk or grout, deposits a bead of sealant in joint.

Power drill and ceramic-tile bit
Bores holes through ceramic tile for removal or cutting.

Keyhole saw
Used to cut away damaged backing.

Tile cutter
Scores and snaps tiles mechanically; may be rented for cutting a large number of tiles.

Glass cutter
Sharpened wheel or carbide blade at tip scores glazed surface of tile for snapping.

Hacksaw with tungsten-carbide blade
Cuts holes and irregular shapes through center of tile.

Straightedge
For tracing guidelines on drywall or tiles.

TROUBLESHOOTING GUIDE

SYMPTOM	POSSIBLE CAUSE	PROCEDURE
Film, haze or water spots on tile	High mineral content in water	Dry tile wall after showering; wash wall regularly *(below)* □○; install a water softener
Opaque white deposits on tiles or encrusted along joints	Soap scum caused by high mineral content in water	Rinse and dry tile wall after showering; wash wall regularly *(below)* □○; store soap away from shower; install a water softener
Black spots, especially along grout joints and caulk	Mildew growing in area of high humidity	Wash away mildew with solution of 1 cup chlorine bleach in 1/2 gallon water *(below)* □○; ventilate room; if damaged, replace caulk *(p. 109)* ▣● or grout *(p. 110)* ▣●
Red or brown stains, especially around plumbing fixtures	Rusty water	Wash stained area with vinegar *(below)* □○; for stubborn stains, wash with solution of 1 part oxalic acid to 20 parts water; install a water softener
Tile surface looks dirty or dingy	Glaze worn off tile, leaving surface porous	Wash with solution of 1 cup chlorine bleach in 1/2 gallon water *(below)* □○; or apply paste of trisodium phosphate and water, let set a few hours and rinse with vinegar; seal tiles with silicone sealant *(p. 110)*; replace tiles *(p. 112)* ▣● if badly damaged
Grout joints stained	Grout is naturally somewhat porous and absorbent	Scrub joints *(below)* □○ using cleaner for type of stain listed above; then apply sealant to joints *(p. 110)* □○
Tile surface pitted	Abrasive or corrosive cleaners; acids in foods	Wash tile *(below)* □○ and apply silicone sealant *(p. 110)*; replace tiles *(p. 112)* ▣● if badly damaged or admitting water to backing
Tiles crazing (network of tiny cracks); wall sound	A symptom of old tiles	No need for repair; if very unsightly, remove *(p. 114)* ▣● and replace *(p. 116)* ▣●
Grout loose or worn away	Friction from abrasive cleaners or water	Regrout wall *(p. 110)* ▣●
Caulk cracked, loose or missing	Caulk old or improperly applied	Remove and replace caulk *(p. 109)* ▣●
Tile cracked	Accidental blow; tile incorrectly installed; house framing shifted	Remove and replace cracked tile *(p. 112)* ▣●; inspect backing for water damage
Ceramic fixture broken	Accidental blow	Replace ceramic fixture *(p. 113)* ▣●
Tiles or fixture loose or fallen off	Poor installation; water damage to backing	Remove all loose tiles *(p. 114)* ▣●; check backing for damage and replace if necessary *(p. 115)* ■●; reinstall tiles *(p. 116)* ■●
Tile wall warped or gives when pushed	Major water damage caused by seepage through tile joints or leaking pipes within wall	Remove tiles in damaged area *(p. 114)* ▣●; check backing for extent of damage and replace entire damaged area *(p. 115)* ■●; reinstall tiles *(p. 116)* ■●

DEGREE OF DIFFICULTY: □ **Easy** ▣ **Moderate** ■ **Complex**
ESTIMATED TIME: ○ **Less than 1 hour** ◖ **1 to 3 hours** ● **Over 3 hours** *(Does not include drying time)*

CLEANING TILE WALLS

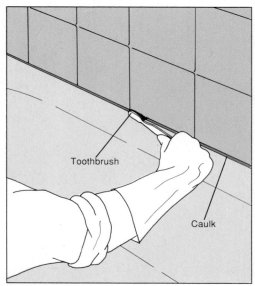

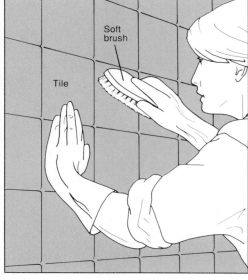

Cleaning tiles, grout and caulk. To remove a tenacious buildup of soap scum, mineral deposits, rust stains or mildew, use the household cleaner recommended in the Troubleshooting Guide, above. For stubborn stains, apply the cleaner to caulk or grout with an old toothbrush *(far left)* or nailbrush; scrub tiles gently with a soft-bristled scrub brush *(near left)*. Wear rubber gloves and ventilate the room when using caustic chemicals, and remember never to mix bleach and ammonia; the combination releases a deadly gas. Weekly washings prevent grime from gaining a toehold. For normal maintenance, apply one of the commercial non-abrasive cleaners with a moist sponge, and rinse well. Abrasives, such as scouring powder or steel-wool pads, remove the tiles' glazed surface and eat away at the grout and caulk, eventually allowing water to seep through to the wall behind them.

RECAULKING AROUND A TUB

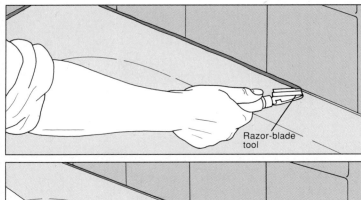

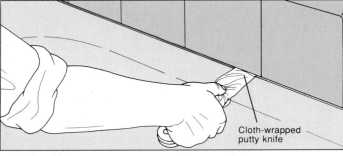

1 Removing old caulk. Draw a razor-blade tool along the edges of the old caulk to break its bond with the tub and the tiles *(above, top)*, using special care to avoid marring their surfaces. Pull out rubbery silicone caulk in strips; to chip out harder caulk, you may need an old screwdriver or a putty knife. Clean the caulk joint with a non-abrasive cleaner and a toothbrush *(page 108)* and rinse well. To remove all traces of moisture and soap film, wipe the joint using a cloth-wrapped putty knife moistened with alcohol *(above, bottom)*.

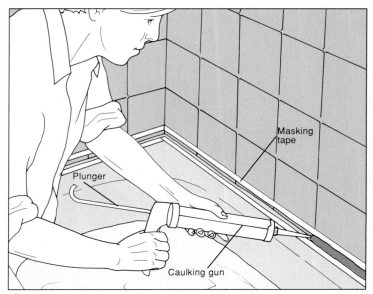

2 Applying new caulk. Fill the bathtub with water to expand the joint; this will make for a tighter caulk seal. If desired, stick lengths of masking tape above and below the joint, as shown, to maintain straight edges. Cut the tip of the caulk tube at a 45-degree angle, making an opening slightly smaller than the joint width. Insert the tube in the caulking gun. Starting at a corner, squeeze the trigger to eject a continuous bead of caulk along the joint, holding the gun in front of you at a 45-degree angle to the joint *(above)*. To stop the flow quickly, snap the plunger lever or turn the plunger handle down. Perform step 3 immediately.

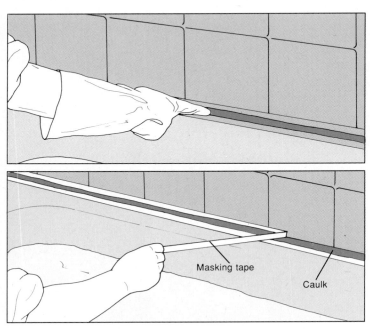

3 Smoothing the caulk. Wearing a rubber glove, run a wet finger along the caulk to press it into the joint and give it a slightly concave surface *(above, top)*. Moistening your finger with a detergent solution will keep caulk from sticking to it. If you applied masking tape, strip off the tape by pulling it straight out *(above, bottom)*. If the edges of the caulk pull away from the joint, smooth them down lightly with a wet finger. Let the caulk set for 24 hours before draining the water from the tub.

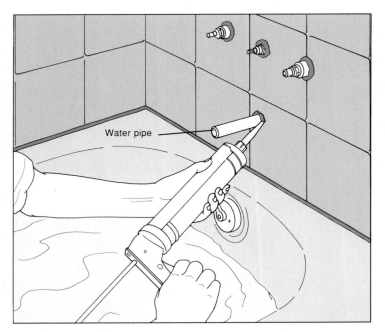

4 Caulking around pipes. Remove faucet handles, escutcheons, tub spout and other plumbing hardware—if screws are not visible, they may be hidden behind decorative plates. Turn a spout or a shower arm counterclockwise to unscrew it, or remove a setscrew. Scrape off old caulk and clean the area *(step 1)*. Squeeze caulk into the space between the pipe and the tiles *(above)* until the space is filled and caulk oozes out over the tiles. Replace the escutcheons before the caulk sets.

REPAIRING A SMALL AREA OF GROUT

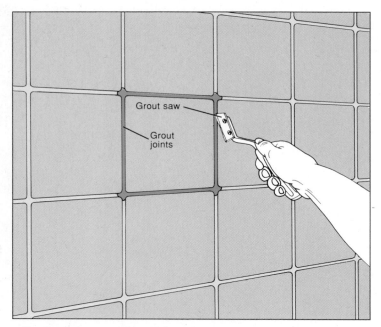

1 **Scraping out the old grout.** Use a grout saw to scrape porous, cracked or disintegrating grout out of the joints by gently pulling the blade along the joint *(above)*. Depending on the width of the joint, you may use an old screwdriver, a nail, a putty knife or a similar scraper. Take care not to mar adjacent tile edges. Scrub out any remaining grout particles with a moistened toothbrush and let the area dry.

2 **Mixing and applying new grout.** Use ready-mixed grout or mix powdered grout with water according to the manufacturer's instructions. To increase its water resistance, substitute a liquid grout additive for the water. Make the grout slightly thinner than the basic recipe to fill narrow grout joints; mix it slightly thicker for wide joints. Stir the grout gently to avoid introducing air bubbles. Press the grout into the joints with a gloved finger *(above)*. Watch for air pockets and gaps, filling them as necessary.

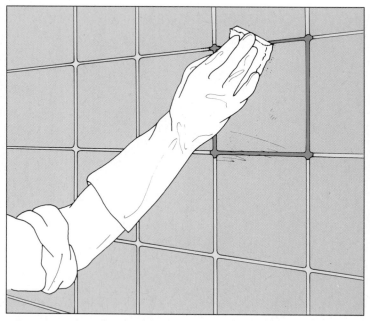

3 **Wiping away excess grout.** Moisten a sponge with clean water and wipe excess grout from the tile surface in diagonal strokes *(above)*, frequently rinsing the sponge in a bucket of water. Do not rub the grout out of the joints—leave them smooth and slightly concave. When you have wiped as much grout from the surface as you can, allow the grout to set for 15 minutes, then polish off the remaining haze with a soft cloth. Clean tools outdoors with a garden hose. Never flush grout down the drain—it clogs pipes.

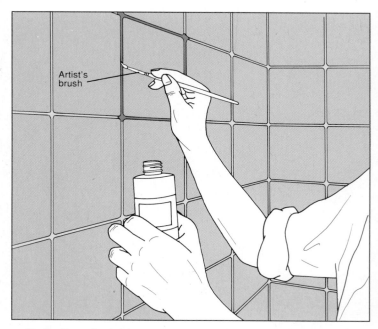

4 **Sealing the joints.** To protect the tile wall from stains and water seepage, apply a silicone sealant to the grout joints. Allow the grout to cure completely before applying the sealant; this may take as long as 4 weeks, depending on the grout or sealant manufacturer's instructions. Thoroughly wash and rinse the old grout joints. Then, using a small artist's brush, apply sealant along all the joints *(above)*. Avoid dripping the sealant on the surrounding tiles. Wait 24 hours before wetting the tile wall.

GROUTING AN ENTIRE TILE WALL

1 **Applying the grout.** Close the tub drain and lay a drop cloth in the tub to catch debris. If there is old grout in the joints, scrape it out *(page 110, step 1)*. Use ready-mixed grout, or mix powdered grout as on page 110, step 2. Working on one 4-foot-square section at a time, use a grout float to spread grout diagonally across the tiles *(above, left)*. After grouting the joints around a corner, press grout into the corner with a gloved finger *(above, right)*.

2 **Scraping away excess grout.** Immediately after completing each 4-foot-square section, pull the long edge of the grout float upward diagonally across the tile surface *(above)*, scraping off as much excess grout as possible without disturbing the grout in the joints. After each stroke, wipe grout off the float with a rag or sponge.

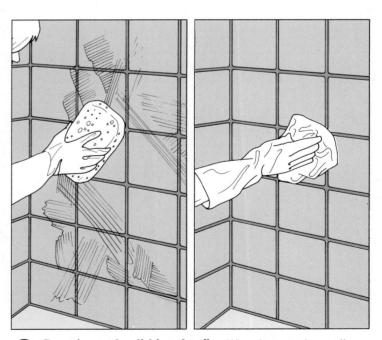

3 **Sponging and polishing the tiles.** Wipe the grout haze off each 4-foot section of the wall *(above, left)*, using a large sponge moistened in a bucket of clean water *(page 110, step 3)* and rinsing it frequently. When you have finished grouting, scraping and sponging the entire wall, polish the surface of the tiles with a soft cloth *(above, right)*. Apply a silicone sealant to the grout joints *(page 110, step 4)*. Discard leftover grout in the garbage, not down the drain, and clean tools outdoors with a garden hose.

REMOVING AND REPLACING A BROKEN TILE

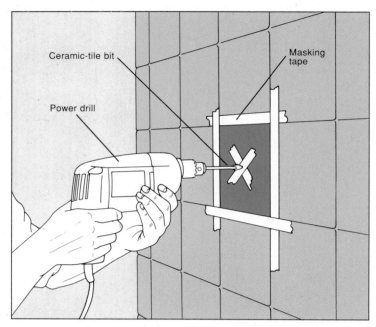

1 Drilling a hole in the tile. Close the tub drain and lay a drop cloth in the tub. Scrape out the grout around the damaged tile *(page 110, step 1)* and protect the edges of the adjacent tiles with masking tape. If the tile is loose or cracked, go to step 2. If not, stick a masking-tape X in the center of the tile. Wearing safety goggles, use a power drill fitted with a ceramic-tile bit or a carbide-tipped masonry bit to drill a hole through the center of the X into the tile with gentle, even pressure. Peel off the tape X.

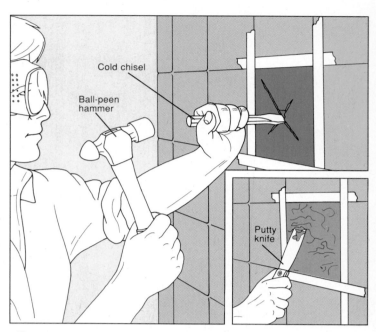

2 Removing the tile. Wearing safety goggles, use a cold chisel and a ball-peen hammer to chip out pieces of the tile *(above)*, starting at the drilled hole or at a crack near the center and working towards the edges. Scrape shards of tile and tile mastic off the wall using a stiff putty knife *(inset)*, leaving a perfectly level surface for the replacement tile. If part of the wall comes away with the old mastic, fill the valleys with mastic or joint compound and let it set 24 hours.

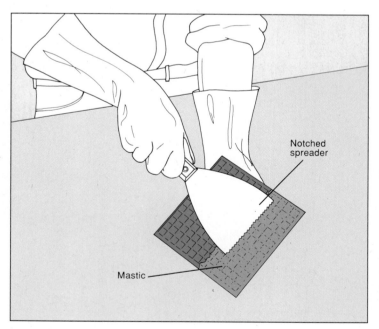

3 Buttering the tile with mastic. Wearing rubber gloves and working in a well-ventilated room, butter the back of the tile with mastic *(above)*—Type I, or water-resistant, for use in a bathroom. Use a notched spreader or trowel with teeth of the size and spacing recommended by the mastic manufacturer. Set the tile firmly in place on the wall, giving it a slight twist without sliding it. Wipe away any adhesive that oozes into the tile joints. If the tile sags on the wall, install spacers to keep its joints even *(page 117)*.

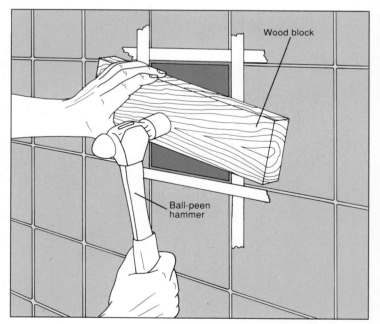

4 Leveling the tile. Set a block of wood long enough to span three tiles over the new tile. Tap gently on the center of the block with a mallet to seat the new tile level with those around it *(above)*. Do not pound too forcefully; you may unseat or damage surrounding tiles. Check that the tile joints are properly aligned; shift the tile slightly to correct them. Allow the mastic to dry for 24 hours. Strip off the masking tape and regrout the tile *(page 110)*.

REMOVING AND REPLACING MOSAIC TILES

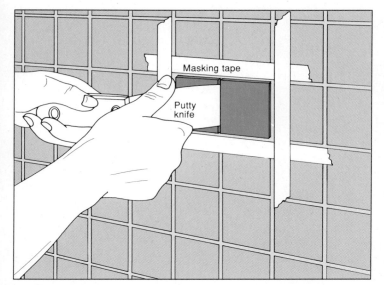

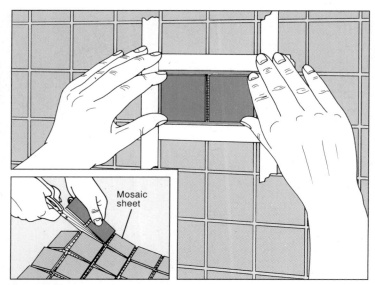

1 Removing the damaged tiles. Because they are small and very hard, mosaic tiles can be pried off in one piece. Protect undamaged tiles by covering their edges with masking tape. Scrape out grout around the damaged tiles *(page 110, step 1)*. Slide the end of a putty knife under the edge of a damaged tile and pry it up *(above)*. Mosaic tiles often have a mesh backing; if necessary, cut through the backing with a utility knife to release the tile. Pry out all damaged tiles the same way. Scrape bits of tile, mastic and mesh off the wall and fill any depressions *(page 112, step 2)*.

2 Setting the replacement tiles. Cut out a group of replacement tiles from a matching mosaic sheet, in the right shape to fit the space being filled *(inset)*. Do not remove mesh or paper joining the tiles. Spread a thin layer of Type I mastic on the back of the tiles with a putty knife. Press the tiles into place, aligning them vertically and horizontally *(above)*. Wipe out mastic that oozes into the joints and level the tiles *(page 112, step 4)*. Let the mastic set for 24 hours. If the tiles were joined by paper on the front, wet it with a sponge and peel it off. Regrout and apply a silicone sealant *(page 110)*.

REPLACING A CERAMIC FIXTURE

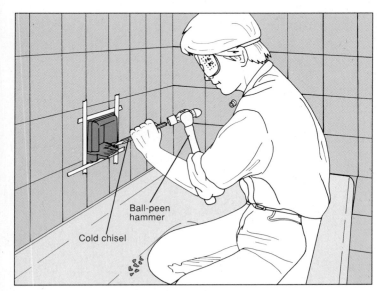

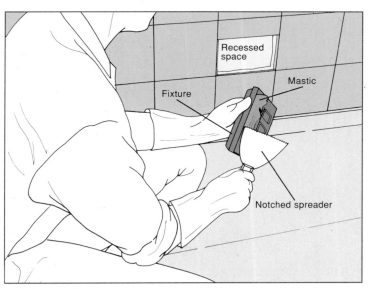

1 Removing a broken fixture. Scrape out grout from around the edges of the fixture *(page 110, step 1)* and protect the surrounding tiles with masking tape. Wearing safety goggles, use a cold chisel and ball-peen hammer to break apart the fixture *(above)*, then pry out the fragments with a pry bar, taking great care not to crack surrounding tiles. Scrape out fragments and old mastic, and smooth the wall surface *(page 112, step 2)*.

2 Installing the new fixture. The original fixture may have been recessed, as shown here, or surface-mounted; the replacement fixture should be of the same size and style. Wearing rubber gloves, spread a layer of Type I mastic on the back and sides of the fixture *(above)*, using the notched spreader specified by the mastic manufacturer. Press the fixture into the space, wiggling it a bit to seat it firmly. Wipe away mastic that oozes out around the edges.

REPLACING A CERAMIC FIXTURE (continued)

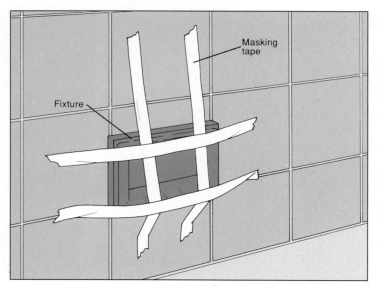

3 **Securing the fixture to the wall.** To secure the fixture while the mastic sets, hold it in place with strips of masking tape placed vertically and horizontally across the fixture. A fixture may also be propped in place with a piece of scrap wood. Let the mastic set for 24 hours before removing the masking tape or prop.

4 **Grouting around the fixture.** Using a wet toothbrush, clean out the grout joint around the fixture and let the joint dry. Following the steps on page 110 for repairing a small area of grout, prepare ready-mixed or powdered grout and push it into the joint with a gloved finger *(above)*. Wipe off excess grout with a moist sponge, let the grout set and protect it with a silicone sealant *(page 110, step 4)*.

REPLACING A DAMAGED BACKING WITH DRYWALL

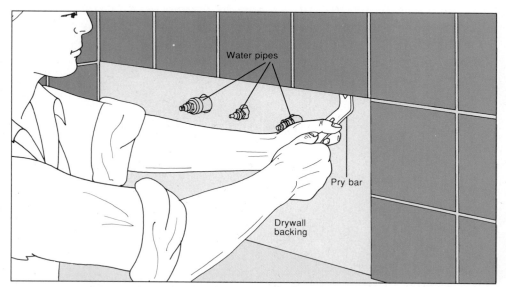

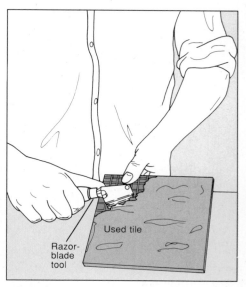

1 **Prying off loose or cracked tiles.** Close the tub drain and lay a drop cloth in the tub. Unscrew any plumbing hardware in the affected area *(page 109, step 4)*. If the wall is badly damaged by moisture, you will be able to pull off the tiles by hand; use a pry bar—very gently—to help release more stubborn tiles *(above)*. Save as many tiles for reuse as possible, but break tiles where necessary *(page 112, step 2)* to gain access to damaged areas of the wall. Remove tiles covering all softened or warped backing, expose sound backing all around and uncover the positions of at least two studs for installing the new section of drywall backing.

2 **Cleaning reusable tiles.** Before reinstalling undamaged tiles, clean their backs thoroughly. Using a razor-blade tool, scrape off old mastic and wall fragments *(above)*, cutting away from the body for safety. If old mastic is difficult to remove, soak tiles in water overnight before scraping.

REPLACING A DAMAGED BACKING WITH DRYWALL (continued)

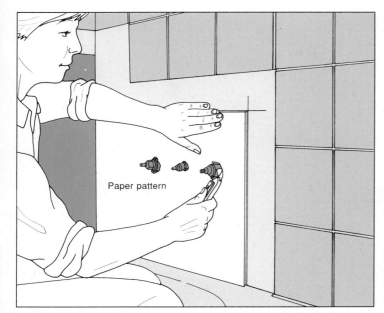

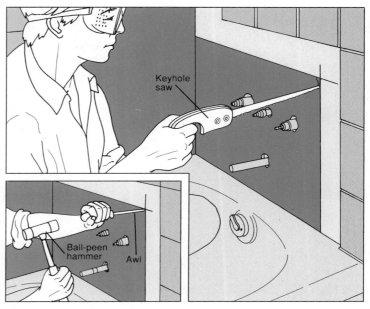

3 **Making a paper pattern for the drywall backing.** Using a straightedge, outline the rectangular areas of the wall to be replaced, making sure the edges of each area overlap at least two studs. If pipes protrude, cut a piece of stiff paper a bit larger than the outlined area and push the pipes through it. Holding the paper against the wall, trim the ragged holes around the pipes *(above)*. Cut the edges of the paper even with the outline on the wall using a straightedge and a utility knife. Take down the paper pattern and save it to cut a new drywall backing.

4 **Cutting out the damaged backing.** Wearing safety goggles, punch the blade of a keyhole saw through the damaged backing near a corner; if the material is very hard (plywood or cementous board), use a mallet and an awl to punch a hole for the saw *(inset)*. Cut as much of the backing as you can with the saw; cut backing that covers studs with a utility knife or a cold chisel and ball-peen hammer. Pull off the backing. Remove drywall screws with a Phillips screwdriver or pry off nails with a pry bar. Scrape the faces of the studs clean and smooth.

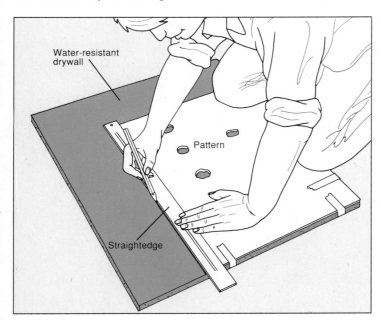

5 **Cutting a drywall patch.** If you made a paper pattern for the wall patch *(step 3)*, tape it to a piece of water-resistant drywall, shown here, or other suitable backing material *(page 106)*, and trace it with the aid of a straightedge *(above)*. For an area without a pattern, measure the area and transfer its dimensions to the drywall, using a carpenter's square to maintain square corners. Score and snap the patch, or cut it out, as described on page 27.

6 **Cutting holes for the pipes.** Lay the pattern on the drywall patch and score around the holes for the pipes with a utility knife *(above)*. Raise both ends of the drywall on wooden blocks, and use a cold chisel and ball-peen hammer to punch out the scored holes *(inset)*. Turn the drywall over and trim the surface paper with a utility knife. Holes that are large enough may be cut out with a keyhole saw.

REPLACING A DAMAGED BACKING WITH DRYWALL (continued)

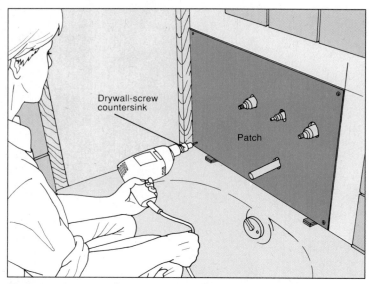

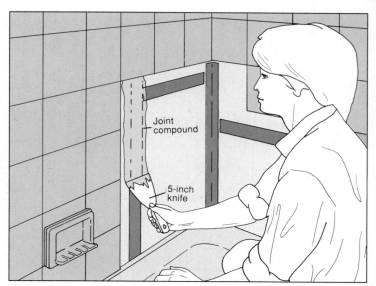

7 **Screwing the drywall patch to the studs.** Insert the patch in its space in the wall. If two patches will meet at a corner, as shown above, install the patch that butts the other last. Fit a power drill with a drywall-screw countersink, and drive drywall screws through the patch into the studs near each corner. Because water-resistant drywall is heavier than ordinary drywall, drive screws at 6-inch intervals to support the additional weight. Caulk around the faucet stems, diverter and tub spout *(page 109, step 4)*.

8 **Sealing the corner joints.** Finish the edges of the patch and the corner with joint compound and paper joint tape *(pages 19, 140)*. Using a flexible 5-inch knife, spread a very thin, smooth layer of Type I mastic over the entire exposed surface of the backing, and allow it to set for 24 hours.

INSTALLING TILES

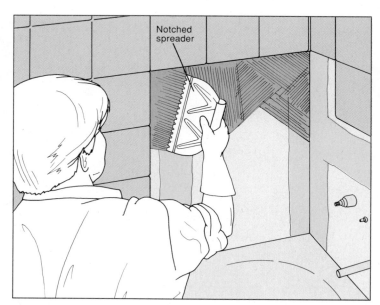

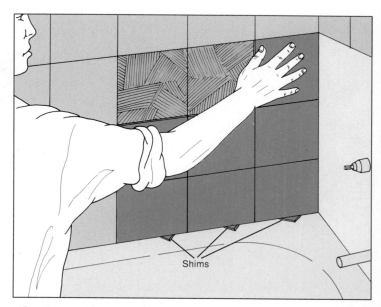

1 **Applying the mastic.** Check that the wall surface is free of bumps or depressions. Sand or cut off bumps and fill small holes with mastic or joint compound. Apply Type I mastic to no more than 10 square feet of the backing surface, applying it first only to those areas of the wall on which you will install uncut tiles. Using the type of notched spreader recommended by the mastic manufacturer, hold the spreader at an angle and spread the mastic with the notched edge *(above)* in short, curving strokes, leaving an evenly rippled coat.

2 **Placing uncut tiles.** Starting at the bottom row, embed a new tile in the mastic with a slight twisting motion, aligning it with the tiles above and beside it. Insert 1/8-inch shims beneath the bottom row of tiles to make a caulk joint along the tub rim. Continue installing uncut tiles this way, working across and up *(above)*. Maintain even spacing between tiles, inserting spacers in their joints *(page 117)* if necessary. Level the surface of the tiles with a piece of scrap wood *(page 112, step 4)*.

INSERTING JOINT SPACERS BETWEEN TILES

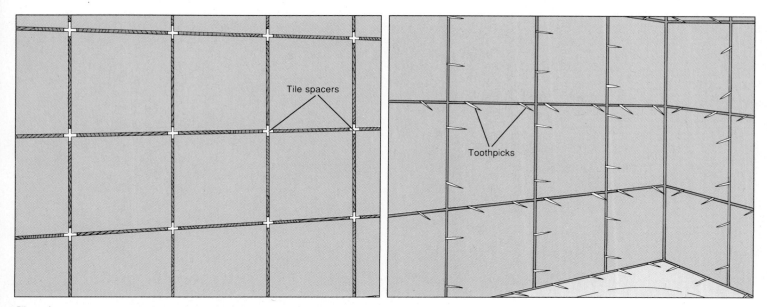

Choosing spacers. Some tiles have tabs called lugs molded into their edges which maintain proper spacing between tiles. Tiles without lugs may need spacers inserted between them to maintain even joints. Manufactured plastic spacers *(above, left)* are available in many shapes, sizes and thicknesses for various styles of tile and grout joints. Varying in size from 1/16 inch to 1/2 inch wide, plastic spacers are usually too large for the narrow joints required in a tub surround. If spacers are needed there, insert round toothpicks *(above, right)* or small finishing nails in the joints.

MEASURING AND CUTTING TILES

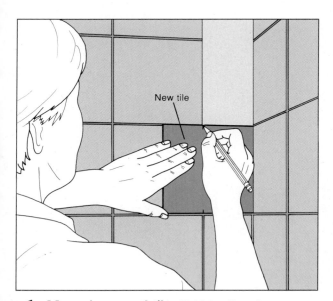

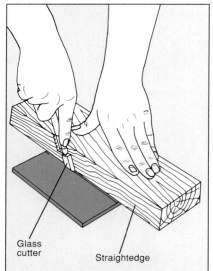

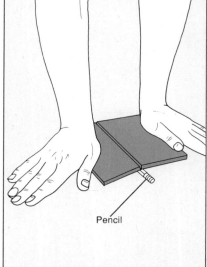

1 **Measuring an end tile.** Hold the tile to be cut on top of the last uncut tile in the row, and push its edge against the corner. Mark the top and bottom of the tile where it meets the edge of the tile beneath it *(above)*. Using a straightedge, connect the marks across the face of the tile to form the cutting line.

2 **Scoring and snapping the tile.** A few tiles can be conveniently cut with a glass cutter, shown above; to cut a large number of tiles, rent a mechanical tile cutter *(page 107)*. Align a straightedge—here, a wood block—along the cutting line. Draw the glass cutter firmly and smoothly along the line *(above, left)*. Lay the tile over a pencil, aligning the scored line with the pencil. Push down on the tile quickly and evenly with the heels of both hands *(above, right)*. The tile should snap along the line, leaving a clean break. When installing the tile on the wall, set the cut edge in the corner.

MEASURING AND CUTTING TILES (continued)

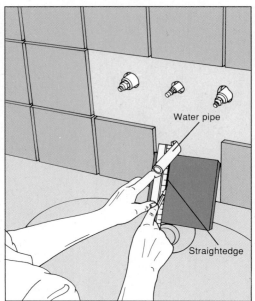

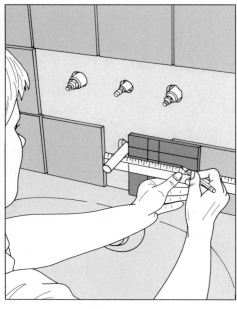

Water pipe

Straightedge

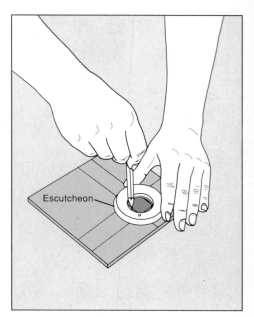

Escutcheon

3 Measuring for a round cut. When tiling around pipes, set all the uncut tiles first. Align the tile to be cut between two installed tiles, its edge against the pipe. Using a straight-edge, draw vertical lines along the tile indicating the width and position of the pipe *(above, left)*. Next, set the tile beside the pipe, flat against the tile underneath. Draw horizontal lines across the tile *(above, right)*, indicating the width and position of the pipe. The four intersecting lines on the tile form a square indicating the location of the pipe.

4 Marking the outline. If the fixture has an escutcheon, or decorative shield, trace its inner dimension over the square as a guideline for cutting the tile *(above)*. If there is no escutcheon, as in the case of a tub spout, simply round the corners of the square to approximate a circle.

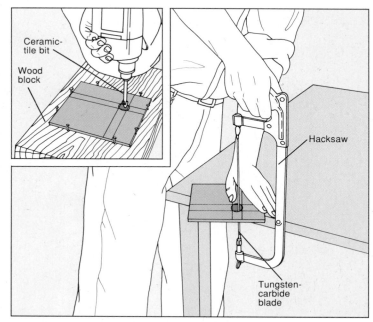

Ceramic-tile bit

Wood block

Hacksaw

Tungsten-carbide blade

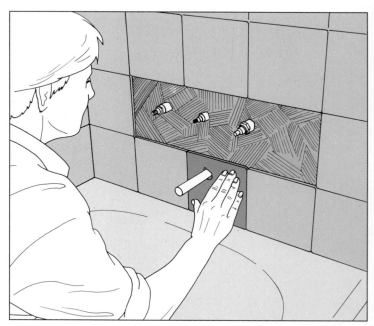

5 Sawing the hole. With the tile supported on a block of wood, use a ceramic-tile bit to drill a hole just inside the circle's edge *(inset)*. Insert a tungsten-carbide tile-cutting blade through the hole and attach it to the hacksaw frame. Hold the tile on a table edge and saw out the circle *(above)*, using a steady up-and-down motion with the entire length of the blade.

6 Fitting the tile. Before applying mastic, slip the cut tile over the pipe *(above)*. If the hole doesn't fit, reshape its edges with a round file. Wearing rubber gloves, apply Type I mastic to the back of the tile *(page 112, step 3)* and install it on the wall. Insert a 1/8-inch shim under the tile if it rests on the tub rim. Repeat steps 3 through 6 to fit tiles around other pipes.

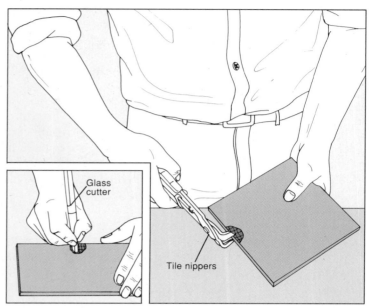

Glass
cutter

Tile nippers

7 **Tracing a notch at the edge of a tile.** If a tile overlaps a pipe without surrounding it, cut a notch in the edge of the tile to accommodate the pipe. Hold the tile against the pipe, its edges aligned with the surrounding tiles. Mark the location of the pipe on the tile as shown, then draw a half-circle connecting the marks.

8 **Nipping the tile to fit.** Using a glass cutter, score the half-circle outline. Score several crisscross lines inside the area to weaken it *(inset)*. Grasping the tile nippers firmly, nibble away small bits of tile *(above)* within the notch. Do not try to cut away large chunks of tile. The fixture escutcheon will hide any ragged edges. Fit and install the tile as in step 6.

INSTALLING MOSAIC TILE

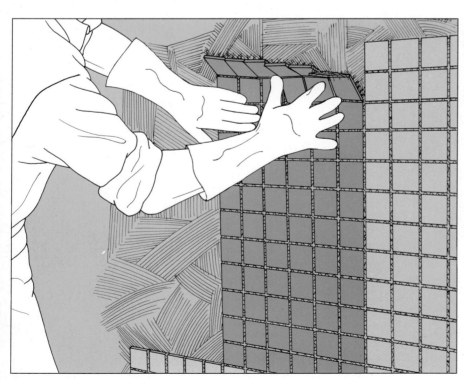

Installing mosaic tile. Mounted on a mesh backing, as shown at left, or glued to a sheet of paper, mosaic tiles (also called sheet tiles) are installed in groups to speed the job. Wearing rubber gloves, apply Type I mastic to the wall surface *(page 116, step 1)*. Roll the sheet of tiles onto the wall from bottom to top *(left)*. Align any crooked tiles with your fingers, working up the sheet. The mesh backing will remain buried in the mastic; a paper facing must be moistened and peeled off after the mastic sets. When installing succeeding sheets, space the joints between sheets to match the joints between tiles; install spacers if necessary *(page 117)*. After the mastic has set, grout mosaic tiles as for individual tiles *(page 110, step 2)*, and apply a silicone sealant *(page 110, step 4)*.

CEILING TILES

Ceiling tiles and panels are a quick, convenient way to reduce noise, disguise an unsightly ceiling, cover exposed pipes and wires or lower a ceiling that's too high. Twelve-inch squares of compressed mineral and wood fibers are permanently nailed, stapled or glued to the ceiling, or to wooden furring strips, through hidden tongue-and-groove edges. Suspended ceiling panels, which may contain fiberglass, measure 2 feet by 4 feet and rest in a metal grid hung by wires from the ceiling. These panels can be lifted out for cleaning or painting.

Regular cleaning should keep ceiling tiles in good condition for many years. Dust them with a rag wrapped around a straw broom, or vacuum them using a soft-bristled dusting attachment. Small stains and water spots on a light-colored ceiling can sometimes be disguised with talcum powder, applied with a cotton ball. An extensively marked or damaged ceiling is best refurbished with a coat of latex paint. Take care not to clog the holes of acoustical tiles. Thin the paint and, if possible, spray it on rather than brushing it. Do not apply latex paint directly over water stains; seal the stain with an oil-based primer and let it dry before you paint over it.

Sometimes suspended ceiling panels warp, usually due to excessive humidity that swells the wood fibers. Improving the ventilation in the room might help, but if you live in an extremely humid area, you are probably better off replacing the old panels with fiberglass panels. Humidity, or pipes that sweat or leak, can also cause the metal grid to rust. Before repairing panels or tiles, be sure to correct any ceiling problems which may be affecting them.

Ceiling tiles and panels flake and crumble when handled, and some may contain asbestos *(page 8)* or fiberglass. Always wear safety goggles when working on any type of tiled ceiling, and wear a respirator and gloves if you suspect that the tiles contain harmful fibers.

TROUBLESHOOTING GUIDE

SYMPTOM	PROCEDURE
Tiles or panels dirty (non-washable)	Clean with wallpaper dough *(p. 92)* □○, or wipe lightly with sponge moistened with solution of bleach and water; if dirt remains, apply latex paint
Tiles or panels dirty (washable)	Wash with detergent-and-water solution and rinse well; if dirt remains, apply latex paint
Small stains	Apply talcum powder with cotton ball; hide with liquid shoe whitener
Extensive stains, burns or water marks	Apply latex paint; replace the damaged tiles or panels *(pp. 120, 121)* ▭●
Tiles or panels warped	Replace warped tiles or panels *(pp. 120, 121)* ▭●
Grid dirty	Remove panels *(p. 120)* ▭○; wash grid with detergent-and-water solution
Grid rusty	Remove panels *(p. 120)* ▭○; rub away rust with fine steel wool; paint grid with rust-inhibiting enamel

DEGREE OF DIFFICULTY: □ Easy ▭ Moderate ■ Complex
ESTIMATED TIME: ○ Less than 1 hour ● 1 to 3 hours

REMOVING SUSPENDED CEILING PANELS

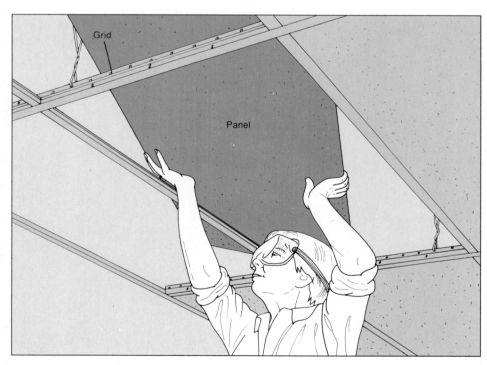

Removing a panel. Wearing safety goggles and standing on a stepladder, gently push up the panel with both hands to free it from the grid. Holding the panel's long edges, turn it sideways *(left)* and tip it, sliding it out of the grid short edge first. Handle the panel carefully; its edges are easily nicked. Remove as many panels as necessary to work on the ceiling, grid or panels themselves. To replace a panel, slide it through the grid, short edge first, align it with the grid and lower it in place, making sure it is properly seated.

REPLACING STAPLED CEILING TILES

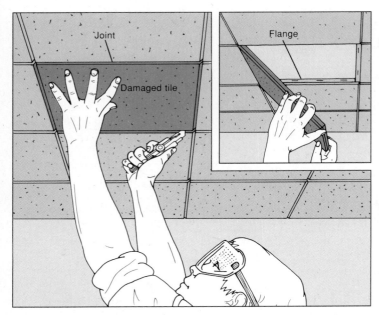

1 **Cutting out the first tile.** Wear safety goggles and stand on a stepladder. To remove a tongue-and-groove tile, insert the blade of a utility knife in the tile's joints and cut through the flanges of the tile on all four sides *(above)*. Pry out the tile *(inset)*, using a putty knife if it does not come loose easily. Remove the flanges left stapled to the ceiling by prying out the staples with an old screwdriver. If you are replacing only one tile, go to step 4.

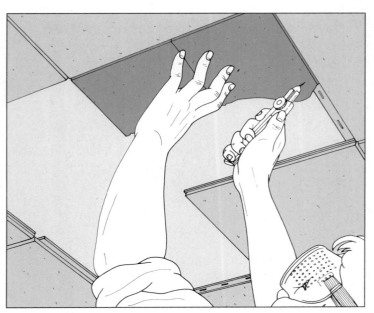

2 **Removing adjacent tiles.** Cut a cross through the center of the next tile. Slide out loose pieces; you may have to cut through some joints and break off pieces of tile to remove the rest *(above)*. Remove all the damaged tiles this way, taking care not to damage good tiles. Pry off any staples and scraps of flange left in the ceiling as in step 1.

3 **Sliding new tiles into place.** Slide a tile into one corner of the space, making sure that the flanges fit together properly. Staple its exposed flanges to the ceiling with a staple gun. Continue inserting and stapling new tiles *(above)* in the order in which they best fit, cutting off protruding flanges only where absolutely necessary *(step 4, inset)*. Install all but the last tile.

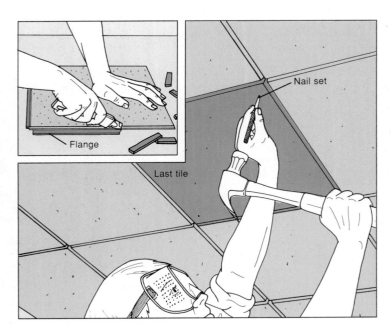

4 **Securing the last tile.** Use a utility knife to cut off all protruding flanges on the last replacement tile *(inset)*. Insert the tile in the ceiling space and drive a finishing nail through it at each corner, using a nail set to recess their heads just below the tile surface.

TIN CEILINGS

Originally a cheap substitute for costly carved plaster, tin ceilings—most of them antique—are now prized in their own right. Rarely made of tin, they are actually thin sheets of steel or copper, stamped with a repeated design. The edges of the sheets are overlapped and nailed either to furring strips or directly to the ceiling. A new or refurbished tin ceiling should be washed with a solution of detergent and water—not an abrasive cleaner— and rinsed and dried thoroughly. Seal the surface with a clear polyurethane or acrylic varnish or an oil-based paint. Spray enamel is handy for touch-ups. A properly sealed tin ceiling that is dusted (and in the kitchen, washed) regularly should need no other maintenance.

Small dents, holes and rust spots can be rebuilt with spackling compound (below). To cover more extensive damage, you can make small replacement sheets (page 123). If you must replace an entire sheet, finding one in a matching design can be difficult. Check the ads in the backs of home renovation magazines for suppliers. If identical sheets are unavailable, buy two sheets in a design similar to the rest of the ceiling. Replace the damaged sheet with one new sheet, and install the other one on the opposite side of the ceiling in a mirror-image position. Another alternative is to take down the undamaged sheets and move them to form a symmetrical arrangement; fill in the empty space with a stamped-metal medallion or sheets of a complementary design. After you have nailed up the new sheets, wash them to clean off the protective oil film. Finish the new sheets to match the rest of the ceiling.

Thin sheet-metal edges are very sharp. When handling the sheets, wear heavy work gloves, and always wear safety goggles when working overhead.

TROUBLESHOOTING GUIDE

SYMPTOM	PROCEDURE
Small dent or hole	Fill with spackling compound (below) □○
Large area of pattern damaged	Reproduce pattern (p. 123); replace entire sheet (above) ■◖
Surface dirty or greasy	Wash with detergent solution and soft brush (left) □○

DEGREE OF DIFFICULTY:	□ Easy ◖ Moderate ■ Complex
ESTIMATED TIME:	○ Less than 1 hour ◖ 1 to 3 hours

FILLING SMALL DENTS AND HOLES

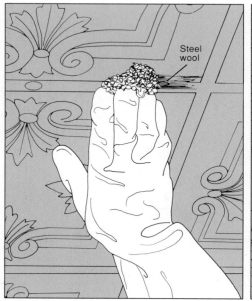
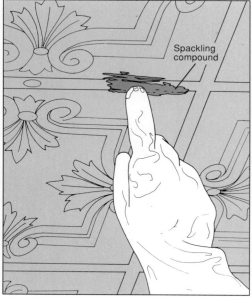

Rebuilding a small area. To restore damaged detail on a painted tin ceiling, rebuild the design with spackling compound. Standing on a stepladder (page 132), polish away rust with fine steel wool (above, left). Dab on spackling compound with a gloved finger (above, center), building it up where the pattern protrudes. After the compound stiffens slightly, sculpt it with any tool that can best shape the missing contours—here, a small manicure stick (above, right). An ice-cream stick or nut pick can also be helpful. Let the compound dry cvernight, then smooth the patch with fine sandpaper; wrap it around a stick to reach awkward crevices. Brush dust from the patch, seal it with shellac and paint it to match the rest of the ceiling.

RECREATING A DAMAGED DESIGN

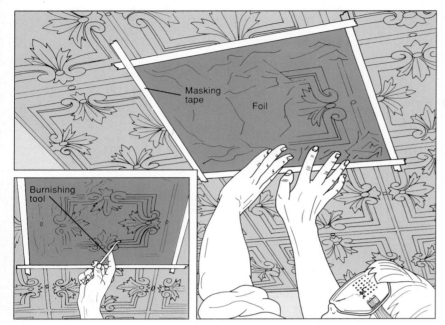

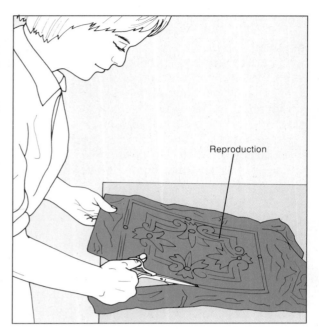

1 **Molding the missing pattern in foil.** The best foil for recreating missing areas of design is artist's burnishing foil, available at art-supply stores. Heavy-duty aluminum foil may also be used. The piece of foil should be large enough to cover the damaged area and reach beyond the edges of a complete section of the design. Wear safety goggles and stand on a stepladder *(page 132)*. Using masking tape, secure the foil over an undamaged portion of the ceiling that exactly matches the damaged area. Press the foil with your fingers *(above)*, molding it into the contours of the ceiling. Finish with a burnishing tool to produce sharp detail *(inset)*.

2 **Cutting the foil to shape.** Remove the foil reproduction from the ceiling without creasing or stretching it, and strip off the tape. Trim the edges of the design with scissors *(above)*. Lay the reproduction on a table protected with newspapers, and spray it with an enamel or clear polyurethane that matches the finish on the ceiling; this also helps stiffen aluminum foil. Allow it to dry overnight, then spray the other side and let dry.

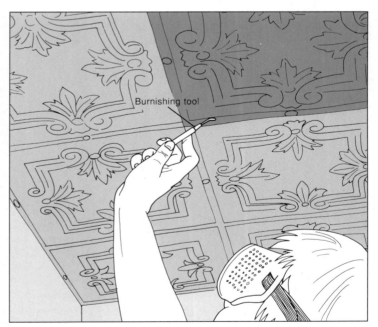

3 **Taping the reproduction in place.** Apply very thin double-sided tape to all four edges of the damaged section. Carefully adjust the foil reproduction over the damaged section *(above)*, feeling with your fingers that its contours fit the contours of the ceiling beneath it, then gently press its edges onto the tape.

4 **Burnishing the edges of the foil.** Use a burnishing tool or a small spoon to press the edges of the foil onto the double-sided tape. Do not drag the burnisher along the edges of the foil because the metal will stretch out of shape. Work from the middle of each edge toward the corner. Trim away any exposed tape with a very sharp razor blade. Seal the foil with polyurethane or paint it to match the rest of the ceiling.

MASONRY

Many a home renovator, in tearing down deteriorated plaster, has discovered hidden treasure beneath it—the warm texture of antique brick. Built of clay bricks or cement blocks laid with portland cement mortar, an interior masonry wall is usually exposed to the out-of-doors on one side. In the case of a cement-block basement wall, water in the surrounding soil can seep through cracks and through the blocks themselves. In the case of exposed-brick house walls, the elements can cause expansion cracks, crumbling mortar joints and a leaching of mineral deposits called efflorescence. The Troubleshooting Guide at right lists some common interior masonry problems and procedures for correcting them.

Cleaning masonry indoors is messy. Tape heavy plastic drop cloths to the floor, and spread newspaper over them to absorb liquids. Some cleaning solutions are caustic—wear long sleeves and rubber gloves, and ventilate the room. Wear safety goggles when chipping masonry.

Damp basement walls can be caused by either the condensation of moisture from inside the house, or moisture seeping through from outside. To discover which, dry the wall and tape a 6-foot-square sheet of plastic to it, sealing the edges securely. Wait 24 hours. If moisture collects under the plastic, the problem is seepage; if moisture forms on top of the plastic, it is condensation. Cure condensation by heating the basement or installing a dehumidifier. To correct seepage, patch all cracks in the wall. If the problem continues, improve drainage around the house. As a last resort, the basement walls may have to be waterproofed from the outside.

TROUBLESHOOTING GUIDE

SYMPTOM	PROCEDURE
Masonry surface dirty	Scrub with a solution of trisodium phosphate and water; rinse well □○
Smoke and soot stains	Scrub with a solution of trisodium phosphate and water, or with commercial scouring powder that contains bleach; rinse well □○
Efflorescence (white mineral crystals)	Brush off crystals, scrub with a solution of 1 part muriatic acid to 9 parts water and rinse well □○; inspect exterior of wall for cause of water seepage
Mildew	Scrub with a solution of 1/2 cup trisodium phosphate and 1 cup chlorine bleach in a gallon of warm water and rinse well □○
Paint spots	Abrade carefully with a wire brush; if necessary, apply a commercial paint remover, scrape it off with a putty knife and rinse well □○
Cracked mortar joints	Fill with mortar *(below)* □○
Brick cracked or broken	Remove and replace brick *(p. 125)* ◨●
Cement block cracked; no leak	Fill crack with mortar *(p. 126)* □○
Cement block cracked and leaking	Fill crack with hydraulic patching cement *(p. 126)* ◨○

DEGREE OF DIFFICULTY:	□ Easy ◨ Moderate ■ Complex
ESTIMATED TIME:	○ Less than 1 hour ◑ 1 to 3 hours

FILLING A CRACK IN A MORTAR JOINT

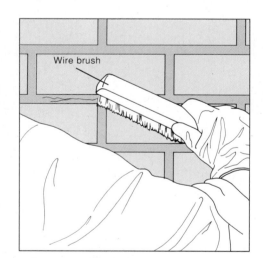

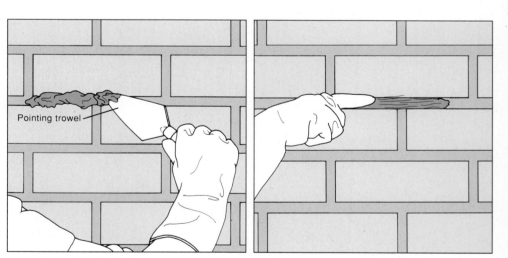

1 Preparing the crack. Using a narrow wire brush, gently abrade the crack in the joint to clear out loose mortar *(above)*. Do not brush the surface of the brick. Dampen the crack by spraying it with water or by scrubbing it with a water-soaked fiber brush.

2 Packing in the mortar. Make a small amount of ready-mix mortar or patching cement according to package directions. Pack the mortar into the crack with a pointing trowel *(above, left)* or a rigid 2-inch putty knife. Scrape excess mortar off the bricks. While the mortar is wet, use a gloved finger, or a shaping tool such as a mason's jointer *(page 125)* or a 3/4-inch pipe, to smooth the joint *(above, right)*.

REPLACING A BROKEN BRICK

1 Chipping out the mortar. Wearing goggles, use a ball-peen hammer and cold chisel to chip out all the mortar around the defective brick. Take care not to damage the surrounding bricks. Pull out the brick; if necessary, break it into pieces using the hammer and chisel *(above)* or a brickset. Chisel out any old mortar that clings to the walls of the cavity.

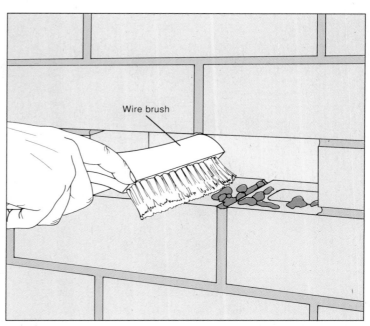

2 Preparing the cavity. Brush debris from the cavity with a wire brush *(above)*, then wipe it out with a wet rag to remove any remaining dust. Soak the replacement brick in water for half an hour. Thoroughly wet the bricks and mortar surrounding the cavity; over the course of half an hour, either use a spray bottle to soak them with water several times, or brush them several times with a wet fiber-bristle brush.

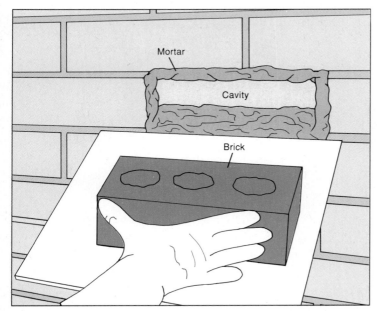

3 Inserting the new brick. Make ready-mix mortar according to package directions. Apply a 1-inch layer of mortar to all four sides of the cavity, covering the entire inside surface. Use a mason's hawk, or a piece of plywood or sturdy cardboard, to hold the replacement brick level with the cavity *(above)*. Firmly push in the brick until its face is level with the other bricks. With a pointing trowel, scrape off any excess mortar that oozes out, and fill in any gaps in the joints.

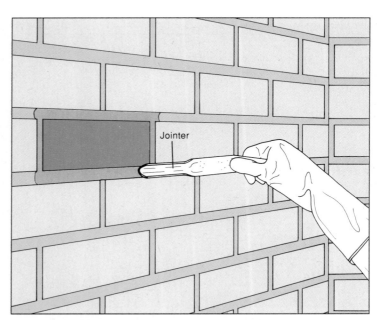

4 Smoothing the joint. To shape the new joints so they match the surrounding joints, use a mason's jointer *(above)*, or a similar tool such as a narrow pipe. Draw the tool along the joints, removing excess mortar.

PATCHING A DRY CRACK IN A CONCRETE BLOCK

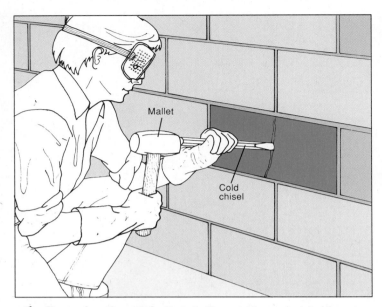

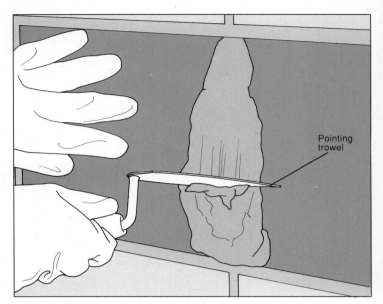

1 Preparing the crack. To help the patching material adhere to the damaged block, use a cold chisel and metal mallet to open out the crack and remove loose bits of masonry *(above)*. Clean out the crack with a wire brush. Thoroughly wet the crack by spraying it with water or brushing it with a wet fiber-bristle brush.

2 Filling the crack. Make a small batch of ready-mix concrete patching compound according to package directions. Using a pointing trowel, pack the crack tightly with patching compound. While the compound is still wet, scrape off any excess *(above)*. You can match the texture of the blocks by stippling the damp compound with a toothbrush, a whisk broom or the tip of a pencil. After the compound has dried, prime the patched area before painting it.

PLUGGING A WET CRACK

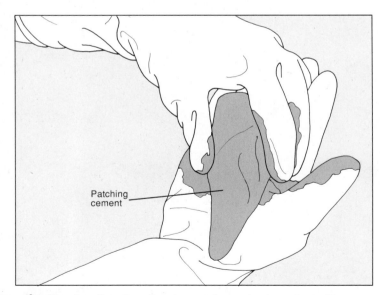

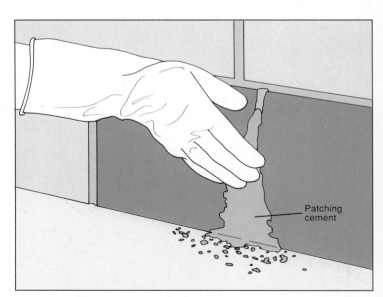

1 Shaping the plug. Seeping cracks are best repaired with a hydraulic patching cement that expands as it dries. Prepare the crack as in step 1, above, chiseling the crack edges to the angle recommended by the cement manufacturer. Mix cement according to package directions and, wearing rubber gloves, shape it into a plug the shape of the crack *(above)*. Work fast; the cement sets rapidly.

2 Plugging the crack. Squeeze the plug deeply into the crack *(above)*. Using a pointing trowel or rigid putty knife, scrape the surface of the plug level with the concrete block. After it has dried, prime the patch before painting it.

MARBLE

A rock formed by heat and pressure inside the earth, marble nonetheless requires surprisingly delicate care. Abrasive cleaners or cleaning tools strip marble's polished surface, leaving the porous core open to stains, and acidic cleaners such as vinegar actually dissolve marble.

Marble panels, which are quite heavy, are usually wired to the wall and held in place with an adhesive; replacing a panel is a job best left to a professional. Unless there is danger of pieces falling, a cracked panel is best left alone; attempts at repair will only damage the marble further.

The procedures listed in the Troubleshooting Guide at right work best on white marble. Colored and variegated marbles are trickier to clean, and different varieties may require special treatments. Try any procedure in a hidden corner before you launch into a full-scale repair job. Such a test will also reveal whether you are dealing with *faux marbre*—wood, plaster or soapstone painted to look like marble. Repairs to faux marbre require professional restoration. Care for synthetic marble (marble dust bonded with epoxy) the same way as for marble, but polish very gently and do not clean with acetone.

For routine washing, sponge marble clean with a solution of lukewarm water and mild detergent, rinse thoroughly and dry with a soft cloth. Polish the surface when necessary *(below)*.

TROUBLESHOOTING GUIDE

SYMPTOM	PROCEDURE
Grease and oil stains	Wash with a solution of detergent or ammonia; for stubborn stains, apply a poultice of acetone and talcum powder *(below)* □○
Organic stains (food, juice, coffee, dye, ink)	Wash with a detergent solution; apply a poultice of talcum powder, hydrogen peroxide and a few drops of ammonia *(below)* □○
Rust stains	Rub stain vigorously with a soft, dry cloth; apply commercial rust-remover jelly (rust remover is acidic; use sparingly and rinse well) □○
Soot and smoke stains	Apply a poultice of baking soda and chlorine bleach *(below)* □○
Marble surface dull	Polish with powdered chalk, pumice powder or tin oxide using a damp buffing pad on a power drill *(below)* □○; use a damp chamois or cloth pad for a spot polish; rinse well and dry, then wax *(below)* □○

DEGREE OF DIFFICULTY:	□ Easy ◪ Moderate ■ Complex
ESTIMATED TIME:	○ Less than 1 hour ◖ 1 to 3 hours

MAINTAINING MARBLE

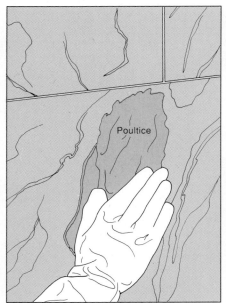

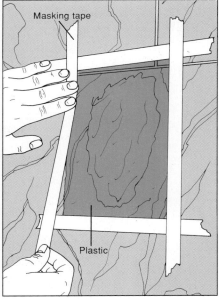

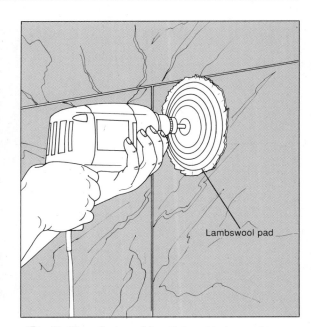

1 **Using a poultice to draw out stains.** Mix into a stiff paste the thickening agent (talcum powder or baking soda) and the cleaning agent recommended in the Troubleshooting Guide *(above)*. Pat this poultice onto the stain. Press a sheet of plastic over the poultice and tape all its edges to the marble with masking tape. In place of the thickening agent, you may instead soak a piece of white blotting paper or a clean white rag in the cleaning agent; cover and tape it as described above. Allow the poultice to work at least 24 hours, then remove the plastic and carefully lift away the poultice with a putty knife. Rinse the area well. Repeat the application if necessary.

2 **Buffing the marble.** Rub a thin layer of top-quality colorless paste wax onto a 3-foot-square section of the marble. Fit a lambswool pad polisher on a power drill (synthetic pads give poor results) and move the drill in circles over the waxed area, buffing it to a high shine. Repeat over the entire surface.

HANGERS AND FASTENERS

Four bare walls never stay that way for long—a plain wall seems to beg for adornment. Hung with bookshelves or towel bars, fine lithographs or exotic plants, walls and ceilings can provide practical storage as well as good looks.

A wall's ability to carry a load depends in part on its condition. Before hanging anything on a wall or ceiling, check that it is sound, and perform repairs shown in this book if necessary. Learn exactly what the wall is made of so that you can choose the right hanger or fastener for the job.

Hanging hardware must be suited both to the construction of the wall and to the weight placed upon it. The chart below lists

common hangers and the types of walls and ceilings to which they are best suited. The load-carrying ratings are listed for comparison purposes only. Follow the weight guidelines listed on the hardware package or ask a hardware professional for assistance.

Several types of hangers are available, and each type supports a load in a different way. Metal expansion anchors and toggle bolts, designed for hollow walls, have wings or leaves that pop open behind the wall when they are screwed in, gripping the wall from behind. Anchors and screw shields made of metal, plastic or fiber come in many styles for use in

	Hollow wall expansion anchor (with sleeve)	Hollow wall expansion anchor (sleeveless)	Hollow wall expansion anchor (hammered type; no drilling required)	Toggle bolt (shank can be headless)	Plastic anchor (also called wall plug)
HOLLOW WALL (includes gypsum drywall and plywood panels over furring or studs.)	Very good for medium loads. Choose sleeve length that matches wall thickness.	Good for light loads in drywall.	Good for light loads in drywall.	Very good for medium to heavy loads. Avoid studs or furring.	Good for light to medium loads.
PLASTER ON LATH	Good if sleeve length matches wall thickness including lath and plaster keys.	Good for light loads.	Not recommended.	Good for medium to heavy loads. Bolt length must clear lath and plaster keys.	Good for light to medium loads.
CERAMIC TILE	Good for tile over hollow wall. Sleeve length must match wall thickness. File off prongs on sleeve.	Not recommended.	Not recommended.	Fair for tile over hollow wall. Do not overtighten; bolt may crack tile.	Good for light loads. Do not force too large a screw into anchor; it may crack tile.
MASONRY (includes concrete, concrete block, brick, and plaster over masonry.)	Good for hollow concrete block. Sleeve length must match block thickness. Not recommended for solid masonry.	Not recommended.	Not recommended.	Very good for hollow concrete block. Not recommended for solid masonry.	Fair for light loads. Do not use in crumbly masonry.
CEILINGS	Very good for hollow ceiling. Sleeve length must match ceiling thickness.	Fair for very light loads only.	Fair for very light loads in drywall ceilings only.	Very good for hollow ceiling. Bolts available with head or headless.	Fair for very light loads only.

hollow, solid or masonry walls. They work by providing a snug gripping surface for a screw or bolt, even in soft material such as gypsum drywall.

Nails can make good fasteners when used with specially angled picture hooks or if driven deeply through the wall into a stud. However, the force of driving a nail can crack a plaster wall or break it away from the lath. A wood screw, driven through a pilot hole into a stud, provides a very strong grip, and is the best fastener for weighty cabinets and bookshelves. To find studs, follow the instructions on page 136. Remember when hanging storage units to include the weight of the con-

tents when calculating the load on the hanging hardware. The total weight may be divided by the number of hangers used, provided the hangers are spaced evenly.

Most hangers and fasteners must be installed through holes predrilled in the wall or ceiling. Choose a drill bit suited to the wall material—an ordinary twist bit will serve for drywall and all but the hardest plaster, a carbide-tipped bit is needed for masonry, and a tile bit is best for drilling ceramic tile. The bit gauge required is usually stamped on the fastener itself or printed on its package; when in doubt, use a small bit and work up to a larger one.

Plastic anchor (hammered type; no drilling required)	Fiber anchor (also called shield)	Lead or alloy anchor (also called shield)	Nailed picture hanger hook	Adhesive picture hanger hook	Wood screw
Good for light loads.	Not recommended.	Not recommended.	Good, especially if nail penetrates stud. Available for a wide range of weights.	Fair for light loads. Wall must be clean and untextured.	Very good in stud or furring. At least half length of screw should penetrate wood.
Good for light loads but may not penetrate hard plaster.	Good for light loads.	Fair for very hard plaster.	Good. Available for a wide range of weights. Masking tape on wall prevents nail from cracking plaster.	Fair for light loads. Wall must be clean and untextured.	Fair in lath. Very good in stud. At least half length of screw should penetrate wood.
Not recommended.	Not recommended.	Not recommended.	Not recommended.	Not recommended.	Not recommended.
Not recommended.	Good for medium loads. Do not use in moist area; anchor will rot.	Very good for heavy loads.	Not recommended.	Not recommended.	Good only if used with fiber anchor.
Fair for very light loads only.	Not recommended.	Not recommended.	Not recommended.	Not recommended.	Good in joist. At least half length of screw should penetrate wood.

INSTALLING ANCHORS IN HOLLOW WALLS

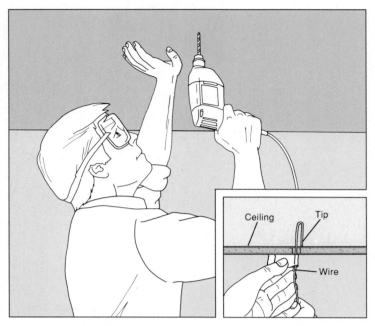

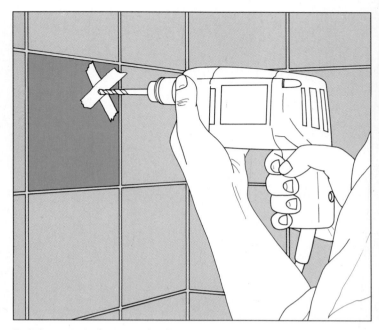

Measuring the thickness of a hollow ceiling or wall. Drill a hole straight through the ceiling or wall at the spot where you will install the hanger *(above)*. Bend a piece of wire into a narrow hook and insert the hooked end through the hole. Pull the wire gently until the tip catches inside. Wrap a strip of masking tape around the wire where it exits the hole *(inset)*, then carefully unhook the wire and pull it out without bending it. The distance between the masking tape and the hooked tip of the wire is the thickness of the wall.

Drilling a hole in ceramic tile. To avoid cracking the tile, select a spot away from its edge, and pad the area with a double layer of masking tape. Fit an electric drill with a ceramic-tile bit or a carbide-tipped masonry bit. Holding the drill with both hands, place the tip of the bit on the masking tape. Drill slowly, without pushing, until the bit starts cutting into the tile *(above)*, then increase the speed a little and gently push the bit through the tile. Find the thickness of the wall as in the step at left.

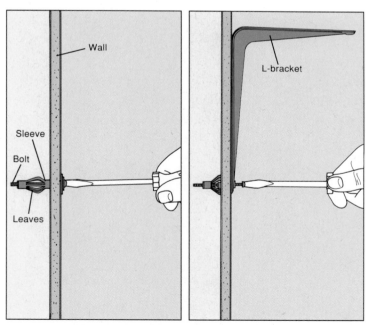

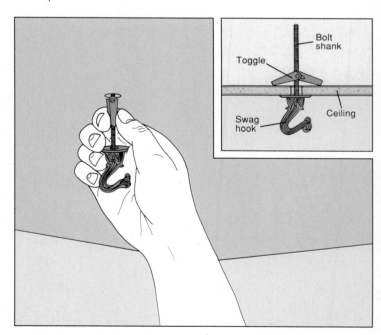

Installing a hollow-wall expansion anchor. Measure the wall thickness *(step above)* and select an expansion anchor with a sleeve of matching length. Push, or gently hammer, the expansion anchor into a predrilled hole and screw in the bolt *(above, left)* until it no longer turns easily, expanding the leaves of the anchor against the back of the wall. Unscrew the bolt, place it through the object to be mounted (in this case, an L-bracket) and screw it back into the anchor.

Installing a spring toggle bolt. First make sure the bolt is the right length: With the wings of the toggle held closed and the object to be mounted (here, a swag hook) installed on the bolt, the bolt shank must be long enough to clear the wall thickness *(step left)*, or the toggle cannot spring open. Squeezing the toggle closed, push it through the hole in the wall or ceiling *(above)* until its wings snap open. Pull the bolt gently while screwing it in by hand, drawing the hook and the toggle flush against the wall *(inset)*.

INSTALLING MASONRY ANCHORS

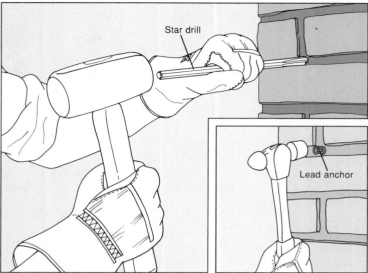

Drilling into masonry. Solid concrete and concrete blocks may be drilled at any spot; a brick wall, shown here, should be drilled only at a mortar joint to prevent the bricks from cracking. Wear goggles to protect your eyes. Fit a variable-speed power drill with a carbide-tipped masonry bit and wrap masking tape around the bit to gauge the depth of the hole. Drill slowly into the wall without forcing the bit *(above, left)*,

until the masking tape contacts the wall. Alternatively, use a star drill—a hardened steel rod with a fluted tip—to drill the hole manually. Place the tip of the star drill on the wall and strike it squarely with a heavy mallet *(above, right)*, giving it a quarter turn after each blow, until the hole reaches the required depth. Blow the dust out of the hole and hammer in the appropriate anchor *(inset)*.

HANGING A LEVEL SHELF

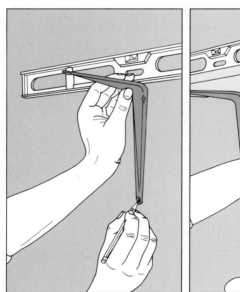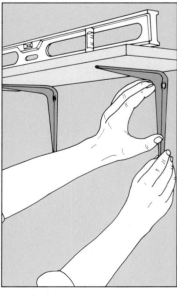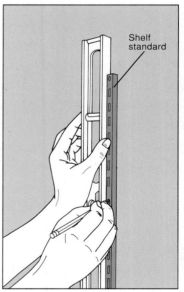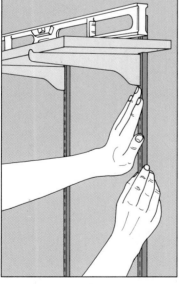

Mounting a shelf with L-brackets. Hold one bracket against the wall exactly where it will be installed. Balance a carpenter's level on top of the bracket and shift the bracket until it is level, then mark its screw hole positions on the wall *(above, left)* and take it down. Drill holes in the wall at the marks and install the anchors and the bracket *(page 130)*. Next, hold the second bracket in place against the wall, and rest the shelf and the level across both brackets *(above, right)*. Level the shelf by moving the bracket up and down, then mark and install the second bracket as you did the first.

Mounting shelves with shelf standards. Hold a shelf standard and a carpenter's level together against the wall and adjust the standard until it is vertical. Mark its screw hole positions *(above, left)* and take it down. Drill holes at the marks, install anchors and mount the standard *(page 130)*. Adjust the second standard the same way, but draw a vertical line along its side on the wall. Snap a bracket onto each standard and set a shelf and the level on the brackets. Move the second standard up and down along the line to level the shelf *(above, right)*, then mark and install the second as you did the first.

TOOLS & TECHNIQUES

This section introduces tools and techniques that are basic to most repairs for walls, ceilings and woodwork, including locating studs and joists *(page 136)*, turning off electrical power *(page 137)* and preparing a room for work *(page 141)*. The systems hidden within walls and ceilings—wiring, plumbing, ductwork, insulation—are illustrated and described on pages 134 and 135.

Since the tools needed for work on plaster are quite different from tools used for wallpapering or for painting, each chapter illustrates and describes the special tools required for the repairs in that chapter. But to accomplish many of these jobs, you will need one or more of the tools pictured at right.

Used singly or in combination, a stepladder, a straight ladder, a pair of sawhorses and several planks are usually all you need to reach ceilings and upper walls safely. Wooden ladders are acceptable for most household repair jobs, but aluminum ladders are preferable for work that doesn't involve electricity; they weigh about 20 per cent less than wood and need little maintenance.

A ladder's strength rating is usually marked on one of its siderails. Experts recommend a Type II, commercial-grade ladder for most repair jobs; better still, use a Type I, industrial-grade ladder.

Even the sturdiest ladder can become dangerous if it is improperly maintained. Before using a ladder, inspect it for cracks and loose parts—do not use a defective ladder. When work is finished for the day, clean the ladder of paint or patching compounds that could cause a slip the next time it is used. Never paint a wooden ladder; paint hides potentially dangerous cracks in the wood. Protect it instead with a coat of clear varnish, shellac or wood preservative. Store ladders horizontally, in a cool, dry place. If a ladder is hung, support it at three or more points to prevent warpage or loosening of joints. Inspect and care for wooden or steel sawhorses the same way as for ladders. Use 2-by-10 or 2-by-12 planks with no cracks; double the planks for added strength.

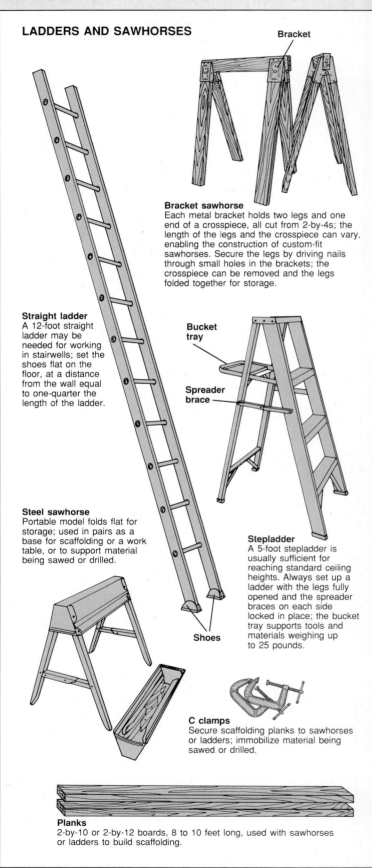

LADDERS AND SAWHORSES

Bracket

Bracket sawhorse
Each metal bracket holds two legs and one end of a crosspiece, all cut from 2-by-4s; the length of the legs and the crosspiece can vary, enabling the construction of custom-fit sawhorses. Secure the legs by driving nails through small holes in the brackets; the crosspiece can be removed and the legs folded together for storage.

Straight ladder
A 12-foot straight ladder may be needed for working in stairwells; set the shoes flat on the floor, at a distance from the wall equal to one-quarter the length of the ladder.

Bucket tray

Spreader brace

Steel sawhorse
Portable model folds flat for storage; used in pairs as a base for scaffolding or a work table, or to support material being sawed or drilled.

Stepladder
A 5-foot stepladder is usually sufficient for reaching standard ceiling heights. Always set up a ladder with the legs fully opened and the spreader braces on each side locked in place; the bucket tray supports tools and materials weighing up to 25 pounds.

Shoes

C clamps
Secure scaffolding planks to sawhorses or ladders; immobilize material being sawed or drilled.

Planks
2-by-10 or 2-by-12 boards, 8 to 10 feet long, used with sawhorses or ladders to build scaffolding.

REACHING HIGH PLACES

Follow basic safety rules when using ladders and scaffolds. Set the feet of a ladder level and never use an unanchored object such as a stone to prop them up. Wear footgear with a well-defined heel for a secure grip on the steps or rungs. Face a ladder when climbing up or down, and use both hands to grasp the steps or rungs—not the siderails. Avoid carrying tools in your hands or pockets; set them on the bucket tray of a stepladder or, if working on a straight ladder, place them in a bucket and hoist it up with a rope looped over a ladder rung. Do not overreach—keep your belt buckle within the limits of the side rails and keep your hips below the top rung of a straight ladder. Never stand on the top step of a stepladder.

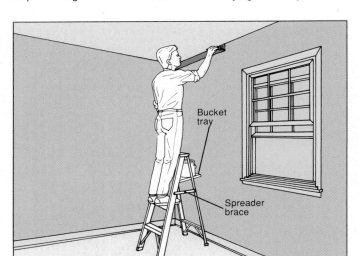

Using a stepladder. Open the legs of the ladder and lock them in place by pushing down on the hinges of the spreader braces. Pull down on the bucket tray to open it. Be sure that all four legs of the ladder are level on the floor. If the ladder is not fitted with rubber shoes or the floor is slippery, set it on a non-slip rug or mat. Work facing the ladder, and never stand or sit on top of the ladder, on the step immediately below it, or on the bucket tray.

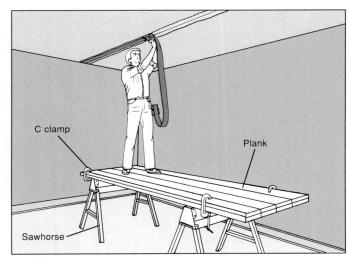

Erecting a scaffold. A scaffold can be built with planks supported by a pair of sawhorses (above) or stepladders. Subtract 3 feet from the length of the planks and set the sawhorses this distance apart. If the distance between the two sawhorses is more than 6 feet, double the planks for strength. Nail planks to wooden sawhorses; use C clamps to hold together doubled planks and to secure planks to metal sawhorses or to the steps of ladders.

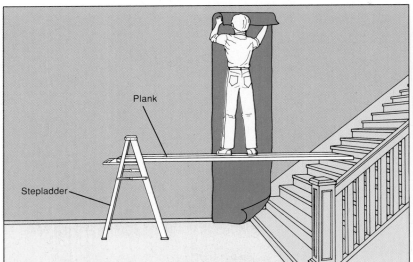

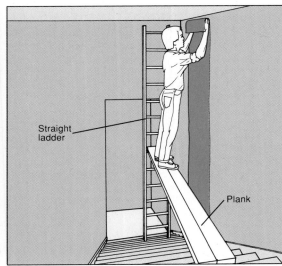

Working over stairs. For work near the bottom of stairs, make a scaffold from a plank and a stepladder (above, left). Butt one end of the plank against the stair riser and extend the other end over the stepladder step by at least a foot. Make sure the plank is level. For work near the top of stairs (above, right), lean a straight ladder against the upper-floor wall or railing and set the feet of the ladder flat on a stair, butted against the riser. Position the plank as described above. For a scaffold with a working length of more than 6 feet, use doubled planks.

WHAT TO EXPECT BEHIND YOUR WALLS AND CEILINGS

Hidden behind the interior walls and ceilings of a typical home is a network of wiring, plumbing, ductwork and insulation. The anatomy at right illustrates some of these systems and indicates where you should be on the lookout for them. Leave nothing to chance; always investigate behind a wall or ceiling before cutting or drilling into it, following the procedure for creating an access opening *(page 139)*.

Wiring in your home runs from the main service panel to all electrical fixtures, switches, outlets and appliances, as well as to the heating and cooling systems. Wires may run parallel to the studs and joists or across them through drilled holes. Shut off the power to any circuit in the vicinity of your work and to any fixtures you plan to remove *(page 137)*.

Between the plumbing service pipe that brings in fresh water and the drainpipe that carries away used water, your home's entire plumbing system is interconnected—the hot water heater, sinks, toilets, tubs and showers, clothes washer and dishwasher, outdoor faucets, and in some homes the hot-water heating system. At least one interior wall in a home is a "wet wall," behind which run most of the pipes; often there is an access panel on the opposite side of the wall from the bathtub. An older home may have plumbing behind an exterior wall. Check for plumbing behind walls by making an access opening *(page 139)*.

Homes with forced-air heating or air-conditioning systems have metal ducts running through the walls and ceilings. These ducts connect the furnace, air conditioner or heat pump to vents in each room. The thin sheet metal of the ducts is easily pierced with a drill or saw. Determine the location of ducts before sawing or drilling into a wall or ceiling, investigating, if necessary, by creating an access opening *(page 139)*.

The insulation in your home helps maintain a comfortable temperature inside, and the vapor barrier keeps out potentially damaging moisture. Within exterior walls and ceilings, or behind a ceiling below an unfinished attic, you can expect to find some form of insulation and vapor barrier. A newer home is most likely to have batts or blankets of insulation consisting of fiberglass or cellulose; these may have a vapor barrier backing of foil, plastic or paper that is stapled to the studs or joists. If the insulation doesn't have a built-in backing, there may be a vapor barrier of overlapping plastic sheets stapled over it to the studs or joists. Occasionally, a foil backing on the drywall itself may act as a vapor barrier. In older homes that have insulation, it may consist of a loose fill of vermiculite, perlite, mineral wool or cellulose; these may have a plastic vapor barrier or, more likely, oil-base enamel, alkyd or special vapor barrier paint may be applied on the interior wall or ceiling surface. Yet another form of insulation and vapor barrier is rigid boards of polystyrene; these are often installed on outside walls in finished basements. Determine the type of insulation and vapor barrier behind an exterior wall or ceiling in your home by making a careful access opening *(page 139)*. After making any hole, repair the vapor barrier and insulation *(page 139)*.

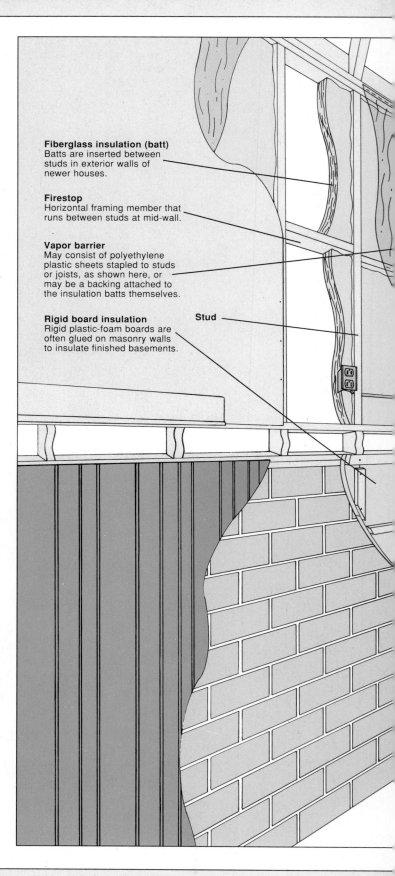

Fiberglass insulation (batt)
Batts are inserted between studs in exterior walls of newer houses.

Firestop
Horizontal framing member that runs between studs at mid-wall.

Vapor barrier
May consist of polyethylene plastic sheets stapled to studs or joists, as shown here, or may be a backing attached to the insulation batts themselves.

Rigid board insulation
Rigid plastic-foam boards are often glued on masonry walls to insulate finished basements.

Stud

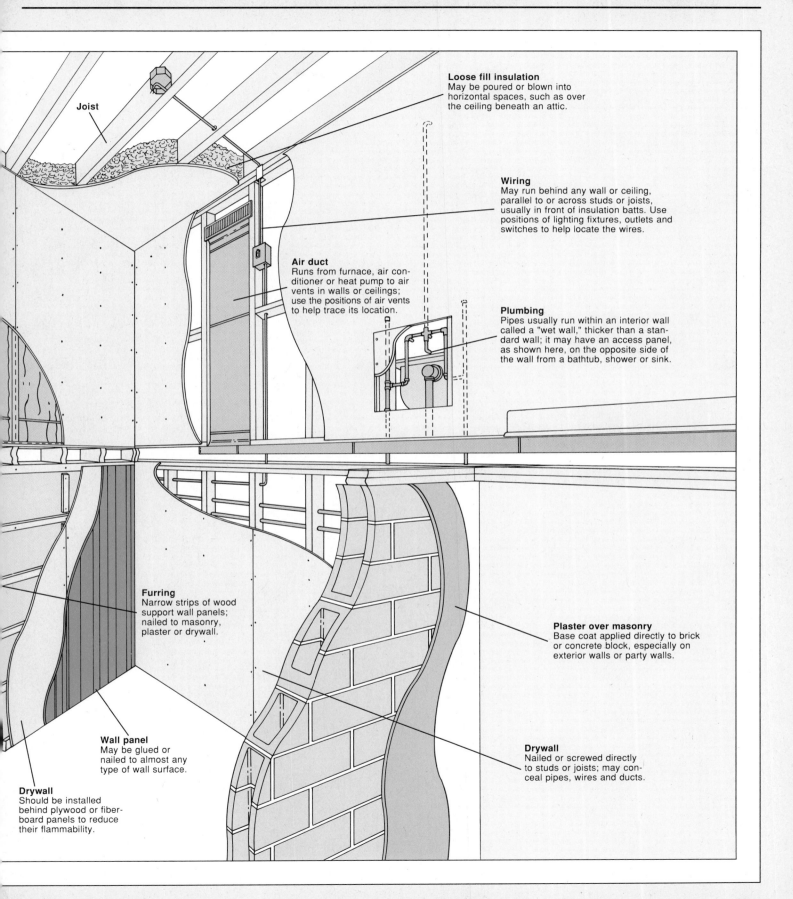

Joist

Loose fill insulation
May be poured or blown into horizontal spaces, such as over the ceiling beneath an attic.

Wiring
May run behind any wall or ceiling, parallel to or across studs or joists, usually in front of insulation batts. Use positions of lighting fixtures, outlets and switches to help locate the wires.

Air duct
Runs from furnace, air conditioner or heat pump to air vents in walls or ceilings; use the positions of air vents to help trace its location.

Plumbing
Pipes usually run within an interior wall called a "wet wall," thicker than a standard wall; it may have an access panel, as shown here, on the opposite side of the wall from a bathtub, shower or sink.

Furring
Narrow strips of wood support wall panels; nailed to masonry, plaster or drywall.

Plaster over masonry
Base coat applied directly to brick or concrete block, especially on exterior walls or party walls.

Wall panel
May be glued or nailed to almost any type of wall surface.

Drywall
Nailed or screwed directly to studs or joists; may conceal pipes, wires and ducts.

Drywall
Should be installed behind plywood or fiberboard panels to reduce their flammability.

LOCATING STUDS OR JOISTS

You can often find a stud or joist by tapping along a wall or ceiling and listening for a change from a hollow to a solid sound about every 16 inches. Alternatively, skim an electric razor along the surface and listen for a change in pitch. A magnetic compass needle may shift when passed over a nail in a stud or joist. Slight ridges or depressions at stud or joist positions can be detected in the oblique glare of an exposed light bulb. Another method is to remove a fixture, switch, or outlet *(page 137)* and inspect behind it; electrical boxes are usually fastened to a stud or joist. If you must remove a baseboard to do a repair, look behind it for studs.

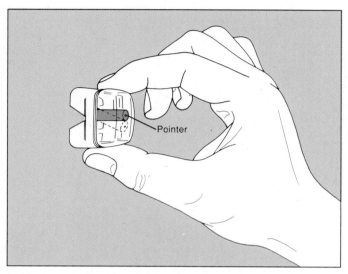

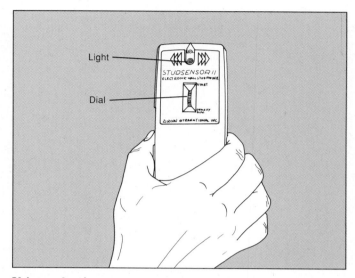

Using a magnetic stud finder. The magnetic pointer responds to metal fasteners driven into a stud or joist. Place the tool flat on the surface with the notched edge to one side, letting gravity pull the pointer downward. Slowly slide the tool along the surface until the pointer stands up straight, signaling a fastener. The center of the stud or joist is indicated by the basepoint of the notched edge on the tool. On a ceiling, find two or more fasteners to determine the direction the joist runs.

Using a density sensor. Roll the dial upward to the "Start" position and place the tool flat on the surface. Press the two buttons on the sides of the tool, turning on the red light, and slowly roll the dial downward until the green light comes on and the red light goes off. Still pressing the two buttons on the sides, slide the tool slowly along the surface. The edge of a stud or joist is indicated when the red light comes on; the other edge is indicated when the green light comes on and the red light goes off.

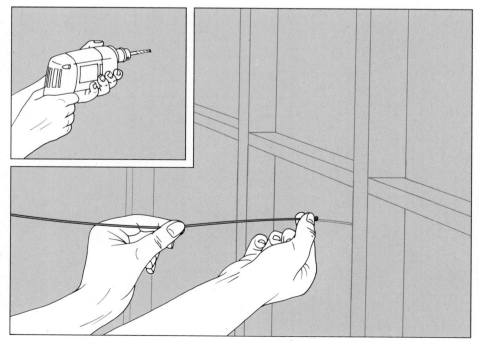

Checking the position of a stud or joist. Using a power drill, drill a small hole about 3/4 inch deep into the wall or ceiling *(inset)*. If the drill bit meets resistance or draws wood shavings, you have found a stud or joist. In a plaster wall, continue to drill a little deeper after getting wood shavings or meeting resistance to be certain that you have found a stud or joist, and not just wood lath. If the drill bit passes through into the hollow behind the surface, enlarge the hole enough to slip in a length of flexible wire. Slide the wire into the hole *(left)*, keeping it as close against the inside surface as possible. When the wire touches a stud or joist, measure the distance between it and the hole by pinching the wire at the point where it enters the hole. Still marking this point on the wire, pull the wire out from the hole and retrace the distance along the outside surface. Test again with the drill to confirm that the end of the wire marks an edge of a stud or joist.

TURNING OFF ELECTRICAL CIRCUITS

Turn off the electricity to any fixture, switch or outlet that must be removed for repair work. Power should also be shut off in rooms where you will be cutting or drilling near wiring in a wall or ceiling. Also turn off a circuit serving the other side of a wall that will be cut or drilled. Newly-wired homes have a circuit-breaker panel *(below, left)*; older wiring systems have fuse panels *(below, right)*. A voltage tester or a lamp is used to verify that the power to a circuit has been turned off. Many rooms are wired with more than one circuit—be sure to shut off all circuit breakers or fuses serving the area being worked on.

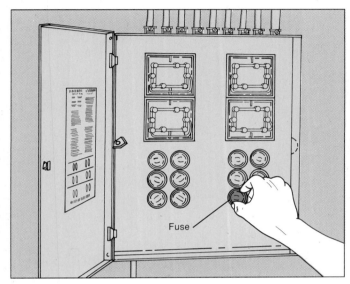

Tripping a circuit breaker. Locate the circuit breaker for the room and flip the toggle switch to OFF *(above)*; it may spring back to an intermediate position. If the circuit breaker for the room is not identified on the panel, test each breaker until the power to the room is off; take the opportunity to label the breakers for future reference. To restore power to the room after a repair is completed, flip the circuit breaker toggle switch back to OFF, then ON.

Removing a fuse. Locate the fuse (or fuses) for the room and turn it counterclockwise to remove it from the service panel. If the fuse for the room has not been identified, unscrew each fuse until the power to the room is off; take the opportunity to identify the room served by each fuse for future reference. To restore power to the room after a repair is completed, screw the same fuse or one of identical amperage back into the socket.

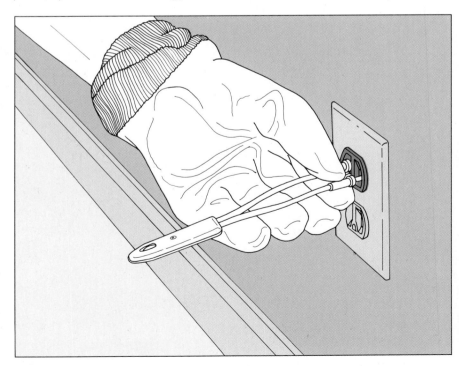

Testing for voltage. A voltage tester lights only when it contacts electricity. To check that the voltage tester is working, try it in a functioning outlet—one in which a lamp works, for example. Turn off the lamp and unplug it; holding the probes of the voltage tester by their insulation—never by the exposed metal—insert a probe into each of the two straight slots *(left)*. If the bulb of the voltage tester glows without flickering, the tester is working. To check that power to an outlet is off, insert the probes of a working tester into its slots as above. The tester should not light. (If you do not have a voltage tester, plug the working lamp into the outlet and turn it on; this time, it should not light.) To verify that power is off to a fixture or switch, remove its cover plate *(page 138)* and pull it out enough to expose the wires. On a fixture, twist off the wire caps with one hand, without touching the wires; on a switch, leave the wires attached to the terminals on the box. Touch one probe of the voltage tester to the bare end of the black wire and one probe to the bare end of the white wire. If there are more than two terminals, test each pair of wires. If the power is off, the bulb of the voltage tester should not light.

DISCONNECTING FIXTURES, OUTLETS AND SWITCHES

It is rarely necessary to disconnect a lighting fixture, outlet or switch entirely in order to work on the wall or ceiling around it. In most cases, the cover plate is removed or lowered and the fixture, switch or outlet shifted out of the way. Always turn off power to the fixture's circuit at the service panel before removing it *(page 137)*.

Techniques for removing two typical fixture cover plates are shown below. The method shown for removing a cover plate and outlet applies to a switch as well, except that a switch cover plate has two screws. Reverse the procedure shown to reinstall the cover plate after a repair, then turn on the power.

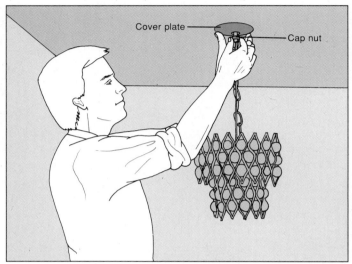

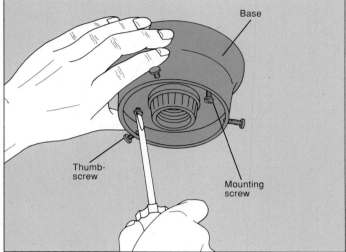

Removing the cover plate of a lighting fixture. A typical swag fixture has one or more lock nuts or cap nuts threaded onto shafts that extend through the cover plate. To remove the cover plate on this type of fixture, turn off power to the circuit *(page 137)* and then unscrew the lock nut or cap nut and slide the cover plate off the shafts *(above, left)*; support a heavy fixture with one hand.

Tape the nuts to the coverplate. A globe-style fixture has mounting screws in its base that may be accessible only with the globe and bulb removed *(above, right)*; loosen the thumbscrews holding the globe to remove it, unscrew the bulb and take out the mounting screws. Place the screws inside the globe for safekeeping. Use a voltage tester *(page 137)* to verify that power is off.

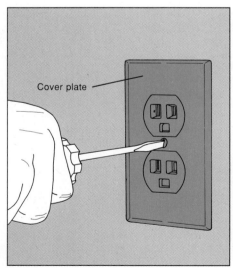

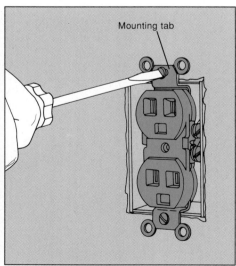

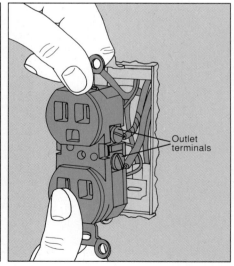

Unseating a switch or outlet. Turn off power to the switch or outlet circuit *(page 137)*. To take off the cover plate, remove the screw or screws holding it in position *(above, left)*; tape the screws to the back of the cover plate to prevent losing them. Remove the screws from the mounting tabs at the top and bottom of the switch or outlet *(above, center)*; tape them to the cover plate. Unseat the switch or outlet by pulling it gently out of its box, partly exposing the wiring *(above, right)*. Verify that power is off with a voltage tester *(page 137)*.

CUTTING AN ACCESS HOLE

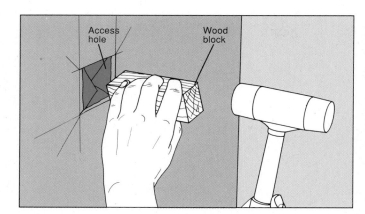

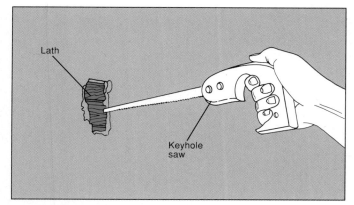

Punching into drywall. Locate a pair of studs or joists *(page 136)*. Midway between them, use a utility knife and straightedge to score a 4-inch square. Score a cross corner to corner. Place one end of a wood block in the center of the square and rap it sharply with a mallet, snapping the drywall along the scored lines *(above)*, then remove the pieces. Inspect inside the opening, using a flashlight if necessary, for any obstructions *(pages 134, 135)*. Enlarge the opening, using a keyhole saw only if the blade has clearance; otherwise, use a utility knife.

Cutting through plaster and lath. Locate the edge of a stud or joist *(page 136)*. Start the access hole at this edge and work toward the next stud or joist. Wearing goggles and work gloves, use a cold chisel and ball-peen hammer to chip off plaster until you're able to check behind the lath for obstructions *(pages 134, 135)*. If necessary, carefully cut away a small piece of lath using the tip of a keyhole saw *(above)*. If the area behind the lath is clear, chip away plaster to the intended size of the hole and cut the lath around the edges of the hole with the keyhole saw.

REPLACING INSULATION AND VAPOR BARRIERS

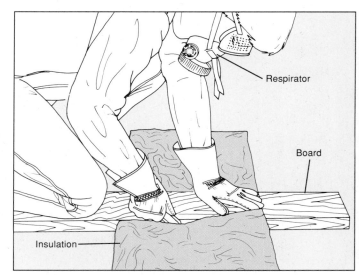

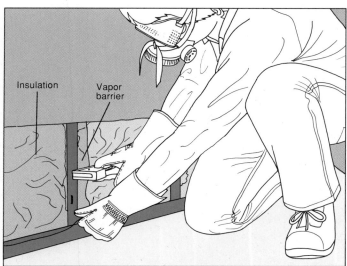

Cutting and installing insulation and vapor barrier. Glass fibers can damage lungs and irritate skin; wear a respirator, goggles, work gloves and long sleeves. Measure the opening along the stud or joist; measure the width only if it is other than the standard 16 inches. Place the insulation batt on the floor and compress it with a board along the line to be cut. Using the board as a guide, cut through the insulation with a utility knife *(above, left)*; it may take several passes. Fit the insulation between the studs or joists; if it has a vapor barrier backing, position the backing side out with the flanges over the studs or joists. If the insulation has no backing, cut a plastic vapor barrier large enough to extend over the studs or joists, overlapping the existing vapor barrier by 2 to 3 inches. Staple the vapor barrier about every 4 to 6 inches along the centers of the studs or joists *(above, right)*.

TAPING AND FEATHERING A DRYWALL JOINT

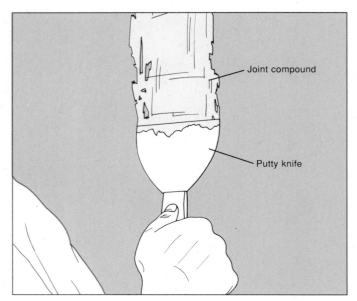

Joint compound

Putty knife

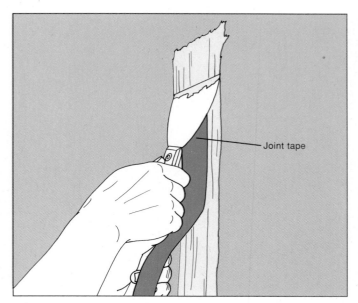

Joint tape

1 **Applying a thin bed of compound.** Use a flexible 4-inch knife to apply a shallow bed of joint compound over the joint; work on a 2-foot length at a time. Load compound evenly across the tip of the putty knife blade. Starting at one end of the joint, press the knife blade against the surface at a 45-degree angle and draw it smoothly along the length of the joint, depositing a 4-inch-wide strip of compound.

2 **Smoothing in the tape.** Holding a roll of tape in one hand and the putty knife in the other, center the tape over one end of the joint. With the knife blade at a 45-degree angle to the surface, press the tape into the compound, drawing the knife along the length of the tape to embed it. If the tape puckers, creases or shifts, carefully lift and recenter it. At the end of the joint compound tear off the tape, and do not overlap it; scissor-cut or overlapped edges of tape are difficult to conceal.

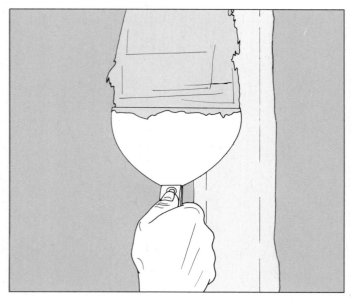

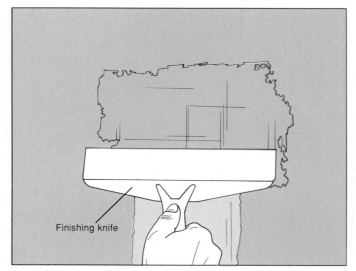

Finishing knife

3 **Embedding the tape.** Load a 6-inch putty knife evenly with joint compound. Position the knife blade at an end of the joint, the corner of the blade even with the center of the tape. Maintaining a 45-degree angle to the surface, draw the knife along the length of the tape in a long, smooth stroke *(above)*. Repeat on the other side, overlapping along the center of the tape. Scrape off excess compound along the edges of the tape and let the compound dry for 24 hours.

4 **Feathering a finishing coat of compound.** Lightly sand the compound with medium-grit sandpaper on a sanding block and brush away dust. Load a 10-inch finishing knife with compound and draw it smoothly along the joint. Wipe the knife clean, position it slightly off-center and draw it along the joint again, applying more pressure to the outside edge of the blade to feather—or taper—the layer of compound. Wipe the knife again and feather the other side of the joint. Let the compound dry for 24 hours; if necessary, follow this step again to apply another finishing pass of compound. Seal the surface with primer.

DRAPING AND MASKING A ROOM

Illustrated below is a room ready for major work on the walls, ceiling or woodwork. Of course, not all of these precautions are necessary for every repair in this book—choose from the techniques pictured to best protect the area where you are working. Keep in mind that dust and fumes spread; close doors to other rooms in the house, sealing entrances with sheets of plastic if necessary. Move to other rooms all easily-carried furnishings—pillows, lamps, pictures, curtains, portable televisions. Roll up rugs and move them out of the way. Push sofas, large chairs and dining tables to the middle of the room and drape them with drop cloths or sheets of plastic. Cover carpeted and wood floors with overlapped drop cloths; plastic tends to slide, making it dangerous to walk on. Wood floors may also be covered with newspapers—the ink may rub off on light-colored carpeting. On stairs, tack a drop cloth into the corners of the treads and risers or use masking tape to hold down newspapers. Over a banister, radiator, or window that's not being painted, drape a drop cloth or tape sheets of plastic or newspaper. Tape newspapers to a baseboard to protect it as well. Remove the cover plates from lighting fixtures, switches and outlets *(page 138)*. Cover fixtures and other permanent accessories such as thermostats with newspaper or a plastic bag. Remove hardware—doorknobs or curtain rods, for example—that is easy to take off; use masking tape to protect hardware that is left in place. If necessary, mask window panes with masking tape, leaving a 1/16-inch gap between the tape and the wood or metal frame of the window. Strip off masking tape as soon as a job is completed, or it may stick permanently.

INDEX

Page references in *italics* indicate an
illustration of the subject mentioned.
Page references in **bold** indicate a
Troubleshooting Guide for the subject
mentioned.

ACKNOWLEDGMENTS

The editors wish to thank the following:
Eric Anderson, Anderson Insulation Co. Inc., Abington, Mass.; Cecil O. Blakney, DiversiTech General, Columbus, Miss.; Larry Brandon, Red Devil, Inc., Union, N.J. and Pryor, Okla.; David Byrd, Montreal, Que.; Ronald M. Clark, Clark Tile Co. Inc., Addison, Ill.; Jean-Luc Devirieux, Montreal, Que.; Roland Dionne and Luc Parent, Canadian Gypsum Company Limited, St. Laurent, Que.; Glenn Eldridge, Chelsea Decorative Metal, Houston, Tex.; Ellis Hospital, Poison Control Center, Schenectady, N.Y.; Leo Frenette, H.R. Cassidy Ltd., Laval, Que.; William Groah, Hardwood Plywood Manufacturer's Association, Reston, Va.; Gennaro Guerra, Guertec Inc., St. Leonard, Que.; Lt. Irwin N. Kingsbury (Retired), Baltimore City Fire Department, Baltimore, Md.; George Kleevic, Geo/Resource Consultants Inc., Washington, D.C.; Raymond McBride, Pierrefonds, Que.; Dr. Michael McCann and Christine Proctor, Center for Occupational Hazards, New York, N.Y.; Peter McGrath, Spray-On Systems Inc., Newton, Mass.; Norman Migdol, Roman Adhesives Inc., Bloomfield, N.J.; New York State Department of Environmental Conservation; John Oberle, Benjamin Moore & Co., Newark, N.J.; Ronald Passaro, American Society of Home Inspectors Inc., Washington, D.C.; Warren K. Porter, Director of Health Sciences Laboratories, U.S. Consumer Product Safety Commission, Bethesda, Md.; Quebec Poison Control Centre, Sainte-Foy, Que.; Mark Quitno, Norman Co., Nevada, Mo.; Yvon Simard, Fiberglas Canada, Montreal, Que.; United States Gypsum Company, Chicago, Ill.; John Yelle, Benjamin Moore & Co., Montreal, Que.

The following persons also assisted in the preparation of this book:
Marie-Claire Amiot, Fiona Gilsenan, Serge Paré, Barbara Peck, Natalie Watanabe, Billy Wisse.

Typeset on Texet Live Image Publishing System.